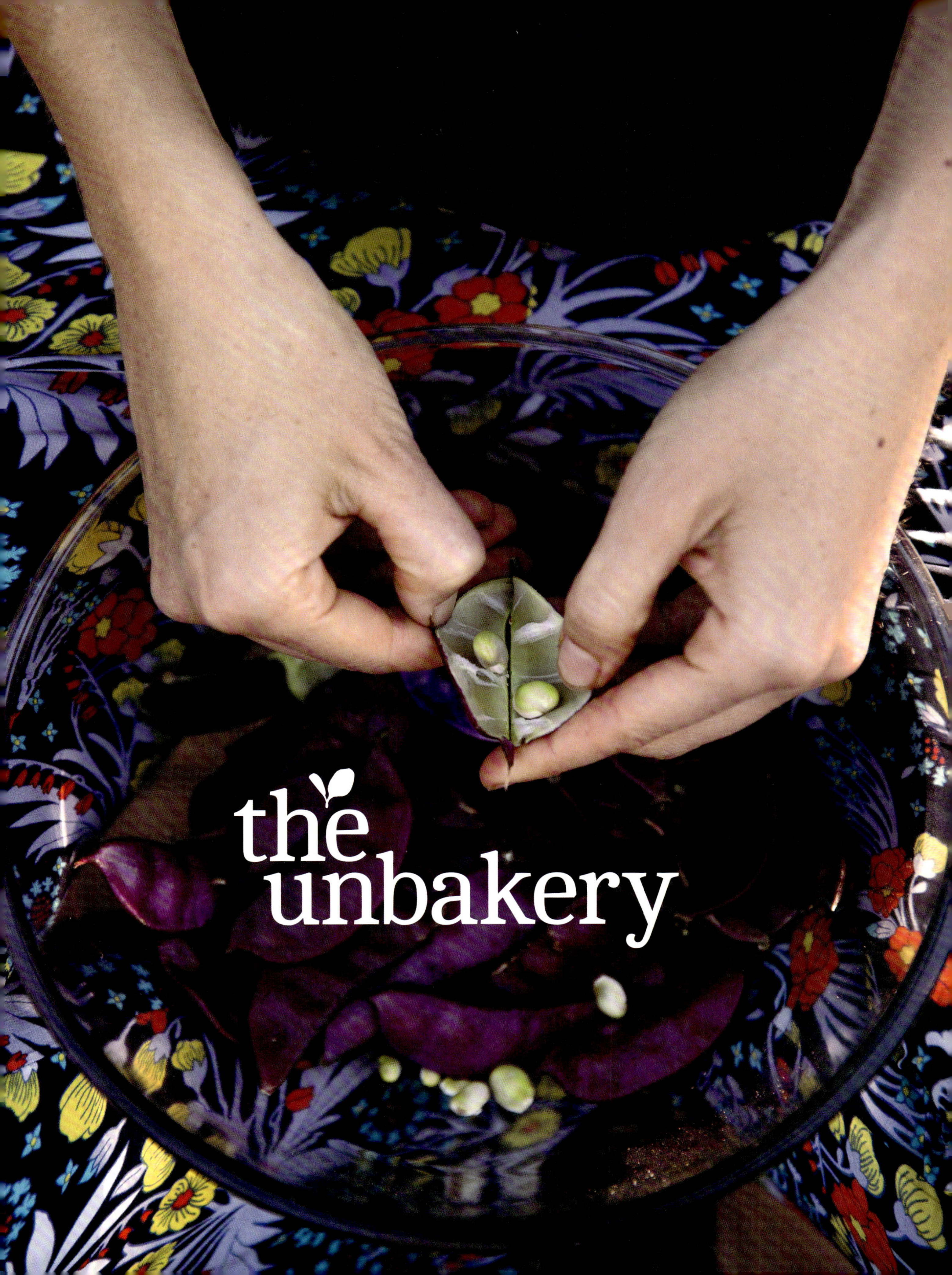
the unbakery

Published in 2015 by Murdoch Books, an imprint of Allen & Unwin
First published in 2014 by Beatnik Publishing

Murdoch Books Australia
83 Alexander Street
Crows Nest NSW 2065
Phone: +61 (0) 2 8425 0100
Fax: +61 (0) 2 9906 2218
murdochbooks.com.au
info@murdochbooks.com.au

Murdoch Books UK
Erico House, 6th Floor
93–99 Upper Richmond Road
Putney, London SW15 2TG
Phone: +44 (0) 20 8785 5995
murdochbooks.co.uk
info@murdochbooks.co.uk

For Corporate Orders & Custom Publishing contact
Noel Hammond, National Business Development Manager,
Murdoch Books Australia

Art Direction: Jeremy Bennett
Design: Kitki Tong
Recipe Development, Food Styling & Testing: Nicole Majsa, Lucia Plowman, Maria Fernandez Salom, Carter Were, Harriet Were
Chefs & Bakers: Megan May, Xander Cameron, Rejina Yoon

IMPORTANT: Those who might be at risk from the effects of salmonella poisoning (the elderly, pregnant women, young children and those suffering from immune deficiency diseases) should consult their doctor with any concerns about eating raw foods.

MEASURES GUIDE: We have used 15 ml (3 teaspoon) tablespoon measures for recipes in this book.

the unbakery

OVER 150 RECIPES FOR BEAUTIFUL RAW FOOD

megan may

photography lottie hedley

MURDOCH BOOKS

contents

Welcome to the unbakery book.

This is a celebration of organic, raw, plant-based food; a collection of recipes that reflects a lifelong love affair with creating and sharing food for wellbeing and pure pleasure.

Packaging it up into one perfect bundle of recipes was no mean feat. This is a treasure chest of recipes from home, from our little bird unbakery and cafés, and from our talented chefs. I wanted to make the recipes accessible to anyone beginning to experiment with raw foods, while still revealing how varied and truly delicious they can be.

While these recipes are 100 percent raw and plant-based, this book is not designed for only those on a purely, or even predominantly, raw diet. Few people would argue that eating more fresh fruits and vegies is not a good thing. These recipes are to inspire you to get creative with raw, plant-based goodness – how far you want to take it is entirely up to you.

megan's story

I grew up in Waimauku, West Auckland, on an organic market garden and small farm, surrounded by an abundance of beautiful food. It was heaven – what kid doesn't love eating fresh strawberries and sugar snap peas straight from the vine? Looking back I realise how lucky I was to learn from the outset that the freshest, most fragrant and amazing food comes from the ground – and not from a tin or a box.

But food wasn't just an early passion – it was a poison too. At the age of six I was diagnosed with allergies to gluten, dairy and sugar – an unfortunate predicament for a child in 1980s New Zealand. Per capita, this country is one of the largest producers of dairy products in the world – if you couldn't eat cereal drowned in milk, a cheese sandwich or hokey pokey ice cream, what could you eat?

As a six-year-old, I preferred to suffer from tummy aches and endless colds than eat a special diet, so when Mum wasn't looking I rebelled. (Sorry Mum!) This meant I was often unwell, but at least my sneaky pleasures were somewhat balanced by all the fresh produce I was enjoying.

And we didn't just eat the best of fruit and vegies. My mum and grandmother made everything from scratch; there were no sauces from tins or packets of pastry.

We made butter from fresh cow's milk, eggs came from chickens and meat from our own animals. I'd try any food and I was lucky to be able to indulge my curiosity. My father helped farmers in Third World countries receive organic certification so they could negotiate better trade prices (in fact, my parents still do this), so we would often have people from exotic cultures staying at our house, sharing their different perspectives on cooking and ingredients.

I've been making food since I was big enough to stand on a stool. Baking was always a favourite activity. We were independent children who prepared our own lunches and, as I grew older, I started making the family dinners. Even in my flatting years, I carried on making everything from scratch using organic ingredients.

It was then – when I'd left home to study environmental sciences at university – that I realised mine was not an ordinary passion for food. My peers weren't making gluten-free pizza bases or whipping up their own sauces. Nor were they spending their student loans at organic and gourmet food stores.

Still, sometimes it takes a while to recognise your passion – even when it's staring you in the face. I was twenty-four and working in the planning department of the Auckland City Council when I realised I was far more excited to win the office baking competition than I was about anything else at work. I decided to turn my back on my chosen career and take the plunge into a different one. I resigned nervously and went to work for minimum wage as a commis (junior) chef at Heron's Flight Matakana vineyard.

Being in a kitchen, creating food and learning from professionals felt exhilarating and right. Keen to prove myself, I embraced the lifestyle of high stress and long shifts. I also ate the food everyone else in the kitchen was eating – regardless of my allergies. Needless to say I soon became exhausted and unwell.

I took a couple of weeks off work thinking I just needed a break. Those two weeks would turn into almost three years. I had done such a swell job of depleting my body that one thing after another simply stopped functioning.

At around this time my partner Jeremy and I moved to London. I was already in a bad way physically but, being in my mid-twenties, was determined to ignore that and try to cut it as a chef in London. Unfortunately it was there that I realised the extent of my ill health. I had, in no particular order, malignant melanomas, the bone density of a sixty-year-old, hormone imbalances (or just no production of them), adrenal fatigue, parasitic infections and depression.

Getting well was a gradual and often frustrating process. Every step forward seemed to result in two steps back. I was incredibly lucky to have Jeremy who stood by me and supported me, while I had only enough energy to work part-time. The rest of my hours were spent visiting an array of medical professionals and alternative specialists. All of these believed they knew what was wrong with me, but each was focused on only one aspect, when my whole physical ecosystem was clearly a mess. I was spending thousands on specialist tests that invariably made the story more complex and sent me down yet another garden path. I was despondent, depressed and had large parasites coming out of my body of their own accord. That was the final straw. I decided I'd had enough of other people telling me what was happening in my body. I was in a very rough place, about as low as I could get, but the decision to take my health into my own hands felt good. I knew the only person who could fix me was me.

While I wasn't a qualified expert, my family background and poor health as a child had given me a solid understanding of the connection between food and wellness. And of course for the past two years I'd been my own living case study and experiment – while I didn't agree with all the expert information I'd heard, I had learned a lot. I knew my body inside out and decided to pay attention to what it was telling me.

I got more confident in my food choices, drinking green smoothies and juices without thinking of the doctor who said diet wouldn't change a thing, nor of the Chinese medicine practitioner who believed I needed to rebuild my strength with meat and hearty cooked meals. My instincts told me that a high percentage of my diet should be raw and my approach was well informed – I wasn't standing in the snow eating pineapples, because eating tropical fruits in a London winter is just wrong. Occasionally I would get some watermelon on a cold day (because I love it) and afterwards I'd start shivering. Each food has different properties and they're fun to experience and learn about. I truly began to understand the importance of eating local seasonal produce – nature is pretty damn clever. It generally gives us what we need, when we need it.

My instincts proved right. I was overjoyed to find that, with the gradual introduction of more and more raw food into my diet, I was feeling positive and clearer in my head and much better physically, too. In fact, I could literally feel my body re-energising and re-building with every mouthful of living food I ate.

This was a revelation. While I'd always been into good organic food, I had a more macrobiotic approach – I cooked everything! It wasn't until I went to SAF,

a restaurant in London by Chad Sarno, and did one of Chad's chef courses that I realised I could take my kitchen prowess and convert it into some seriously good raw food. The skills were totally transferable; there were just a few tools I would need to acquire and a few I'd no longer be using, but the foundations were the same: combine delicious flavours using good organic ingredients. Chad wasn't fanatical about being raw, he was just doing his thing and doing it well. I scribbled down the name of every cookbook on his shelves.

My previous raw experiences hadn't been so casual or inspiring. They were more along the lines of 'eat 100 percent raw or you will kill yourself with every bite of that evil cooked food'. This was not an approach I connected with. If my lifelong allergies had taught me one thing it's that we all respond to food in different ways. We need to be inclusive and open-minded about different approaches.

Back in New Zealand, I saw that the raw food movement was pretty much non-existent. If I wanted to enjoy interesting combinations of raw ingredients, I would need to create my own. That wasn't a problem – I was still in the process of rebuilding my health and had time on my hands. I began to develop the recipes for 'grawnola' and macaroons that were to become a staple of our little bird brand.

The grawnola was a really important product to me. As I am gluten-free, breakfast is probably the hardest meal. A lot of gluten-free foods in the supermarket are highly refined and lacking in sustainable energy or nutrition. I had tried one sprouted buckwheat grawnola in the UK; it didn't taste great but it did sustain and nourish me for the morning. So I went to work creating grawnolas that would have that effect, and taste amazing too.

I'd been perfecting the grawnola and macaroons for around six-to-eight months when someone encouraged me to sell some from a stand at a talk David Wolfe (the American raw food pioneer) was giving. I almost didn't show up. I felt sick with nerves to be sharing my work with other people. Raw was so new at this time in New Zealand that a sprouted cereal was not a food many would want to try, let alone buy. Jeremy, who is talented at everything except making food, created packaging and labels two nights before. I turned up quivering like a leaf and set up my stand. After about an hour, I stopped shaking each time I poured nut milk into a grawnola sample and I had sold out by the end of the night. Everyone loved it! And several of the large organic store buyers were there and wanted to stock it.

And so, almost by accident, little bird began. I developed more products and set myself up in a production facility in Kingsland, everything made with minimal machinery. We didn't have a lot of money – actually, we didn't have any money. My not working for several years and endless expensive doctors had left us skint. It's a difficult yet satisfying way to build a company, the no-money way: you become very resourceful.

At the front of our small factory was an internal garage that opened onto busy New North Road. After a few years of steady progress with little bird products, I started to eye up this area as a potential space for a raw café.

Flashback to age twenty-two: I was a flight attendant for a stint after finishing university. I worked the international routes and grasped the opportunity to visit restaurants, food stores and cafés all over the world. I clearly remember chatting to someone on the plane and saying I planned to open my own organic café. At the same time I was telling myself this was a pipe dream and I needed to get more realistic – neither my experience of handing out plastic trays on a 747 nor my environmental science degree were exactly stepping stones to running an organic food business.

But … sometimes dreams become reality. We opened our first little bird unbakery with fifteen seats in the garage in front of our factory. Within a week there were queues out the door, and many of Auckland's famous faces and media personalities were making their way to Kingsland to try our raw menu. I couldn't have been more blown-away or more terrified. I had only employed one person to help; we needed more staff and quickly – unbaking into the night became a regular activity for some time.

During this thrilling but scary time I was very aware of the need to preserve my hard-won health. For a while I ate an almost 100 percent raw diet, with a predominance of greens, keeping it nutrient-dense and light. I stayed away from all sweet food and stimulants – anything that might put me on an energy rollercoaster. And instead of the long days (and nights) taking their toll, I thrived.

With the success and learnings from our first unbakery came our second a year later, a much bigger space in Ponsonby's Summer Street. Jeremy, now my husband, left his job as an architect to join me in my mad pursuit. When it comes to fitting out a space he does a beautiful job. With its brick walls, wooden floor boards, lovely natural light and abundance of plants, the Summer Street unbakery is a fusion of our passions and skills – I guess that's pretty special.

food: a love affair

I'm sure there have never been more theories about diet as there are right now. From Paleo to vegan, the philosophies vary greatly and all have their die-hard converts. Raw food isn't new but lately it has become a buzzword and, increasingly, you hear people advocating a 100 percent raw diet – the blogosphere is rife with them. I've experimented with quite prolonged periods of eating 100 percent raw myself, and I agree that it can be a powerful and healing approach.

These days, however, I prefer not to put a percentage figure on what I eat, and nor would I advocate that anyone eat exactly the way I do. Eating is a highly personal pursuit. Our bodies are all different and cultural and emotional factors also come into play. I can only share what I've learned through my experience, which is that a mostly raw, mostly plant-based diet has tremendous health benefits. I'm not rigid about it. Stressing about every mouthful you eat is a bore and, ironically, quite unhealthy – I've been there!

There are four basic factors to the diet I follow: it is mainly raw, mainly plant-based, it's organic and it consists of whole (as opposed to processed) foods. Beyond that, I'm open-minded. Food is to be celebrated, explored and shared. And the beauty of learning to create delicious snacks, satisfying dinners and indulgent desserts from raw plants is that even your most carnivorous guests will devour them with pleasure.

why raw?

The official definition of raw food is that which hasn't been heated above 46°C (115°F). The goal of eating food in this state is to maximise our assimilation of its vitamins and minerals. Enzymes, which aid the digestive process, tend to be killed in the cooking process. And digestion is not something to take lightly – it is how you access your body's nutrition. Being lactose intolerant and a coeliac, I know how detrimental malabsorption of food is. Rebuilding your health after that is no walk in the park.

Once you begin to increase the raw, plant-based foods in your diet, you probably won't worry too much about the science behind it because, quite simply, you'll feel great. You can look forward to benefits such as increased energy and clarity, a more light-hearted outlook, stronger immunity, glowing skin and strengthened nails. And the more of these foods you eat, the more you will crave them – I promise. You will feel satisfied with less of the cooked, processed foods you were eating, because your body is getting all the nutrients it needs.

Forget those old jibes about 'rabbit food'. When you attune your taste buds to a raw diet, you will be blown away by the flavours. You'll find yourself contemplating the subtle differences between tomato varieties and salad greens the way you would between fine wines. And it's impossible to exhaust the cornucopia of delicious plant-based foods on offer. You will never get bored.

about organics

A lot of food is grown and preserved with the use of pesticides and a great many other chemicals. Once consumed, our bodies do their best to process and eliminate these toxic substances – a stressful process best avoided altogether.

These chemicals have a long-term effect on the soil, the people working on farms and the environment at large. For this reason, when you support organic farmers, your decision affects far more than just the quality of the food in your refrigerator.

Organics were just everyday life for our family, although that was rare in the 1980s. Growing up on an organic farm, with my dad teaching organics at the local polytechnic, we were surrounded by farms that used an array of sprays – a totally different approach to that of my dad, although he never preached about it.

Organic farmers take the long view, nurturing the soil so that it will be able to feed generations – and not just provide a bumper crop this summer. To do it well requires patience and a lifetime of knowledge. These farmers are so important to our planet and our individual health. As with all farmers (organic or not), theirs is a risky business; they toil and can lose a year's work overnight in a deep frost or storm. Supporting them is easy – try to seek out organic produce wherever you can. The benefits are so profound – and mutual.

the whole truth

You hear a lot about processed foods. Well, wholefoods are basically the opposite. Refining foods down to their least fibrous state, not to mention adding a host of chemicals so that they'll last a decade, is a pretty new thing. The industrial revolution has a lot to answer for; its impact on the health of developed countries has been nothing short of disastrous. With diabetes (to name just one modern disease) reaching epidemic levels in many countries, including New Zealand, even the most mainstream health professionals are questioning the modern diet of highly processed convenience foods.

The fact is that what is billed as 'convenient' often just means 'profitable'. It's seldom necessary to add chemicals to food for longevity. Foods can be preserved by dehydrating, pickling and fermenting – often adding nutrient value, rather than depleting it.

Avoiding heavily processed foods is easy. If you would struggle to name the plant or animal that a food is derived from, don't eat it. Likewise if it has a use-by date in the far-flung future or a list of ingredients that sound more scientific than culinary. And if the first ingredient listed is sugar or refined cornflour (cornstarch), run for the hills.

Nature is no simpleton. Wholefoods are already complex and neatly packaged bundles of complementary goodness. Take a kale leaf. It has many macro and micro nutrients working in perfect harmony; it is an abundant source of iron, an important mineral best consumed with vitamin C – and kale delivers plenty of that, too. Wholefoods seem to have been designed by nature for maximum nutritional benefit. The more you can pack into your diet, the more alive you'll feel.

plants rule

Plants are amazing foods. I can vouch that you feel pretty damn good when you eat a lot of them.

Whether you are a vegan, a vegetarian or someone who enjoys meat and dairy products, you'll benefit hugely by increasing the percentage of plant-based foods in your diet. And if you're someone (or the parent of someone) for whom vegies can be a challenge, this book offers myriad ways to sneak plant foods into everything from smoothies and juices to crackers, desserts and bread.

Plants contain an abundance of antioxidants as well as phytonutrients such as anthocyanins, carotenoids, ellagic acid, flavonoids, glucosinolates and resveratrol. These all work to boost the immune system, make our cells sparkle and slow the ageing process.

the raw lifestyle

Embarking on a new journey with your eating often means some lifestyle changes. Here are some tips and ideas to help you maximise the goodness you're doing for your body.

start slow

If you're brand new to this, please start gently. Don't try and be 100 percent raw overnight, hitting numbers is not the point here. Take small steps, perhaps aiming to add a juice or smoothie to your food intake each day. And maybe replace your store-bought salad dressing with a delicious one filled with goodness from one of our recipes.

The weekend is a good time to play around in the kitchen experimenting with nut cheeses, wraps, activated seeds and breads. This will pay off during your busy week when you'll be able to assemble a healthy, delicious meal in a flash.

But above all, try to let go of the all-or-nothing approach. You are far more likely to make permanent and healthy changes if you are realistic and kind to yourself. Embracing wellbeing is a life-long process, with many ups and downs. Forget the quick fix.

stress less

Reducing your stress levels can impact your health as much as changing your diet. I've certainly had my periods of feeling overwhelmed, but I've learned in recent years that some subtle shifts in perspective can turn those times into an interesting challenge. Relaxation is like a muscle that gets stronger the more you use it. Running two cafés and a manufacturing business provides me with endless opportunities to give this muscle a work out …

Embracing plant-based foods will reduce the stress on your digestive system and give you a mood lift – so that's one box ticked. Just beware of letting it become a source of stress itself – so tonight you ate enough pizza to feed an extended Italian family? Big deal! Put some extra kale in your smoothie tomorrow.

As you are what you eat, you are also what you think. See if there's a way you can find moments of joy in things (or people) you find challenging. There is always energy and clarity to be found with just a small tweak in the way you view a situation or relationship.

One of the best things you can do for your stress levels is schedule some relaxation time. I know, scheduling stress relief sounds ironic – but it won't happen unless you make time for it. Decide what makes you feel most serene: taking a long walk, listening to music, seeing friends, dinner with your partner, a massage – and book it in.

move your body

There's no such thing as a healthy and sedentary body. Exercise can earn us a nice physique, but much more importantly it increases circulation and makes your cells more receptive to insulin (helping to stabilise blood sugar) thereby aiding them to function better and detoxify waste.

Sadly, exercise has become for many another source of competitive feelings and guilt. Gyms make a killing off all those unused memberships. It doesn't have to be that hard – if the bright lights and loud music of the gym aren't your thing, never set foot in one again. You don't even need to take up yoga or jogging. Just put on some music and mop the floor, weed the garden, swim in the sea or take a walk in the park on your lunch break. Do whatever gives you pleasure, just move your body every day.

drink water

Drinking several glasses of filtered water daily is as essential as eating a healthy diet. Our bodies are comprised of around 70 percent water – it flows through the blood, carrying oxygen and nutrients to cells and flushing waste. If we're not hydrated it's also difficult for our bodies to digest and absorb nutrients.

Natural water contains a vast array of minerals but most of our water is processed with chemicals to make it safe to drink, which tends to strip those minerals away.

If you have access to natural spring water, that's the ultimate. For most of us though, finding a good filtration and remineralisation system is the best option. Many wholefood stores sell filtration jugs and carbon sticks quite inexpensively. In all of our recipes we use filtered or living water, including with soaking and sprouting. Otherwise, we've found sprouts spoil more easily, especially buckwheat.

create a healthy home

So many products that we have in our homes – from lipstick to fabric softener – expose our largest organ (our skin) to harsh and unnecessary chemicals.

Replacing these products with their non-toxic alternatives has a wide-reaching impact, similar to that of organic farming. It will not only benefit you and your family, it will benefit the people who make your products (reducing their exposure to chemicals) and the greater environment – all that stuff eventually ends up in our waste water system.

Making this change is incredibly easy now. There's an ever-increasing range of excellent non-toxic products for your home and your body. These alternatives are affordable and they work.

about detoxing

Everything outlined above – eating well, reducing stress, exercising, drinking quality water and limiting toxins in your home – will provide an effective daily detox. Our bodies and cells create waste constantly so detoxing shouldn't be an annual thing to get in shape for summer, it's something to consider every day. Bodies are incredible; they actually want to function well and will do just that with regular encouragement.

But sometimes we need a detoxing boost or just to give our digestive system a rest. At little bird we provide a cleanse that consists of smoothies and juices and one meal per day. We focus on filling your body with highly functional nutrients from vegetables, fruits and superfoods to revitalise your cells as well as eliminate toxins, along with some herbal teas to support your main cleansing organs (liver and kidneys). I've tried many cleansing experiences and many left me feeling even more depleted. For that reason I developed our cleanses to be revitalising as well as detoxifying, so you don't need a week to recover afterwards.

There are many cleanses and detoxes that work well for different people. I would advise finding a good nutritionist, naturopath or practitioner with detoxing knowledge who can guide you toward a program that will work for you.

when you need something extra

I believe there's a place for supplementation although high doses of fractionised vitamins and minerals, without the proper co-factors and enzymes to digest them, for the most part just create very expensive poop. There are many wonderful companies that do produce wholefood supplementation – sometimes we need some extra support but we need the kind that our body can thrive on. If you feel your diet needs a boost, I recommend you consult with a good nutritionist or naturopath.

the raw kitchen

This short introduction to some of our favourite ingredients is by no means comprehensive but it will hopefully inspire you to try something new. Of course the best way to get to know ingredients is to try different recipes and then to experiment with them on your own …

Vegetables are number one in a raw kitchen – everything else is there to enhance them.

Choose fresh organic vegetables that look vibrant and healthy; if they look a bit sad, they've probably lost some nutritional goodness. If you can't get organic vegetables, soaking them in a little apple cider vinegar will help remove some pesticides and other water-soluble chemicals.

Farmers' markets are the best place to shop for freshness as well as a greater variety of vegetables. Don't ever feel limited by the vegies you know – there are hundreds I had never tried before I switched to a more raw, plant-based diet.

You might find you enjoy raw a vegie you never had time for cooked – the flavours can differ hugely. One that surprised me this way was brussels sprouts. Every child's nightmare when cooked, they're surprisingly good raw and finely shredded with a little olive oil, lemon and sea salt.

Some other vegies you might prefer raw include kohlrabi, parsnip, Jerusalem artichoke, cauliflower, peas, yacon, the many varieties of radish, tomatillo, sweet corn, celeriac, bok choy (pak choy), choy sum, wild garlic shoots, turnips and asparagus.

I really encourage you to broaden your vegetable repertoire. Maybe try a new variety of an old favourite such as beetroot (beets) (try new colours – the flavours are all unique) or heirloom tomatoes. Baby veg also have a different texture and flavour to their grown-up versions; baby carrots, turnips and radishes are some of our favourites. We like to dip them into nut cheese as a snack – they're rather beautiful too, when served in a dish.

Green leafy vegetables are essential. They pack a nutritional punch containing a wide range of vitamins, minerals and proteins (iron, calcium and vitamin K to name a few). I challenge you to increase your intake of raw, leafy greens and not notice an almost instant improvement in mood, wellbeing and appearance (greens are great for glowing skin, hair and eyes). And for anyone who has never been a huge fan of the leaves on their plate, drinking them in smoothies will be a revelation.

Green leaves also make excellent wraps; with any of our wrap recipes in this book you could substitute nori or a taco shell with a big leafy green such as a collard, iceberg lettuce or Chinese cabbage (wong bok).

Kale is the king of greens. It's one of the most nutrient-dense foods available, is easy to grow and is definitely having a fashion moment. But make sure you mix it up – there are plenty of others vying for the crown and variety is key to getting all the nutrients your body thrives on. Try English spinach, cavolo nero, collard greens, silverbeet (Swiss chard), cabbages, mustard greens, sorrel, witlof (chicory), rocket (arugula) and cos (romaine), iceberg, frisée and buttercrunch lettuces. And that's just a start.

Fresh fruit is nature's original treat. The sweet side of raw can be very attractive when transitioning to a raw food diet but remember it's vegies that your body will thrive on the most.

Focus, if you can, on the less-sugary fruits: green apples, berries, kiwifruit, cranberries, lemons, limes and grapefruit. Some of the highest in sugar are cherries, grapes, tangerines, bananas and mangoes. Fruit is not processed sugar by any stretch, it is a wholefood full of goodness – but still best enjoyed in moderation. Listen to your body and get to know which foods increase your energy and which take it away. I found that as my own body regained its health, and I ate more greens and fermented foods, my capacity to eat fruit increased dramatically.

Dried fruits have had most of their moisture removed, leaving much of their nutritional goodness intact. Their sweetness is concentrated so beware of eating them by the handful. As a sweetener and binder in raw desserts, dried fruits are fantastic. Good-quality dates, figs, sultanas (golden raisins), currants, apricots, sour cherries, apple and goji berries are staples in our little bird unbakery pantry. If you have a dehydrator, you can make your own of whatever fruit is cheap and in season.

Freeze-dried fruits have had all their moisture content removed using very low temperatures. The tiniest amount adds an intense burst of fresh flavour to many sweet treats and desserts. Berries that are difficult to dehydrate because of their high water and low sugar content are best preserved this way – almost all dried berries, organic or non-organic, have added sweetener to them to plump them up.

Nuts and seeds are packed with protein and good fats that will leave you satisfied with hours of energy. They also have essential vitamins such as A and E – great for glowing skin. However, you don't need to consume a lot of these dense little nutritional powerhouses every day – it can put stress on your digestive system and make it sluggish. As with many of the ingredients here, you want to use nuts and seeds to complement your vegies, rather than as the main event.

Activating or soaking nuts and seeds (see pages 26–27) is a great way to make them more digestible.

In our pantry we have almonds (the only alkalising nut), walnuts, pecans, pine nuts, pistachios, Brazil nuts, cashews, hazelnuts and macadamia nuts. Seeds include sunflower, pumpkin, sesame, hemp, chia and flax.

In New Zealand we don't have great access to pecans, pine nuts and pistachios. We only use them in a few recipes for that reason but if you have them growing in your area feel free to substitute them for other nuts in other recipes. Keep it local and seasonal where you can.

Grains aren't a huge part of a raw food diet but there are a few grains and 'pseudo grains' that we like to have in the pantry. Our favourite pseudo grain is buckwheat which, despite its misleading name, is in fact a seed and a member of the rhubarb family. We use it in our grawnolas and in many sweet treats. Sprouted and dried, it can provide texture and nutrition to a dish in which you don't want the richness of nuts. Buckwheat is a saviour to the gluten-intolerant – it is completely devoid of all things wheat-related, including gluten.

Wild rice is actually an aquatic grass that you can sprout. It is a fantastic food containing a much broader range of vitamins and minerals and more protein than most grains. Combine a little sprouted wild rice with massaged kale, crushed garlic, olive oil and sea salt and you have a delicious, very nutritious side salad.

Oats are a comforting and nourishing grain that we use in some of our sweet treats. A wonderful wholefood, they are a much better choice for the gluten-free than many gluten-free flours, which tend to be heavily refined.

To clarify a common confusion: oats don't contain gluten but are often processed in facilities that use gluten. You can get certified gluten-free oats. For severe coeliacs, oats can still be a problem as they contain a potentially disagreeable protein called avein.

Other grains we use in small amounts include millet, quinoa and amaranth. These each have wonderful nutritional qualities and help contribute to a well-balanced diet.

Sea vegetables are a true superfood. At the unbakery we love our sea vegies! You can add them to your meals without even noticing the sea vegetable flavour while still getting all the goodness. Try a sprinkle of korengo, sea lettuce, wakame or dulse on a salad or a wrap. Keep kelp mixed in with your salt. Nori, used for sushi, will wrap around anything; no need for rice, grab some vegies, maybe a few pieces of avocado, a touch of umeboshi vinegar and tamari, and you have yourself a quick and delicious sea vegie wrap.

Sea vegetables are quite special. They contain the fifty-six elements essential for human health, including calcium, magnesium, potassium, iodine, iron and zinc, together with important trace elements such as selenium, which have often been depleted from our soils and, in turn, from our vegies.

They are also said to help detoxify the body and help protect it from radiation. Studies show that populations with a regular intake of sea vegetables have less mineral depletion than those without. The well-documented longevity of the people of the Japanese island Okinawa is believed to be due to their regular consumption of sea vegetables.

Sweeteners are a hot topic right now! Every era has its diet demon and it seems sugar has become to this decade what fat was to the 1980s and 1990s.

White sugar is not a wholefood. It plays havoc with blood sugar and offers little for the body to thrive on, so there is good reason to steer clear of it. Wholefood sugars are a different thing and sweet treats have always had a place in the little bird unbakeries. Wholefoods sugars contain vitamins and minerals as well as other nutritional properties that, consumed in small amounts, can be good for us.

We encourage people to use sweeteners minimally and use a wide variety to see which work for them. Wholefoods sweeteners we use in the unbakery include: dates and other dried fruits, raw honey, lucuma, mesquite, whole leaf stevia and yacon powder.

Other sweeteners we use that have been minimally processed and have some great properties and flavours include: maple syrup, raw agave (look for the high-quality, less-refined versions), coconut sugar, coconut nectar, yacon syrup and birch xylitol (we don't use the corn-derived version).

Confused? Don't be. Any of the above are worth enjoying in moderation.

'Superfoods' is a pretty loose term. I use it to mean a food that has exceptionally high concentrations of phytonutrients and antioxidants, and I like to think of them as nature's supplements, concentrated goodness in a wholefoods form for those times you feel your body needs a little extra TLC.

Camu camu is a great example – this antioxidant-rich berry from the Amazon is also a good source of minerals, amino acids and powerful phytochemicals. Its most outstanding property is a whopping amount of vitamin C – sixty times more than that of an orange. I regularly add it to smoothies and love it so much I put it in our little bird macadamia and berries grawnola so people can start the day with a superfoods boost without even thinking about it.

Other favourite superfoods include: chia seeds, hemp seeds, bee pollen, acai, maqui, goji berries, blue green algae, cacao, maca powder, bee pollen, aloe vera, sea vegetables and medicinal mushrooms (reishi, chaga, cordecyps). And there are many more. I encourage you to explore what adding a few superfoods to your diet can do for your health.

Fats are good for you! Your body – in particular your brain – needs fats to function. You need to get a good ratio of omega 3 fats to omega 6 fats (1:2) so variety is key. Getting enough omega 6 is easy when you're eating lots of plant-based foods. Flax, chia and hemp seeds and walnuts are all great sources of omega 3s.

Intensely processed trans-fats and hydrogenated oils are far from being healthy fats. The processing of oils is a terrible business. To extract extra oil from seeds and olives, hexane is often used. Yes, that's the stuff your car runs on, not you. Used in the processing then burnt off, hexane isn't listed as an ingredient. These abrasive processes remove nutrients such as vitamins E and A, damage molecules and create free radicals. So please, stick to high-quality, cold-pressed, organic oils. These can seem crazy expensive but they're worth it.

Oils we love: number one is coconut! Unrefined raw coconut oil has so many health-giving properties. The lauric acid in it has anti-viral, anti-fungal and anti-bacterial qualities; it boosts your metabolism, lowers blood pressure, helps with the absorption of minerals and is a great source of energy. You can buy it in bulk at good prices, it is delicious in a huge number of recipes, and it doubles as a lovely body moisturiser too.

Other oils we use include: cold-pressed olive oil, and oils made from flaxseed, hemp, walnut, hazelnut, chia seed, avocado, pumpkin seeds and cacao butter.

Whole avocado is another fat that makes many appearances in our raw food cuisine. It's high in vitamin A and protein, it's great for your skin and it has anti-ageing properties. Avocado is easy to digest and its fat content helps keep you satisfied.

Protein is one of the things you will be quizzed about most if you are eating a plant-based diet: 'That's great but where will you get your protein?' The answer is easy: the same place you get all those vitamins and minerals and micronutrients from – plants. Good sources of plant-based protein include green leafy vegetables, peas, chickpeas, sprouts, nuts, seeds, buckwheat, cacao, oats and goji berries.

If you thrive on a high protein diet or just need a protein boost then you could add some excellent clean protein powders to your smoothies such as sprouted rice protein, sacha inchi or hemp.

Fermented foods are fashionable right now – with good reason. They are amazing for you. Try incorporating at least one fermented food into your diet every day such as sauerkraut (see page 58) and coconut yoghurt (see page 34). When recovering my own health, fermented foods were central to getting my gut functioning and absorbing nutrients again.

Fermented foods are living probiotics that help bring balance back to the bacteria in the gut. They are a great source of enzymes for better digestion and absorption, and help to increase immunity and prevent intolerances and allergies.

Fermented foods we use include: sauerkraut, kimchee, coconut kefir, raw coconut yoghurt, miso paste and kombucha.

Activating and sprouting a seed (or grain or legume) unlocks many of its nutritional advantages. These are otherwise blocked by anti-nutrients such as phytic acid. Once you start the germinating process, a dormant seed becomes a tiny live plant and phytic acid is reduced. The process of changing seeds into little plants is simple while the nutritional change is huge and complex – check out our rough guide to sprouting on page 26. It's incredible to think how much potential life there is in seeds; it takes

a handful to make a field of broccoli – that's some serious energetic potential.

Activating nuts and seeds doesn't go as far as sprouting but it's very beneficial in helping to remove the natural enzyme inhibitors that make it difficult for our bodies to digest nuts and some seeds. We activate all our nuts and seeds that benefit from it (see pages 26–27) in the café.

Drying activated nuts and seeds with spices creates a brilliant snack or a salad ingredient that adds a little flavour and crunch.

Salt must be good! If I'm going to get a little crazy and dogmatic on an ingredient that you shouldn't use, it's bad salt. That stuff is highly refined, it's the white sugar of the savoury world. When we refer to salt we mean unrefined sea salt or Himalayan crystal salt. There are many boutique salts that are locally harvested – you may find one from your area. If you're worried about getting enough iodine, add kelp to your salt to create a natural version of iodised salt. Good salt has many essential minerals, it's relatively inexpensive and a small packet will last ages. The tiniest pinch can transform a sweet or savoury dish, making each flavour pop and become more defined. I find with spicy food in particular, if you don't add a little salt, you can't taste all those beautiful layered flavours. The same can go for dishes featuring chocolate – a little salt will make those flavour notes shine.

Nut butters are indispensable in the raw kitchen, adding wonderful flavour and richness to raw milks, smoothies and treats. You can make your own or buy good raw, organic ones; there are great brands on the market such as Artisana and Dastony.

Our favourite butter is almond for its versatility – but we're also fans of hazelnut, Brazil nut, cashew, sesame, coconut, pumpkin seed, hemp and sunflower.

At the unbakery we also make our own, using a stone grinder for the ultimate silky smooth variety, or a food processor if we're in a rush. Check out the recipe for making your own with a food processor on page 78 – it's really simple and a great way to know you are eating it fresh.

Spices are a passion of mine. Raw dishes are transformed by the clever use of them – in fact, that process was what made raw food click for me. Bringing the knowledge about flavours I'd gained in professional kitchens to the freshest of produce was exciting – and created the best food I'd tasted in my life.

I particularly love the rich history behind spices. Eating flavour combinations enjoyed hundreds, sometimes thousands, of years ago is like culinary time travel. If you are fascinated by different cuisines and cultures, a good book such as *Spice Notes* by Ian and Kate Hemphill (or their new edition *The Spice and Herb Bible*) is invaluable.

Herbs pack fresh flavours into a dish while also providing you with a nutritional kick. They are an integral ingredient in many of our raw dishes – wonderfully fragrant, they leave your taste buds enlivened and your body feeling good.

Herbs contain many unique antioxidants, essential oils, vitamins and phytosterols that help boost your immunity and detox your cells. We put basil or parsley (a blood cleanser and full of iron and vitamin C) in many of our smoothies; coriander (cilantro) can also provide flavour and a health boost to a smoothie, especially when paired with pineapple. (Coriander (cilantro) is known to help detox the body of heavy metals as well as providing you with vitamins like A and K.)

If there are flowers on a herb like rosemary or thyme, use them in your dish as well. They carry some of the same flavour as the leaves and add a little floral elegance to your plate.

getting equipped

Decking out your kitchen with new toys when you embark on a raw journey is not necessary. When I started experimenting with raw dishes, we didn't have a lot of money; I wasn't working and Jeremy was not convinced we needed to spend $1000 on anything that might only be used now and then. So I made do with what I had – essentially a good stick blender and a spice mill (a spice mill is fantastic, you just have to do things in small batches). Later I had a machine that contained a blender, food processor and spice mill attachment, which worked hard for me until it literally ended up in flames. It was difficult to get things totally smooth in the blender so I sieved a lot of the sauces – that was a little labour intensive but got good results.

If you're not someone who enjoys that kind of mucking around, I would recommend you get a good-quality blender, a food processor and a mandoline. A good place to start if you're on a budget is second-hand websites. And if you really feel you're going to embrace making gourmet raw dishes, focus on quality. Getting the very best equipment with warranties is essential.

blender

This is at the top of the raw kitchen list. Do your research as it is a big investment, find one that suits your needs – and remember the length of a warranty is a telling sign of how durable your machine really is.

We use the Vitamix, Blendtec and Thermomix and have found these to be the best of the bunch, in that order. The Thermomix is a great all-rounder for home and makes excellent nut butters, but will not make your sauces and smoothies as silky smooth as the Vitamix or Blendtec.

There are many great personal blenders and stick blenders on the market such as the Tribest. If you're only cooking for one or two people one of these might suffice and it doesn't come with the hefty price tag of a full-scale blender.

juicer

Juicing is a wonderful way to absorb nutrients. We make lots of juices from vegetables, which are less juicy than fruits. A juicer that extracts the most from your produce will save you money in the long run.

Juicing is popular right now and there are new juicers coming out all the time, so do your research and check those warranties.

We use a cold-press juicer (as opposed to a centrifugal juicer); they are slower but retain many more nutrients and enzymes from the produce and the juice will not oxidise as quickly. We have had six different juicers at home over the years and have found the vertical and horizontal auger juicers from Oscar to be excellent. With all juicers, be prepared to change some of their parts every few years; they will wear out but the motor will keep running like a champ.

The Angel and Norwalk juicers are tried and tested health-nut favourites but they come with a hefty price tag and unless you are juicing a lot I would recommend you stick to a more affordable choice.

If you want to make juice quickly and are going to consume it straight away, a centrifugal juicer should suffice – the Breville Juice Fountain™ is a good affordable choice in this category.

food processor

For making raw desserts, brownies, breads and crackers, a food processor is essential. A mid-range model usually suffices, although processing a lot of dried fruit to make bars and cookies will put extra wear and tear on the motor. You can also get some great mini food processors from good brands – these can be a good choice as you will seldom fill the food processor and larger loads can be done in batches.

Our favourite food processor is the Magimix. Cuisinart and KitchenAid are also brands we'd recommend.

dehydrator

A dehydrator is not something to buy straight away. It usually takes people a while to start using them. Dehydrating isn't labour intensive but it does require patience and organisation – waiting two days for crackers to be ready requires a different way of looking at things.

I use the dehydrator a lot, especially in the winter. It's like my oven now, I use it for so many things; nutrient-rich dishes served straight from the dehydrator can be deliciously warming in the cooler months. I use it in lots of little ways; I've never really liked raw mushrooms, for example, but dehydrating them for an hour transforms them into something delectable.

We use the Excalibur and Sedona dehydrators, they are both excellent and reliable models.

spiraliser/mandolines

These are two of my favourite things in the kitchen and you can pick them up pretty cheaply.

The spiraliser will let you make noodles out of many vegetables; carrot, beetroot (beets), zucchini (courgette) and parsnip are some of the main ones. Check out the picture on page 167 showing it in action. In summer when zucchini are abundant we use our spiraliser a lot! Zucchini pastas are delicious – it's funny how often people think it's traditional pasta and ask where the zucchini is in the dish. Creating versions of familiar dishes is a wonderful way to get people interested in trying more raw food.

The mandoline is incredibly handy. You can julienne and slice vegetables finely and quickly, creating interesting texture that can transform simple dishes into something quite sophisticated – see the beetroot ravioli page 200.

Mandolines can be a bit scary – that blade is sharp! There are techniques that will help keep your hands safe (don't ever curl you fingers around the item you're cutting, you want to press down on the palm of your hand and keep the fingers pointing skyward away from the blade). Mandoline gloves are available; they are a fabric version of a butcher's glove and will keep your pinkies safe.

For mandolines and spiralisers we use the Benriner brand. They are reliable and sturdy and you can replace the blades when they get dull. The horizontal spiraliser is our preferred one and I wouldn't recommend any of the vertical ones we have tried from different brands.

some more handy items

Nut milk bags or cloths – cheap and great to have. They will enable you to make your own nut milks and you can also use the bags for sprouting. Any good kitchen store will sell them.

Kitchen axe or cleaver – for coconuts! You don't want to be using your good chef's knife for that job.

Small hand citrus squeezer – helps you get more juice from your citrus. Fresh lemon and lime juice are used in dressings and many of our dishes.

Microplane – the long zesting grater is a valuable tool, for zesting citrus and grating ginger and garlic very finely into dishes.

Lettuce spinner – awesome for keeping lettuce and herbs fresh after you've washed them.

Coffee grinder – if you don't have a good blender, a coffee grinder makes flax and other small seeds into flours easily.

Palate knife/offset spatula – good for spreading mixtures onto dehydrator sheets.

Garlic press – it's not pleasant eating chunks of raw garlic; a garlic press or crusher is a great tool to have.

Vegetable peeler – an old-fashioned metal-hinged peeler is so useful. Don't waste your money on fancy peelers, the old-style ones are best.

Storage containers – airtight storage containers are an absolute must and should probably be at the top of the list. If you are taking the time to make delicious fresh food and dehydrated treats, you want to store them properly; humid air is not your friend.

Jars – mason and AEG jars are an inexpensive tool for sprouting and are handy for soaking nuts and seeds.

Nut cracker – if you are able to get hold of fresh unshelled nuts you will enjoy being able to crack them. It's also a much cheaper way of eating nuts. If you've got kids, this can be a great job for them.

Slice (slab) tin – several recipes call for a slice tin. We use a moveable slice tin so we can adjust the size according to how large we want to make our dish.

Tart (flan) tin – a French fluted tart tin is useful for making our sweet and savoury tarts.

Loose-based cake tin – for our cakes we use loose-based tins; you can also use spring-form cake tins. Raw cakes are very filling, there are no crappy fillers in anything so you only need a small amount – if you don't have a large family to feed you should get smaller tins and halve recipes to match the size of your tin.

Ice cream maker – so not essential – but fun to have in the summer months. Raw ice cream is delicious. After years of eating soy ice cream substitutes as a kid, I find raw coconut and cashew-based ice creams are heaven!

a few tips for using these recipes

Read the recipes thoroughly before you use them. We have tried to give you a good indication of what time and equipment will be required. If there are recipes referred to from other pages, check them out too. Familiarising yourself with the processes required will prevent serving your guests dinner at 10 pm. Eating late is not good for you!

Adjust to fit. We have indicated the number of serves each dish makes, but feel free to adjust them to your own needs. Our cakes and desserts are quite large so, unless it's for a party or you have a large family, by all means reduce the size – raw deserts are very satisfying and you'll only need a small piece. The cheesecakes and many of the desserts can also be frozen and rolled out on a later occasion.

Don't turn off your taste buds. Fruit and vegies vary greatly in flavour and size, so you needn't follow these recipes religiously – use your own judgement too. A good rule of thumb with fruit and vegies is to start small and add more as you see fit. The same goes for sweetening and seasoning: always taste as you go. For example, if you have very sweet fruit and there is another sweetener in the recipe, add it cautiously, tasting all the way.

Substitute ingredients as needed. If you can't get hold of an ingredient or we suggest one that isn't right for your body, find an alternative or use an ingredient that you know works for you.

The dehydration times we indicate are only guides. Your dehydrator, the time of year, humidity and the ingredients will all cause variations. If you are making bread, you want it to be dried but flexible and have some moisture to it. Crackers and activated nuts you want super crispy.

Invest in storage containers. I rant about this one a bit; I can see some of the staff rolling their eyes now. But … it is really important to store your foods in sealed airtight containers in order to keep dehydrated products (which you've waited two days for) crisp and your beautiful home-made nut cheese fresh.

A note about rawness: the recipes in our unbakery collection are raw (meaning nothing is heated above 46°C/115°F), organic and made from plants. We have used the occasional ingredient that is not raw, namely coconut sugar, maple syrup, smoked paprika and toasted sesame oil. You can omit these if you are following a strictly raw diet.

Plan ahead and make sure you shop for ingredients in advance. You will probably be learning new techniques, so having the right ingredients on hand will make that process fun rather than stressful. A good idea is to decide on a few recipes you want to try each week and then organise how to fit the required shopping, soaking, sprouting and dehydrating etcetera into your schedule. The rest is easy.

For greater detail on superfoods, sweeteners, nuts and seeds, supplementation and more, please check out the information page at littlebirdorganics.co.nz

the basics

Raw cuisine works best when built on a solid foundation of 'basics'. These are the things that will turn a bunch of green leaves into an amazing salad, and help you start to replace conventional versions of your favourite things with healthy alternatives that are no less tasty.

Some people think raw cuisine is complicated and time consuming (and, like certain dishes in any cuisine, sometimes they are correct!) But, the basics section is actually just that: basic. These are all easy things to make, and often quick to make as well.

If you can become an expert at preparing the items in this section alone, then the challenge of adding more raw to your diet is already half met.

activated nuts & seeds

Sprouting is a mini miracle – tiny greens grown without soil and maturing in 1–5 days. Sprouts grow all year round with very little effort and provide you with vital, very locally grown nutrition.

Almost any nut, seed, grain or bean can be sprouted (germinated) for a tremendous boost in vitamins, minerals and enzymes. The process of germination breaks down the complex nutritional matrix of the seed (nut, grain or bean) into simpler compounds. The nutrition is then easier to digest, as in this simple form they are more bioavailable for your body to use.

This is a brief guide to getting started with sprouting. If you're totally new to sprouting there are numerous books and online resources with in-depth information to trouble-shoot any questions you might have. The main thing is knowing it's really easy! (And that you need to wash your sprouts regularly.)

getting started

AEG jar or other **wide-mouth jar**

sprouting lid (you can buy them at most health food stores or use a piece of mesh or muslin and a rubber band to form a top cover on your jar.)

or **sprouting bag** (cotton, linen or plastic mesh), instead of the jar-and-lid/muslin combo

fresh filtered or **spring water**

any **seeds**, **nuts**, **beans** or **grains** that take your fancy

seeds

When purchasing seeds – try and always buy organic seed – ensure they are viable and free of chemicals (chemicals can inhibit the sprouting process).
Store seeds in airtight containers in a cool cupboard.

method

Remove stones, sticks, foreign seeds, broken seeds. Rinse the seeds and place in your jar or bag.

Sprouting in jars:
Put seeds in jar, add water to soak and put the mesh lid or cheesecloth on. Soak seeds in filtered water for specified time (see table). When soak is over, invert jar and drain water, then fill with water and drain again to rinse. Tilt jar at a 45° angle and prop in this position on your sink (so that filtered water may drain thoroughly). Keep out of direct sunlight. Rinse seeds in the jar 2–3 times per day until ready (see list), always keeping it angled for drainage.

Sprouting in bags:
Place seeds in an appropriate sprouting bag. Soak seeds and bag in filtered water for specified time (see list). When soak is over, hang up inside a plastic bag (this forms a little greenhouse). Wash the sprouting bag and the sprouts 2–3 times per day until ready (see list). Leave in a light area but out of direct sunlight.

Other sprouting methods:
Seedling trays – these are very good for growing micro greens (use organic potting mix).

Clay saucer – used for mucilaginous seeds like flax, psyllium, chia.

Commercial sprouting tiers – wide variety available. These are generally expensive and a lot of them don't work as well as jars and bags.

When your sprouts are ready to harvest:
Small seeds like alfalfa are ready when the hull begins to break away from the two tiny leaves that unfold. Grains and bean sprouts are ready when the tail is as long as the grain or bean.

use

Once sprouted, rinse seeds and drain well. Store in the refrigerator in a container lined with paper towels. Eat while super fresh – this is what makes sprouts so cool; you have your own little garden in the kitchen to harvest from. If you are only sprouting for a few people make small batches regularly. Sprouts are best eaten within 3–4 days.

Some sprouts like buckwheat may be dehydrated and stored in an airtight container for up to several months.

activating/soaking:

Activating nuts and seeds doesn't go as far as sprouting but it's very beneficial as it helps remove the natural enzyme inhibitors that make them difficult for our bodies to break down and digest.

Different varieties of nuts need different soaking times to activate. Here is a general guideline for common nuts and seeds that require soaking. You don't need to be too pedantic on the times; use them as a minimum guide but remember not to over-soak them, especially in warm climates as they will start to turn.

Wash all your nuts and seeds thoroughly after soaking and drain well. They may be stored in the refrigerator for up to 2–3 days in an airtight container, wash again before use. Or, preferably, dehydrate at 46°C (115°F) for 2 days and store in an airtight container in your pantry for several months.

High fat nuts like Brazil nuts and macadamias benefit some from soaking, but the nutritional difference of soaked vs. unsoaked is small.

soak times for activating

almonds	10–12 hours
cashews	2–4 hours
hazelnuts	4–6 hours
pecans	4–6 hours
pumpkin seeds	4–6 hours
sesame seeds	4–6 hours
sunflower seeds	4–6 hours
walnuts	4–6 hours

sprouts to try at home

Buckwheat – soak 2 hours | sprout 1–2 days
Use hulled buckwheat groats. Wash very thoroughly as they let off a mucilaginous substance. Each time you wash them you want to rinse until they are clean of it.

Millet – soak 8–14 hours | sprout 1–2 days
Unhulled millet sprouts best (but the hull is very crunchy and the sprout is rather bland).

Quinoa – soak 2–4 hours | sprout 12 hours
Rinse seeds multiple times to get off soapy tasting saponin in seed coat.

Rye – soak 8–14 hours | sprout 1–2 days

Mustard – soak 6–14 hours | sprout 1–2 days

Wheat – soak 8–14 hours | sprout 1–2 days
(including kamut and spelt)

Radish – soak 8–14 hours | sprout 1–2 days

Sesame – soak 8–14 hours | sprout 1–2 days
Use unhulled sesame seeds for sprouting; hulled seeds can be soaked to improve flavour and digestibility.

Sunflower – soak 8–14 hours | sprout 18 hours
Use hulled sunflower. Skim off seed skins at end of soaking. If you leave them in, they can spoil your sprouts.

Alfalfa and clover – soak 4–14 hours | sprout 1–1½ days

Chickpea – soak 12–18 hours | sprout 2–3 days

Lentils, brown/green and red –
soak 8–14 hours | sprout 1 day
You must use whole lentils.

Mung beans – soak 8–14 hours | sprout 18 hours–1 day

Adzuki beans – soak 8–14 hours | sprout 1 day

Peas – soak 12–14 hours | sprout 1–2 days
Be sure to buy whole peas, not split peas.

basic nuts & seeds

Keeping a selection of activated nuts and seeds on hand in the refrigerator or pantry gives you the ability to jazz up any salad, dessert or breakfast dish in an instant.

Any good-quality raw nuts will do but I can never resist a bag of fresh whole nuts at a farmers' market. Cracking nuts is a lovely meditative pursuit, similar to shelling peas. It's also something children love doing and a great way to get them interested in the kitchen.

standard sprouting & dehydrating process

Make time: 10 minutes | Soak time: varies | Dehydrating time: 1½–2 days | Equipment required: dehydrator

Soak seeds, sprouts or nuts in filtered water for the specified time (see page 27). Drain and rinse well. Spread seeds onto a dry towel and blot dry.

Spread thinly on dehydrator trays (with dehydrator sheet) and dry at 41°C (106°F) for 1½–2 days (depending on humidity levels). When they are ready they will be very crunchy, almost like a roasted nut. They shouldn't be soft in any way.

If you don't have a dehydrator you could spread onto a baking tray lined with baking paper and put in oven at the lowest possible temperature on a fan bake setting with the door slightly ajar. Check every few hours and remove when they are completely dry and crunchy. (Everyone's oven operates differently. The main points are; use it on a fan bake setting to help air circulate and have the oven at its lowest possible temperature. If you have a kitchen thermometer you can check the temperature – see page 270 for more details.)

Store in an airtight container in a cool cupboard or refrigerator.

Check littlebirdorganics.co.nz for more details and tips on using an oven for dehydrating.

paprika pumpkin seeds

Adding spices to nuts and seeds before drying them leaves you with a very tasty snack. Adding a mixture of seeds like sunflower and sesame to this recipe would make a delicious, nut-free savoury trail mix.

Make time: 10 minutes | Soak time: 4–6 hours | Dehydrating time: 1½–2 days | Equipment required: dehydrator

300 g (10½ oz/2 cups) **pumpkin seeds** (soaked 4–6 hours)

½ tsp **paprika**

¼ tsp **smoked paprika**

2 tbsp **cold-pressed olive oil**

¼ tsp **sea salt**

Drain the soaked pumpkin seeds and rinse thoroughly.

Spread seeds onto a dry towel and blot dry. Place in a bowl and toss with paprika, olive oil and sea salt.

Follow the standard dehydrating process from here on (see above).

Store in an airtight container in a cool cupboard or refrigerator.

caramelised walnuts

We keep these on hand for adding an extra sweet and spicy crunchy note to many of our breakfasts (chia bircher, see page 72) and salads (peach salad, see page 152).

Make time: 10 minutes | Soak time: 4–6 hours | Dehydrating time: 1½–2 days | Equipment required: dehydrator

230 g (2 cups) **walnuts** (soaked 4–6 hours)

50 g (1¾ oz/¼ cup) **coconut sugar**

pinch **sea salt**

optional – ½ tsp **cinnamon**

Drain the soaked walnuts and rinse thoroughly.

Spread nuts onto a dry towel and blot dry. Place in a bowl and toss with the coconut sugar, sea salt and cinnamon (if using).

Follow the standard dehydrating process from here on (see page 28).

caramelised hazelnuts

A sweet and delicious crunchy nut to add to your desserts and salads. We use these to garnish desserts like our hazelnut mousse cups (see page 220).

Make time: 10 minutes | Soak time: 4–6 hours | Dehydrating time: 1½–2 days | Equipment required: dehydrator

270 g (9½ oz/2 cups) **hazelnuts** (soaked 4–6 hours)

115 g (4 oz/⅓ cup) **organic maple syrup**

pinch **sea salt**

Drain the soaked hazelnuts and rinse thoroughly.

Spread nuts onto a dry towel and blot dry. Place in a bowl and toss with the maple syrup and sea salt.

Follow the standard dehydrating process from here on (see page 28).

spiced cashews

Originally devised for our pad thai recipe, we also use these on many of our other Southeast Asian dishes for an extra flavour hit.

Make time: 10 minutes | Soak time: 4–6 hours | Dehydrating time: 1½–2 days | Equipment required: dehydrator

310 g (11 oz/2 cups) **cashews** or **cashew pieces** (soaked 2–4 hours)

50 g (1¾ oz/¼ cup) **coconut sugar**

¾ tsp **chilli powder**

1 tsp **kaffir lime powder** or **lime zest**

½ tsp **sea salt**

Drain the soaked cashews and rinse thoroughly.

Spread nuts onto a dry towel and blot dry. Place in a bowl and toss with the coconut sugar, chilli powder, lime and sea salt.

Follow the standard dehydrating process from here on (see page 28).

milks

Making dairy-free milks from nuts and seeds is so quick and easy. If you keep soaked/activated nuts in the refrigerator, it only takes a few minutes to make up a litre (35 fl oz/4 cups) of milk – much easier than popping down to the store when you've run out.

Activating nuts and seeds: soak or sprout your nuts and seeds in order to get the best out of them. Just note they have different soaking times (see page 27). This starts the sprouting process and enables most of the phytates, enzyme inhibitors and complex starches to be broken down, making it easier for you to absorb the goodness.

We use nut milk in many ways – on our cereal, in our smoothies, flavoured milks and many of our amazing desserts. We also use the leftover pulp in recipes like chocolate layer cake (see page 252) so don't throw the nut pulp away if you're planning on working your way through the book.

nut milk

Almond milk is our kitchen's staple milk. We use it in many of our drinks and dessert recipes; almonds are one of the only alkalising nuts and a great source of vitamin E, which helps your skin look lovely.

If you don't have almonds, you can substitute any of your favourite nuts or seeds. Hazelnuts, Brazil nuts, cashews and macadamia nuts can be substituted in this recipe.

Make time: 5 minutes | Soak time: 12 hours | Makes: 550 ml (19 fl oz) | Equipment required: blender

110 g (3¼ oz/⅔ cup) **almonds** (soaked 12 hours) or 4 tbsp **almond butter** (see page 78)

500 ml (17 fl oz/2 cups) **filtered water**

pinch **vanilla bean powder** or ½ tsp **vanilla extract**

pinch **sea salt**

optional extra if you like it sweet
– 1 tsp **sweetener** (maple syrup, raw agave, coconut crystals, raw honey) or 1 **pitted date**

optional extra – ¼ tsp **sunflower lecithin** or **non–GMO soy lecithin** to help emulsify and not let the milk separate over time (if it separates just shake the bottle until it remixes before using)

Drain the soaked almonds and rinse thoroughly, then blend all ingredients on high in a blender for 1–2 minutes until well combined.

Strain through a fine cheesecloth/muslin or a nut milk bag. The result should be a lovely, smooth milk that doesn't contain any grainy pieces. Strain again or use a finer weave cloth if this has happened.

Place in a sealed jar or bottle. Will keep in the refrigerator for 2–3 days.

Keep the leftover nut pulp from your nut milks to use in some of our dessert and cake recipes, or place in your dehydrator at 41°C (106°F) to make nut flour.

You can add more filtered water to make your milk thinner or more nuts to make it more like a cream.

You can also make milks with nut butters. Blending a few spoonfuls of raw almond or cashew butter with filtered water is an effective timesaver, although nothing compares to the rich creaminess of lovingly prepared fresh milk.

coconut milk (nut free)

Our other staple milk, used in many recipes we want to keep nut free. It has a delicious flavour that works well in savoury and sweet recipes.

Make time: 5 minutes | Makes: 550 ml (19 fl oz) | Equipment required: blender

115 g (4 oz/1¼ cups) **desiccated (shredded) coconut**

1 tsp **coconut butter**

pinch **vanilla bean powder** or ½ tsp **vanilla extract**

pinch **sea salt**

optional extra if you like it sweet
– 1 tsp **sweetener** (maple syrup, raw agave, coconut crystals, raw honey) or 1 **pitted date**

Soak desiccated coconut in 625 ml (21½ fl oz/2½ cups) of filtered water for 1 hour.

Blend all ingredients on high in a blender for 1–2 minutes until well combined.

Strain through a fine cheesecloth/muslin or a nut milk bag. The result should be a lovely, smooth milk that doesn't contain any grainy pieces. Strain again or use a finer weave cloth if this has happened.

Place in a sealed jar or bottle. Will keep in the refrigerator 2–3 days. Shake well before using. Some of it will solidify in the refrigerator, but a really good shake and leaving it out of the refrigerator for 10 minutes before using will bring it back together.

You can add more filtered water to make your milk thinner or more coconut to make it more like a cream.

hemp milk (nut free)

Hemp is one of the most amazing foods. It's high in protein and contains all ten essential amino acids (protein building blocks that your body doesn't make itself and must get from the food it consumes). Hemp is up there with chia seeds and leafy greens as a superfood that you should be getting in your diet most days.

Hemp milk by itself is not as delicious as the nut milks or coconut milk. But it's one that works well underneath other flavours and as a base for smoothies.

If I'm making hemp milk for a cereal or drinking milk, I mix it with almonds or coconut to make the flavour less dominant. Hemp milk also benefits from a small amount of sweetener, so if you're not blending it with another milk base add a teaspoon of sweetener or a date.

Make time: 5 minutes | Makes: 500 ml (17 fl oz/2 cups) | Equipment required: blender

60 g (2¼ oz/½ cup) **hemp seeds**

500 ml (17 fl oz/2 cups) **filtered water**

pinch **vanilla bean** or ½ tsp **vanilla extract**

pinch **sea salt**

optional extra if you like it sweet
– 1 tsp **sweetener** (maple syrup, raw agave, coconut crystals, raw honey) or 1 **pitted date**

Blend all ingredients on high in a blender for 1–2 minutes until well combined.

Strain through a fine cheesecloth/muslin or a nut milk bag. The result should be a lovely smooth milk that doesn't contain any grainy pieces. If this has happened strain again or use a finer weave cloth.

Place in a sealed jar or bottle. Will keep in the refrigerator for 2–3 days.

You can add more filtered water to make your milk thinner, although hemp milk is thinner than other milk recipes.

irish moss paste

Irish moss is used in recipes as a gelling agent. It's a wonderful food in its raw form (not the heavily processed and fractionated form that is used in conventional ice creams and many sauces) and has many health-building properties. It is an excellent source of minerals, helping give strength to connective tissues including hair, skin and nails.

Make time: 20 minutes | Soak time: 12–14 hours | Makes: 3 cups | Equipment required: blender

50 g (1¾ oz/¾ cup) **irish moss**

185 ml (6 fl oz/¾ cup) **filtered water**

Soak Irish moss overnight in a bowl of water.

Pick out any brown parts (for visual affect only) and rinse very well. Irish moss is a sea vegetable and may taste a little like the ocean when not well washed.

Blend the hydrated (soaked) moss with the water in a high-speed blender, then place in bowl in refrigerator to gel.

Will keep in the refrigerator for 1 week.

fresh young coconuts

Coconuts! These little guys offer us so much. Their water is filled with electrolytes and is super hydrating. You can drink it straight or in smoothies or cocktails; you can even ferment it. Then scoop out the flesh and you're off and running again. We use it to make noodles, 'bacon', yoghurt, cream and milk, and it features regularly in our desserts.

Equipment required: small axe (preferable) or large knife, chopping block

fresh young coconuts – these ones have the pale husks (the brown husk versions have thick dried flesh and don't contain water). Avoid ones which appear to be too perfect in their blonde colouration (especially if they have been pre-packaged) as these have more than likely been bleached, and a bleach bath doesn't bode well for the purity of the contents!

Start with a small axe and a chopping block. Have a bowl on hand for the water. You can use a large knife, but don't use a precious one, as you can damage the blade.

Coconuts have a 'crown' and you should be able to pop the top off quite easily. The crown is on the end of the coconut that wasn't attached to the tree. For the ones purchased from a store, this end is usually the pointy end.

Use the heel of the axe (pointy edge of the blade closest to the handle) or knife and strike with a medium pressure – you are aiming to work the crown off gradually rather than in one chop! Work your way around the crown spiking your axe into the nut until the crown is free enough to fold over.

Pour out the water into a bowl. Scoop the flesh out with a spoon and scrape the flesh clean with a knife before using.

coconut yoghurt

A must-have ingredient in the refrigerator, this is an everyday staple. Fermented, living probiotic foods are extremely beneficial for your health; coconut yoghurt is the perfect way to introduce them to your diet in a delectable form.

Make time: 10 minutes | Fermenting time: 7–12 hours | Equipment required: blender

320 g (11¼ oz/2 cups) **young coconut flesh**, scooped and washed clean
(approximately 2 coconuts)

185 ml (6 fl oz/¾ cup) **coconut water**
or **filtered water**
(If your coconut meat is thick then you will need to add more filtered water to the blend.)

30 ml (1 fl oz) **coconut kefir**
or 3 capsules of **dairy-free probiotics**

Blend the coconut flesh with the coconut water or water. Blend until the coconut flesh is smooth and creamy like the texture of runny custard. Mix in the coconut kefir or probiotics; kefir makes a more alive yoghurt with a tarter taste so if you have it available it is preferable to use.

Pour contents of your blender into a clean glass bowl or jar. If using a jar make sure the mix only comes to about half way, as it will expand while fermenting.

Cover the bowl or jar with a lid, place in a warm place like a hot water cupboard or next to your dehydrator for the yoghurt to culture overnight, but no more than 12 hours. In warmer months you should only leave to culture for a maximum of 7–8 hours at room temperature. Keeps in the refrigerator for 4–5 days.

The yoghurt should be white. If it turns pink, discard it.

coconut bacon

You think you've heard it all but then along comes a dish like coconut bacon. It sounds a bit ridiculous but it's delicious as a snack and adds a lovely savoury element to many of our dishes.

I've never been a fan of fake meats. They are so often laden with chemicals and preservatives that for me defeat the purpose of eating a plant-based diet. This bacon is the perfect antidote, using just a few simple ingredients.

Prep time: 15 minutes | Dehydrating time: overnight | Makes: 1 cup | Equipment required: dehydrator

320 g (11¼ oz/2 cups) **young coconut flesh** (approximately 2 coconuts)

60 ml (2 fl oz/¼ cup) **tamari**

2 tbsp **organic maple syrup** or **coconut sugar**

2 drops **liquid smoke** (make sure they are actual drops; this stuff is strong)

pinch **sea salt**

Ideally the flesh will be soft but still have some firmness to it. If it's too thick you can still use it, you will just need to slice it thinly. Slice horizontally to get the thinner pieces around 3 mm (⅛ in) thick, it will taste more 'coconutty' if the meat is thick. If it's too thin you might just need to eat it or find another use for it.

Scoop the flesh out of the coconut and clean any remaining husk off it with a sharp knife. Give it a quick rinse before use.

Slice the coconut meat into 2 cm by 5–6 cm (¾ in x 2–2½ in) strips as best you can and then place in a bowl with all the other ingredients and leave to marinate for 20 minutes.

Place the coconut on some baking paper or a dehydrator sheet, pour over the rest of the marinade and place in a dehydrator overnight for approximately 12 hours.

You can store the bacon in the refrigerator for up to 3 weeks.

caramelised shallots

Used on pizzas, pastas, salads and sandwiches, caramelised onions lend a savoury sweet touch of goodness. They go especially well with dishes containing mushrooms and olives.

Prep time: 10 minutes | Soak time: 3–4 hours | Dehydrating time: 4–5 hours | Makes: ¾ cup | Equipment required: dehydrator, mandoline

235 g (4¾ oz/¾ cup) **pitted dates**

1 tbsp **tamari**

2 tbsp **cold-pressed olive oil**

¼ tsp **sea salt**

4–5 **shallots**

Soak the dates in water for 3–4 hours or until soft, strain off the water and blend with all the other ingredients except the shallots in a high-speed blender until smooth.

Thinly slice the shallots lengthways with a mandoline or a knife. Place in a bowl of filtered water for ½ an hour. Then rinse and drain.

In a bowl, mix the date mixture with the shallots until they are thoroughly covered in the mixture.

Place on a dehydrator sheet and dehydrate for 4–5 hours at 46°C (115°F) until soft and sticky.

Store in the refrigerator for up to 1 week.

bagels & seeded breads

In the cafés we unbake all sorts of breads. This versatile one is used as a base for a range of unbakery staples including bagels, pizza bases and seeded breads.

Breads are an established part of our Western diet, and a bit of a comfort food at times. Eating raw doesn't mean giving up on bread. These raw breads are really useful to have on hand for a quick snack, or to bulk up that salad into a heavier meal.

bagel variation

Make time: 1 hour | Soak time: 12 hours | Dehydrating time: 12–16 hours | Makes: 6 bagels |
Equipment required: blender, dehydrator, food processor

160 g (1 cup) **almonds** (soaked 10–12 hours)

155 g (1 cup) **cashews** (soaked 2–4 hours)

85 g (3 oz/½ cup) **sultanas (golden raisins)** (soaked 2–4 hours)

135 g (4¾ oz/¾ cup) **whole golden flax seeds**

80 g (2¾ oz/1 cup) **psyllium husk**

1 **garlic clove**

1 tbsp **lemon juice**

1 tbsp chopped **rosemary**

40 g (1½ oz) **young coconut flesh**

½ tsp **sea salt**

filtered water

cold-pressed olive oil

Drain the soaked nuts and rinse thoroughly.

In a blender, process the whole golden flax seeds into flour.

In a food processor, blend the almonds, cashews and sultanas into a paste adding water as needed to achieve this.

Add the flax seed, psyllium, garlic, lemon, rosemary, coconut flesh and sea salt to the food processor along with 500 ml (17 fl oz/2 cups) of water and blend until combined.

Shape into 6 bagels 9–10 cm (3½–4 in) round, and brush with some olive oil before drying to stop them from cracking.

Place on a mesh sheet and dehydrate at 46°C (115°F) for approximately 12–16 hours.

You can store in the refrigerator for 2–3 days. Slice in half and warm in a dehydrator before using.

pizza variation

Make time: 1 hour | Soak time: 12 hours | Dehydrating time: 10–12 hours | Makes: 5 pizzas |
Equipment required: blender, dehydrator, food processor

Follow the basic instructions for the bagel bread recipe and make the following adjustments:

Replace the rosemary with oregano.

Shape into 5 thin pizza bases, 15 cm (6 in) round, and brush with olive oil.

Place in a dehydrator on the mesh sheets and dehydrate at 46°C (115°F) for approximately 10–12 hours.

You can store in the refrigerator for 2–3 days. Warm in a dehydrator before using.

seeded fennel & carrot bread variation

Make time: 1 hour | Soak time: 12 hours | Dehydrating time: 10–12 hours | Makes: 2 loaves | Equipment required: blender, dehydrator, food processor

Follow the basic instructions for the bagel bread recipe and make the following adjustments:

Adjust the sultanas (golden raisins) to 60 g (2¼ oz/⅓ cup).

Add 1½ peeled and roughly chopped carrots to the food processor along with the almonds, cashews and sultanas.

Soak 50 g (1¾ oz/⅓ cup) pumpkin seeds and 55 g (2 oz/⅓ cup) sunflower seeds for 4–6 hours. Rinse thoroughly. Add to the mixture after you have finished the food processor steps, along with ½ teaspoon of fennel seeds or caraway (optional).

Shape into 2 loaves, 18 x 10 cm (7 x 4 in) and 7 cm (2¾ in) high.

Place on a mesh sheet and dehydrate at 46°C (115°F) for approximately 14–18 hours.

You can store in the refrigerator for 2–3 days, slice into 8 mm (⅜ in) slices and warm in a dehydrator before using.

caramelised onion & zucchini flat bread

Onion bread is one of the most popular raw foods bread recipes and for good reason; it's a wonderful savoury bread with loads of flavour. In the cafés we serve it as a side with salads and make delicious sandwiches out of it.

I like the addition of zucchini (courgette) for some extra green vegetables, but the variations without work really well if zucchini are not in season. The addition of walnuts makes a beautiful nutty tasting bread perfect for serving on cheese boards.

Make time: 20 minutes | Soak time: 4–6 hours | Dehydrating time: 16–18 hours | Makes: 16 pieces | Equipment required: blender, dehydrator, food processor

3 large **onions**

1 **zucchini** (courgette)

60 g (2¼ oz/⅓ cup) **whole golden flax seed**

120 g (4¼ oz/¾ cup) **sunflower seeds** (soaked 4–6 hours)

4 tbsp **tamari**

5 tbsp **cold-pressed olive oil**

80 g (2¾ oz/⅓ cup) **date paste** (see following recipe)

1 tbsp chopped **rosemary**

1 tbsp **lemon juice**

60 ml (2 fl oz/¼ cup) **filtered water**

pinch **sea salt** (add to taste)

optional – 1 tbsp **coconut yoghurt** (see page 34)

Peel and thinly slice the onions. We do this using a slicing attachment on the food processor; you can also slice lengthways with a knife by hand. Grate the zucchini and place in a bowl with the onions.

Make the whole flax into a flour in your blender and set aside.

Drain the soaked sunflower seeds and rinse thoroughly. Process in your food processor until finely ground; a little texture is ideal but no chunky bits.

Place the rest of the ingredients together into the bowl with the zucchini and onions; mix together by hand. Spread batter out to approximately 6 mm (¼ in) thick over 2 dehydrator sheets (see page 270).

Place in the dehydrator at 46°C (115°F) for 12 hours. Take the bread out and flip onto a mesh sheet and dry for another 4–6 hours or until dry but still pliable.

Place onto a board and cut into 8 pieces per sheet.

Store in the refrigerator in an airtight container for up to 1½ weeks.

Onion Bread Variation
To make onion bread, omit the zucchini and the lemon juice. You will need to add an extra few tablespoons of water to the mixture.

Walnut and Onion Bread Variation
To make walnut and onion bread, omit the zucchini and the lemon juice. Add 120 g (4¼ oz/½ cup) of soaked walnuts (6–8 hours) roughly ground up in a food processor. You will also need to add an extra few tablespoons of water to the mixture.

date paste

Make time: 5 minutes | Soak time: 12 hours | Makes: 1 cup | Equipment required: blender

160 g (1 cup) **pitted dates** (soaked overnight)

Strain and blend the dates into a paste with a little of the soaking water (aim for consistency of tomato paste (concentrated purée)).

Store in an airtight container in the refrigerator for 5–6 days.

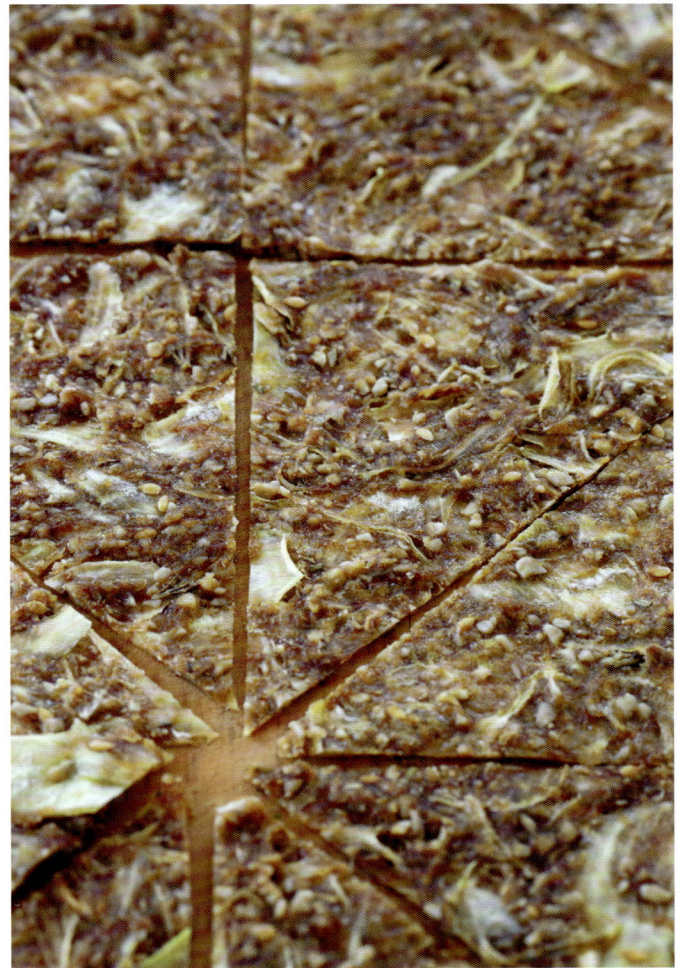

nut cheeses

Cultured nut cheese is well worth the effort. When we used to sell our cheese at the morning market, people couldn't get enough of it; no matter how many we made, we would sell out each day. So many people avoid dairy products for various reasons and the thing they miss most is nearly always cheese! Nut cheeses are too delicious to be solely the domain of those avoiding dairy. Our cheeses are fit for any cheese board.

Culturing the nuts brings out their goodness and provides you with wonderful living probiotics.

macadamia & cashew cultured nut cheese

Make time: 30 minutes | Soak time: 4–6 hours | Culturing time: 16–24 hours | Dehydrating time: 16–18 hours | Makes: 2 rounds of cheese | Equipment required: dehydrator, food processor

155 g (1 cup) **macadamia nuts** (soaked 4–6 hours)

155 g (1 cup) **cashews** (soaked 2–4 hours)

250 ml (9 fl oz/1 cup) **filtered water**

2 **probiotic capsules**
or 1 tsp **dairy-free probiotic powder**

½ tsp **sea salt**

2 tsp **nutritional yeast**

Drain the soaked nuts and rinse thoroughly. Place in a food processor with the water. Blend until totally smooth; you may need to do this for a minute at a time so you don't overheat the mixture. There should be no lumps or graininess in the mixture at all. Stir in probiotic powder at the end.

Line a sieve with cheesecloth or use a nut milk bag and place over a bowl. Place the nut mixture into the cloth – fold cheesecloth over the top of the mixture ensuring that it is well wrapped in – you need to be able to place some weight on top. If using a nut milk bag, form a twist in the top to seal it in tightly. Take a small flat plate and place on top of the mixture, then add some weight – at home I use a pestle and mortar. The weight should not be so heavy that the cheese pushes through the cloth. You want only the water to come out of the mixture.

Leave at room temperature to culture for 16–24 hours. The time it takes will depend on the temperature of your room – if you live in a warm climate it will culture faster than in a colder climate. The mixture is ready when there is some activity in it, there should be some fluffiness in the centre of the mix and it should no longer taste just of puréed nuts.

Transfer to a bowl and stir in sea salt and nutritional yeast.

Shape into 2 rounds approximately 3 cm (¼ in) high and 7 cm (2¾ in) wide, (of course you can make smaller or larger ones as well).

Place in a dehydrator for 16–18 hours at 41°C (106°F) to form a rind. The culture and flavour continues to develop while drying.

Once dried, wrap with baking paper and store in an airtight container in the refrigerator for up to 1 week.

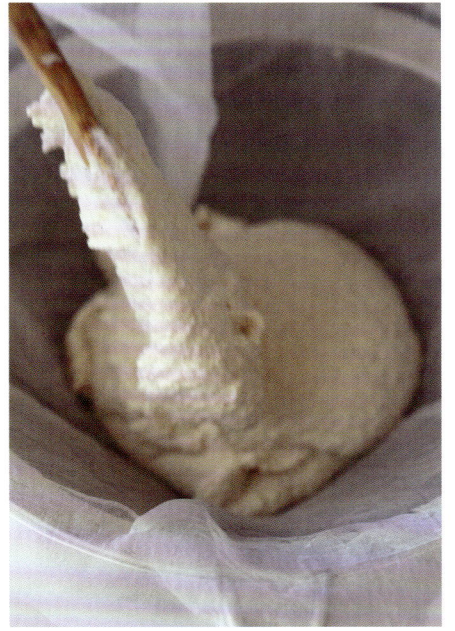

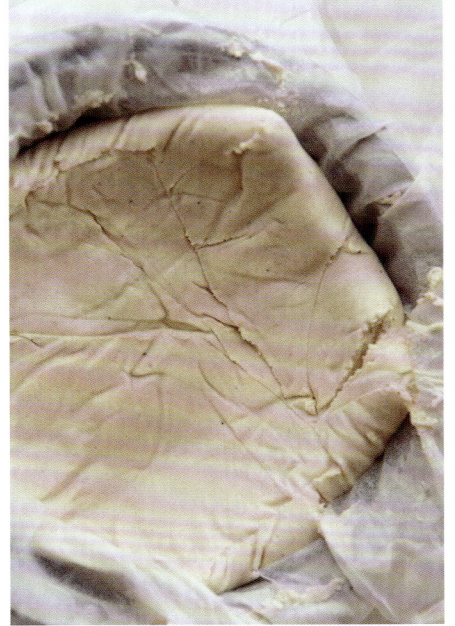

macadamia & cashew herb cheese

This is a fresh herbed cheese similar in flavour to a herbed Boursin™ cheese. You can use it in lots of ways: as a dip, spread, in ravioli and in our zucchini cannelloni (see page 188).

Make time: 20 minutes | Soak time: 2–4 hours | Equipment required: blender or food processor

155 g (1 cup) **cashews** (soaked 2–4 hours)

75 g (½ cup) **macadamia nuts** (soaked 2–4 hours)

125 ml (4 fl oz/½ cup) **filtered water**

60 ml (2 fl oz/¼ cup) **lemon juice**

2 tsp **nutritional yeast**

1 tbsp finely chopped **chives**

1 tbsp finely chopped **tarragon**

1 tbsp finely chopped **parsley**

1 tbsp finely diced **shallot**

1 tbsp finely chopped **chervil**

⅓ tsp **sea salt**

Drain the soaked nuts and rinse thoroughly. Place in a food processor (you could use a blender but this will require more water to get it moving and create a runnier cheese) with the water, lemon juice and nutritional yeast and mix until smooth. Finely chop all the herbs and fold in, add sea salt.

Add any additional sea salt and cracked pepper to taste.

Will keep in the refrigerator for 3–4 days.

macadamia feta

This has a lighter, fresher taste than our parmesan. We like to sprinkle it over salads and use it as a crumble on many of our dishes.

Make time: 10 minutes | Soak time: 2–4 hours | Dehydrating time: 12–16 hours |
Equipment required: blender, dehydrator

230 g (1½ cups) **macadamia nuts** (soaked 2–4 hours)

170 ml (5½ fl oz/⅔ cup) **filtered water**

80 ml (2½ fl oz/⅓ cup) freshly squeezed **lemon juice**

2 tsp **nutritional yeast**

½ tsp **sea salt**

Drain the soaked macadamia nuts and rinse thoroughly. Put all ingredients in a high-speed blender (for a small amount like this you could also use a stick blender or the spice mill attachment on a food processor).

Blend on high until smooth, scraping down the sides as necessary (a little texture is fine so don't worry if you can't get it super-smooth).

Add more sea salt or lemon juice to taste; you want it to have the taste of a fresh cheese with a hint of citrus and saltiness to it – remember the flavour will intensify as it dries.

Spread mixture approximately 4 mm (³⁄₁₆ in) thick on a dehydrator sheet and place in the dehydrator overnight at 41°C (106°F) for around 12–16 hours. There should be no wet patches in it.

Peel cheese from sheet and break into pieces. Store in an airtight container in the refrigerator for several weeks.

cashew parmesan

This raw cheese is great sprinkled over salads and many other raw or cooked dishes in place of parmesan.

Make time: 10 minutes | Soak time: 2–4 hours | Dehydrating time: 12–16 hours |
Equipment required: blender, dehydrator

235 g (8½ oz/1½ cups) **cashews** or **pine nuts**
(soaked 2–4 hours)

125 ml (4 fl oz/½ cup) **filtered water**

4 tbsp freshly squeezed **lemon juice**

2 tbsp **nutritional yeast**

¾ tsp **sea salt**

Drain the soaked nuts and rinse thoroughly.

Put all ingredients in a high-speed blender (for a small amount like this you could also use a stick blender or the spice mill attachment on a food processor).

Blend on high until smooth, scraping down the sides as necessary (a little texture is fine so don't worry if you can't get it super-smooth).

Add more sea salt or lemon juice to taste; you want it to have a mild cheesiness because the flavour will intensify as it dries.

Spread mixture thinly on a dehydrator sheet and place in the dehydrator overnight at 41°C (106°F). Peel cheese from sheet and break into pieces, store in an airtight container in the refrigerator for several weeks.

sauces

A rich, creamy sauce can add a lot to a dish, and it is totally possible to create these without using dairy. Nuts, avocado, even coconut can easily be used instead, and will make sauces that often keep longer than a dairy-based version might. These are a few of our favourites, which we will use throughout the book, but they can be made by themselves and used on whatever you like.

cashew mayonnaise/aioli

When you think about raw food, you don't often consider mayonnaise or aioli, but this recipe is seriously good. Try using it instead of ordinary aioli or mayonnaise, whether the dishes are raw or not.

You can use cashews or avocado as the base – they are both great, although the cashew base tastes more like traditional aioli.

Soak time: 2–4 hours | Makes: 1½ cups | Equipment required: blender

155 g (1 cup) **cashews** (soaked 2–4 hours)
or **avocado**

3 tbsp **lemon juice**

1 tbsp **apple cider vinegar**

½ tsp **sea salt**

2 crushed **garlic cloves**

½ **shallot**

125 ml (4 fl oz/½ cup) **filtered water**
(add as needed)

5 tbsp **cold-pressed olive oil**

1 tsp **wholegrain organic mustard**

Drain the soaked cashews and rinse thoroughly.

Place all ingredients except the olive oil and mustard in a high-power blender – blend until creamy and smooth. With the blender running slowly, pour in the olive oil. Now add the mustard, pulse until incorporated into the aioli.

If you want to make more of a mayonnaise, add a little more water and olive oil, this creates a more fluid mix.

Aioli flavour ideas – omit the mustard and add a pinch of saffron or 1 teaspoon of preserved lemon for a more Middle Eastern touch, or 1 teaspoon of wasabi to give it a Japanese one.

sour cream

A simple sour cream recipe that can be used as a condiment with many dishes, raw or otherwise.

Soak time: 2–4 hours | Makes: 1½ cups | Equipment required: blender

155 g (1 cup) **cashews** (soaked 2–4 hours)

60 ml (2 fl oz/¼ cup) **filtered water**

1 tsp **cold-pressed olive oil**

60 ml (2 fl oz/¼ cup) **lemon juice**

1 tbsp **lime juice**

½ tsp **sea salt**

Drain the soaked cashews and rinse thoroughly.

Blend all ingredients in a blender until completely smooth – you can add a little more water if needed. You can also sieve the mixture if you find your blender is not making it smooth enough.

Add extra sea salt and lemon or lime juice to achieve a sour cream flavour. Chill in the refrigerator or freezer before using.

sweet soy sauce

Dehydrating time: 12–16 hours | Makes: ¾ cup | Equipment required: dehydrator

200 g (7 oz/1 cup) **coconut sugar**

80 ml (2 ½ fl oz/⅓ cup) **tamari**

Place ingredients in a heatproof bowl and stir together. Place the bowl in a dehydrator for 12–16 hours at 46°C (115°F). Stir the mixture to see if it's ready; it should have a consistency similar to molasses. Store in a sealed jar in the pantry for up to 1 month.

alfredo sauce

This raw alfredo sauce has a lovely, creamy texture like a traditional alfredo sauce. It would also work great on non-raw dishes.

Soak time: 2–4 hours | Makes: 1½ cups | Equipment required: blender

155 g (1 cup) **cashews** (soaked 2–4 hours)

125 ml (4 fl oz/½ cup) **filtered water**

½ tsp **sea salt**

½ crushed **garlic clove**

¼ **shallot**

freshly cracked pepper

optional – ¼ tsp **nutritional yeast**

Drain the soaked cashews and rinse thoroughly.

Place all the ingredients in a high-power blender – blend until creamy and smooth. Add more water as needed.

This recipe works really well with zucchini (courgette) pasta or to use for making creamy mushrooms for a hearty brunch meal.

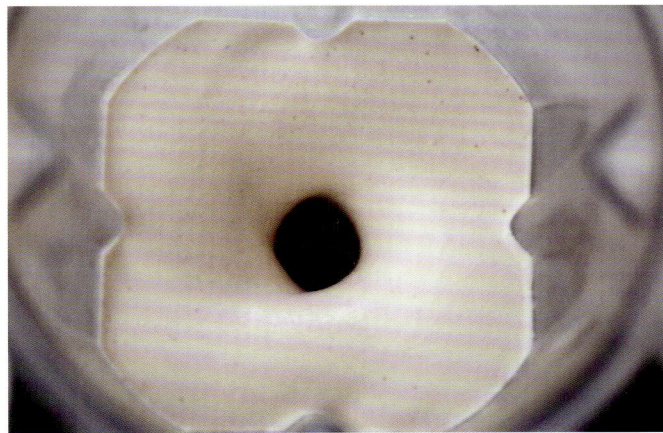

dressings

Having some good dressings on hand is essential when you want to make quick, easy salads. Our chef Xander is renowned for his dressing prowess. The recipes here are an accumulation of his years of experience in many great kitchens in New Zealand and the United States.

All of these recipes make around 2 cups of dressing; adjust the recipes to quantities that suit your household needs.

caesar dressing

Soak time: 2–4 hours | Makes: 625 ml (21½ fl oz/2½ cups) | Equipment required: blender

50 g (1¾ oz/⅓ cup) **cashews** (soaked 2–4 hours)

¼ cup **macadamia and cashew cheese** (see page 42)

2 **pitted dates**

1 tsp **korengo flakes** or finely chopped **nori sheet**

1 heaped tsp **capers**, plus juices

⅓ **shallot**

1 **garlic clove**

1 tbsp **tamari**

3 tbsp **white wine vinegar**

4 tbsp **lemon juice**

125 ml (4 fl oz/½ cup) **filtered water**

60 ml (2 fl oz/¼ cup) **cold-pressed olive oil**

¼ tsp **sea salt**

½ tsp **freshly cracked black pepper**

Drain the soaked cashews and rinse thoroughly, combine all ingredients in a blender. Blend until smooth, around 1 minute, adding more water as needed if the dressing is too thick. Add more sea salt and pepper to taste.

Store in the refrigerator for 3–4 days.

Traditional caesar uses anchovies – we are using the sea vegetables, shallots and tamari to create a similar flavour.

red wine vinaigrette

Makes: 625 ml (21½ fl oz/2½ cups) | Equipment required: blender

1 small **garlic clove**

1 large **shallot**

185 ml (6 fl oz/¾ cup) **red wine vinegar**

60 ml (2 fl oz/¼ cup) **filtered water**

5 **pitted dates**

1½ tbsp **sea salt**

1 tbsp **coconut sugar**

½ tsp **fresh thyme**

½ tsp **fresh oregano**

375 ml (13 fl oz/1½ cups) **cold-pressed olive oil**

Peel the garlic and shallot and roughly chop. Combine all ingredients except oil in a blender and blend on high for 30 seconds.

Turn speed down to medium and slowly drizzle in the olive oil.

Use immediately or keep in the refrigerator for 2–3 weeks.

balsamic vinaigrette

Makes: 625 ml (21½ fl oz/2½ cups) | Equipment required: blender

1 small **garlic clove**

½ medium **shallot**

80 ml (2½ fl oz/⅓ cup) **filtered water**

170 ml (5½ fl oz/⅔ cup) **balsamic vinegar**

2½ tbsp **coconut sugar** or **raw honey**

2 tbsp **dijon mustard**

½ tsp **paprika**

1 tbsp **sea salt**

375 ml (13 fl oz/1½ cups) **cold-pressed olive oil**

½ tsp finely chopped **parsley**

½ tsp finely chopped **oregano**

½ tsp finely chopped **basil**

Peel the garlic and shallot and roughly chop. Combine all ingredients except for the oil and herbs in a blender and blend on high for 30 seconds.

Turn speed down to medium and slowly pour in the oil until fully emulsified. Remove from the blender and stir in chopped herbs.

Use immediately or keep in the refrigerator for 2–3 weeks.

garlic tahini dressing

Makes: 500 ml (17 fl oz/2 cups) | Equipment required: blender

80 ml (2½ fl oz/⅓ cup) **filtered water**

135 g (4¾ oz/½ cup) **raw tahini** (use regular if not available)

60 ml (2 fl oz/¼ cup) **apple cider vinegar**

2 tbsp **tamari**

2 tbsp **lemon juice**

½ tbsp **sea salt**

1 medium **garlic clove**

1 tbsp **white sesame seeds**

170 ml (5½ fl oz/⅔ cup) **cold-pressed olive oil**

1 tbsp finely chopped **parsley**

1 tbsp finely chopped **chives**

Combine all ingredients except for the oil, parsley and chives in a blender and blend on high for 30 seconds until smooth.

Turn blender down to medium and slowly pour in the olive oil until fully incorporated. Remove dressing from blender and fold in parsley and chives.

Use immediately or keep in the refrigerator for 2–3 weeks.

preserved lemon dressing

Makes: 625 ml (21½ fl oz/2½ cups) | Equipment required: blender

2 deseeded **preserved lemons** (see page 56)

125 ml (4 fl oz/½ cup) **filtered water**

185 ml (6 fl oz/¾ cup) **lemon juice**

1 large peeled **shallot**

1 tsp **fresh oregano**

250 ml (9 fl oz/1 cup) **cold-pressed olive oil**

Combine everything except oil in a blender on high for 30 seconds or until mixed well.

Turn speed down to medium and drizzle in oil until fully emulsified.

Use immediately or keep in the refrigerator for 2–3 weeks.

tacos & corn chips

Soft taco shells and crispy corn chips made from beautiful, fresh corn are a great alternative to conventional versions, with no nasty oils. I've been known to eat a whole tray of these chips in one sitting. To make them your own you can add a good taco seasoning or chilli and lime to the mixture, or sprinkle it over the top when they are dried.

Make time: 20 minutes | Dehydrating time: 8–10 hours | Makes: 18 taco shells |
Equipment required: dehydrator, food processor

600 g (1 lb 5 oz/3 cups) **fresh corn**
or **frozen** (if out of season)

155 g (1 cup) roughly chopped **onion**

135 g (4¾ oz/¾ cup) finely ground **flax seed meal**
(use ground flax seed or grind some whole flax
seeds yourself in a coffee grinder)

250 ml (9 fl oz/1 cup) **filtered water**

1 tbsp **lemon juice** or **lime juice**

1 tsp **sea salt**

To prepare tacos:
Place the corn and onion in the food processor. Process until almost smooth – a little texture is ideal. Add the remaining ingredients and process in your food processor until completely mixed together. Be careful not to over-blend.

Spread the mixture out onto 2 dehydrator sheets until approximately 3 mm (⅛ in) thick, trying to get it as even as possible.

Dehydrate at 41°C (106°F) for 4 hours then flip the sheets over and continue drying for another 4–6 hours. Remember, dehydrating is an art and depends on lots of variables so be attentive when getting to know a new recipe – if you live in a very dry climate your drying times will be reduced and equally if you live in a tropical humid climate it can take a lot longer for things to dry.

The tacos are ready when they are dry but still flexible – there shouldn't be any crunchy parts. Take the sheets out of the dehydrator and place on a board or bench you can cut on. Cut 9 circles per dehydrator tray. We use a 12 cm (4½ in) cutting circle but you could use a small plate or stencil and cut around it with a knife. The scraps from the tacos we put back in the dehydrator to make chips.

If you have over dehydrated don't worry – there are a few ways of saving them. Firstly, try putting them in the refrigerator overnight – they will soften in there. If they are really dry you can spray with some water and rehydrate the mixture and start drying again.

Tacos keep in the refrigerator for up to 1 week in an airtight container.

To prepare corn chips:
Follow the taco shell recipe above. Spread the mixture slightly thicker on the trays – approximately 4 mm (³⁄₁₆ in).

When they are dry and still flexible, cut into triangular chips instead of circles. Place them back in the dehydrator at 46°C (115°F) for 12 hours or until very crisp. Sprinkle with a little sea salt or Mexican seasoning. We sprinkle ours with some dehydrated lime, chilli powder and sea salt.

beetroot, rosemary & seeds crackers

The subtle flavour of these crackers makes them the perfect base for piled-on flavours or for dipping into delicious spreads such as almond hummus (see page 139). For a punchier flavour, you could add more herbs and some of your favourite spices to the mix.

Make time: 30 minutes | Soak time: 4–6 hours | Dehydrating time: 17–21 hours |
Equipment required: blender, dehydrator, food processor

150 g (5½ oz/1 cup) **pumpkin seeds**
(soaked 4–6 hours)

145 g (1 cup) **sunflower seeds** (soaked 4–6 hours)

225 g (8 oz/1¼ cups) **whole golden flax**

1 **beetroot (beets)**

1 large **carrot**

1 very thinly sliced **red onion**

185 ml (6 fl oz/¾ cup) **filtered water**

1½ tsp **sea salt**

½ tsp **freshly cracked black pepper**

2 tbsp **cold-pressed olive oil**

1½ tbsp chopped **rosemary**

Drain the soaked seeds and rinse thoroughly. Pulse them in a food processor until lightly chopped.

Take 180 g (1 cup) of the flax and blend into flour using a high-speed blender. Leave the remaining 45 g (¼ cup) whole.

Prep the vegetables – peel and grate the beetroot and carrot. Slice the onion lengthways into thin slices.

Place all the remaining ingredients together in a bowl and fold until well combined.

Spread out 4 mm (³⁄₁₆ in) thick on a dehydrator sheet and sprinkle with a little extra sea salt and cracked pepper. Dry for 3 hours at 46°C (115°F).

Take them out of the dehydrator and gently cut into the shape you like – we have cut ours into 7 x 5 cm (2 ¾ x 2 in) rectangular shaped crackers.

Dry for another 14–18 hours at 46°C (115°F) or until they are very crunchy. Store in an airtight container for several weeks.

sundried tomatoes

For our sundried tomatoes we like to use cherry tomatoes, which are small and sweet and have a more intense flavour than larger tomatoes. But any other tomatoes will work great here too.

Make time: 15 minutes | Dehydrating time: 12–16 hours | Equipment required: dehydrator

300 g (10½ oz/2 cups) **cherry tomatoes**

1 tbsp **fresh thyme**

3 tbsp **cold-pressed olive oil**

½ tsp **sea salt**

freshly cracked pepper

Place halved tomatoes in a bowl. Mix with the rest of the ingredients.

Place on a dehydrator sheet and dry for 12–16 hours at 46°C (115°F).

Store in the refrigerator for up to 1 week. Note the drier they are the longer they will keep.

tomato sauce

Raw tomato sauce is quite a revelation. Using sundried tomatoes provides the intensity of flavour that you usually achieve by spending hours over the stove. You can use this sauce in many recipes, like our spaghetti and meatballs (see page 136) and pizza (see page 134).

Make time: 10 minutes | Soak time: 2 hours | Equipment required: blender

75 g (½ cup) **sundried tomatoes**

200 g (7 oz/1 cup) chopped **fresh tomato** (you can use cherry tomatoes)

1 deseeded **red capsicum (pepper)**

1½ tbsp **cold-pressed olive oil**

1 tsp **fresh oregano**

fresh basil (a few leaves)

½ **garlic clove**

½ **fresh red thai chilli**

2 **pitted dates**

2 tsp **apple cider vinegar**

⅓ tsp **sea salt**

freshly cracked pepper

Soak the sundried tomatoes in water for 2 hours or until soft. Rinse well. If you are using your own home-made ones you don't need to soak them.

Place the tomatoes and capsicums in the blender first (they have a high water content and once they start to break down will provide the liquid for getting things blending) then top with the rest of the ingredients except the sea salt and pepper – blend until smooth.

Add the sea salt and pepper to taste – sundried tomatoes are often very salty already so the amount of extra sea salt needed can vary.

Store in the refrigerator for up to 2–3 days.

tomato bombs

Tomato bombs give salads a burst of tomato goodness. We use them in our breakfast salad (see page 68). I have added the garlic here as an optional ingredient as they are equally good without. These are so good it's hard to stop eating them.

Make time: 5 minutes | Dehydrating time: 12–16 hours | Equipment required: dehydrator

300 g (10½ oz/2 cups) **cherry tomatoes**

2 sprigs **thyme**

optional – 2 **garlic cloves**

185 ml (6 fl oz/¾ cup) **cold-pressed olive oil**

Wash the tomatoes and pat dry.

Place the whole tomatoes in a bowl with whole garlic cloves and thyme sprigs and cover with olive oil – you want the olive oil to cover the tomatoes entirely, add more if you need to.

Place in the dehydrator for 12–16 hours at 46°C (115°F).

Serve immediately while warm or store in the refrigerator covered in the oil for up to 5–6 days. Once you have used the tomatoes you can still use the oil for a week in dressings and salads.

pickled ginger & beetroot

This pickled ginger recipe uses the beetroot (beets) to colour the ginger and the ginger to flavour the beetroot – you can use both of them as your sushi ginger or as a lovely addition to a sandwich or salad.

Curing time: 6–12 hours | Equipment required: mandoline

12–15 cm (4½–6 in) piece **fresh ginger**

1 medium **choggia beetroot (beets)**
or **regular beetroot (beets)**

1 tbsp **sea salt**

80 ml (2½ fl oz/⅓ cup) **brown rice vinegar**

4 tbsp **raw agave, xylitol**
or **coconut nectar**

filtered water

optional – 2 tbsp **umeboshi vinegar**

Peel the ginger and beetroot. Slice both very finely on a mandoline – you could do this by hand with a knife but it will be hard to get the same thin effect. Take the ginger and massage with sea salt for 1 minute then leave for 30 minutes for the ginger to soften. Squeeze the ginger to extract some of the juice out of it; you can do this by placing it in a nut milk bag and squeezing.

Rinse the ginger under running water and pat dry. Mix the vinegar and sweetener together until combined. Pour into a jar with the layered beetroot and ginger. Top with a few tablespoons of filtered water, just enough to cover the beetroot and ginger. Allow to pickle for a minimum of 6 hours before using.

Store in the refrigerator in an airtight jar. Will keep for up to several weeks.

preserved lemons

Place lemons and sea salt in a jar, let them spend a few months together, and you have created your own preserved lemons. They are wonderfully fragrant and enhance many dishes.

Curing time: 2 months | Equipment required: blender

12 **lemons**

260 g (9¼ oz/2 cups) **sea salt**

1 litre (35 fl oz/5 cups) **filtered water**

Cut lemons into quarters nearly to the base where the lemon attaches to the stalk.

Open up the lemons so the flesh is exposed and sprinkle in about a tablespoon of sea salt per lemon. Firmly pack the lemons in an appropriately sized container or jar and cover.

After 2 days the lemons should be more pliable and some of the juices should have released. Pack the lemons down in the container or jar, squeezing out even more liquid from the lemons. Take the excess juice that has accumulated at the bottom of your container/jar and put it in the blender with the rest of the sea salt and water.

Blend on high until the salt is dissolved, then pour the mixture over the lemons until fully submerged. Weigh the lemons down with a small plate or whatever you have laying around the kitchen that is suitable. Seal the container or jar and leave in a dry storage space for 2 months. Do not expose to any air.

flavoured oils

Herb oils add a vibrant garnish to many dishes. We haven't specified which herbs to use as most fresh varieties with soft, brightly coloured leaves work well. We most often use basil and chives and these will be referred to throughout the book.

Equipment required: blender

250 ml (9 fl oz/1 cup) of **cold-pressed olive oil** (a neutral or butter-flavoured olive oil is preferable)

2 large handfuls loosely packed **fresh herbs**

Prepare a mixing bowl filled with iced water and place another mixing bowl inside it.

Blend the oil and herbs on high until warm but not hot – this will activate the chlorophyll in the leaf. Pour the mixture into the mixing bowl you have already immersed in ice water (you want to cool it down quickly to lock in the colour that you've activated through blending). Strain through a fine chinois strainer or sieve lined with cheese cloth and leave to strain overnight.

Keep the oil in a jar in the refrigerator for several weeks or until it loses its bright green colour.

pickled shallots

We use pickled shallots in salads and sandwiches for extra texture and flavour.

Curing time: 4–6 hours | Equipment required: mandoline

6 **shallots**

250 ml (9 fl oz/1 cup) **merlot vinegar** or **good red wine vinegar**

Thinly slice shallots lengthways on a mandoline or with a knife. Place in a jar with the vinegar and seal; leave at room temperature for 4–6 hours. These will last several months stored in a sealed jar in the refrigerator.

little bird lox (smoked 'salmon')

180 g (1 cup) **carrot juice pulp** or finely grated **carrots**

2 tbsp **cold-pressed olive oil**

1 tbsp **lemon juice**

½ tsp **salt**

1 tbsp **korengo**, chopped **nori sheets** or **dulse flakes**

2 drops **liquid smoke**

2 tbsp finely diced **shallots**

2–4 tbsp chopped **dill**

1 tsp finely chopped **capers**

Mix all the ingredients in a bowl until well combined.

Will keep in the refrigerator for 3–4 days.

If using grated carrots, be sure to pat dry.

Be careful when adding the liquid smoke to the mixture, it is incredibly strong and adding too much will put out the flavour balance.

Be sure to rinse capers if salted.

sauerkraut

A healthy body needs a healthy gut; you really are what you eat. Sauerkraut is one of the best foods you could possibly eat and it's so easy to make your own. If you have any digestive problems eating lactic acid fermented vegetables is a must. Your gut is the centre of your inner eco system – keeping it thriving with the right bacteria works wonders on every aspect of your health.

Don't worry about needing special equipment like a fermenting crock or making massive batches. It only takes a few days to ferment small batches and you can use any AEG or mason jars you have around.

Make time: 30 minutes | Fermenting time: 10–21 days | Equipment required: mandoline

2 heads **cabbage**

2½ tbsp **sea salt**

10 **juniper berries**

1 large **jar** or **crock**

1 small piece **cotton** or **hemp fabric**

rubber band or **string**

Clean the area and equipment (including your hands) you are using thoroughly. You don't want any extra bacteria to make its way in and ruin your kraut-making efforts.

Remove and discard any of the limp outer leaves of the cabbage. It's useful to reserve a few of the larger leaves for later but make sure they are fresh ones. Shred the cabbage finely on a mandoline or by hand. Place in mixing bowl. Massage in the sea salt thoroughly. Add the juniper berries and let the mixture sit for 1 hour so the sea salt can draw the liquids out from the cabbage (caraway seeds would work well as a replacement for the juniper berries).

Pack the cabbage as tight as you can into an appropriate-sized jar/container; if you don't have a large jar you can use several smaller AEG-type ones. Note: Using a smaller jar may result in a quicker fermenting time, so make sure you check progress regularly if you're doing this.

Pour the cabbage juice that has been released over the packed cabbage in the jar or crock. Place one of the larger outer leaves of the cabbage (or some baking paper) over the surface of the cabbage to ensure it's fully submerged in its liquid. Make sure there is no air hitting the cabbage at any point. You could place a little weight on top of the cabbage leaf, such as a small jar or glass, to ensure everything keeps fully submerged.

Place a thick piece of fabric over the jar and tie securely with a rubber band or some string.

Over the next 24 hours, press down on the cabbage every so often with the weight. As the cabbage releases its liquid, it will soften and you can compact it down further, helping more liquid to rise over the top of the cabbage.

Let the jar sit in a dark room with a temperature of around 18°C (64°F) for 10–21 days. Remember a smaller batch will ferment quickly so check regularly to see if it's ready.

While it's fermenting you may see bubbles coming through the cabbage or foam on the top – sometimes even a white scum. Don't worry, these are all normal. The scum can be skimmed off the top before refrigerating.

If you see any mould, remove it immediately; remember to make sure your cabbage is fully submerged. Do not eat mouldy parts close to the surface, remove and check the remaining kraut to see if it has been affected.

Sauerkraut will keep in the refrigerator for 1–2 months in a sealed jar – make sure it's not exposed to air to maintain freshness. As long as the kraut still tastes good it will be good to eat.

There are some wonderful raw krauts available in stores. I recommend eating these krauts first so you understand what taste to go for (you can then identify healthy kraut versus funky kraut).

art of produce

fantastic fresh fruit and veg

Aldo, Terry, John and the crew at Art of Produce are our go-to guys for fresh fruit and vegetables. They bring in top-quality organic produce from all over the greater Auckland area and deliver it to us every morning.

Aldo has decades of experience in the produce industry, including various stints as a grower of lettuce, tomatoes and mushrooms. He knows the industry inside out, and will always go the extra mile to find us the best-quality products at the most affordable prices.

He is also a surf lifesaver, as fit as a mallee bull and has a handshake that will crumple an unprepared hand.

In short, Aldo is the man, an old-school gentleman and definitely a favourite of the girls at little bird. (I'm not sure he knew that before now – sorry girls, it's out of the bag ...)

These guys are the first people we see every morning, and while we have early starts, they start even earlier.

Currently based in Grey Lynn, they are in a super handy spot to service our unbakeries, and they frequently deliver several times a day to keep us stocked up. I'm sure there are a few sighs at their end when we ring up to say we're out of coriander (cilantro), but they always deliver without complaint!

breakfast

These days everyone should be well versed in the importance of breakfast. Eating a clean, nutrient-dense meal to give you sustaining energy for the day's activities is vital. Raw food is perfect for a morning meal – the nutrition is readily available and easy for your body to recognise and convert (remember that your digestion needs to wake up just like the rest of you). And best of all, with these recipes it should be a meal to look forward to – something to get out of bed for!

chia coconut pudding
with passionfruit coulis & peaches

Chia seeds are one of the most amazing foods out there, so filled with goodness we should eat them every day.

If you like tapioca and rice puddings, you will love this breakfast chia pudding and the chia bircher (see page 72). The passionfruit jam is delicious but if you don't have time, putting fresh passionfruit on top is also good.

While this is a breakfast dish it also works perfectly as a dessert – I serve it in ramekins and make the portions smaller.

Make time: 20 minutes + component recipe | Soak time: 30 minutes | Serves: 4

chia coconut pudding

60 g (2¼ oz/¾ cup) **chia seeds**

685 ml (23½ fl oz/2¾ cups) **coconut milk**

2½ tbsp **raw agave/coconut nectar** or 6 drops **stevia/honey**

1 tsp **vanilla extract**

pinch **sea salt**

passionfruit coulis

1 tbsp **irish moss paste** (see page 33)

125 g (4½ oz/½ cup) **fresh** or **frozen passionfruit pulp** (defrosted)

1 tbsp **raw agave/coconut nectar** or 4 drops **stevia/honey**

½ tsp **vanilla extract**

optional – use **fresh passionfruit** if you don't have time to make this

fruit

2 thinly sliced **peaches**

To prepare the chia coconut pudding:
Mix all the ingredients in a bowl – mix well for a few minutes as the chia starts to absorb the milk to make sure there are no clumps. Leave for 30 minutes until the chia seeds have fully absorbed all the coconut milk.

This mixture will keep in the refrigerator for 2–3 days so you can make enough for a few days at once.

To prepare the passionfruit coulis:
Mix the Irish moss paste with the rest of the ingredients until there are no clumps of the paste – let set in the refrigerator for 2–3 hours to gel up.

To serve:
Place ¼ of the mixture in each bowl and top with sliced peaches and passionfruit jam.

A true superfood, chia seeds were prized by the Aztecs for their endurance-enhancing qualities, giving them the name 'running food'. Chia seeds are packed with energy and contain lots of fibre, which makes them extremely filling and low in calories.

Chia seeds contain the all-important essential omega 3 and 6 oils. They have twice the protein concentration of other seeds and are easily digestible in their whole form. They also contain notable amounts of other important minerals: iron, magnesium and zinc.

They are a brilliant food for everyone, but are especially good for active kids, helping keep their blood sugar levels balanced; athletes for their protein and endurance-enhancing properties; and pregnant woman for their protein, iron and omega 3 content.

ultimate fruit salad
with coconut yoghurt & herbs

In summer this is my perfect breakfast. After a morning walk up the old volcano next to our house, I sit down with a green juice and a big plate of fresh fruits to share. I love mango and papaya and passionfruit so they are often around, but the key to my perfect fruit salad is the addition of sprouts and herbs and coconut yoghurt. For a warming boost in winter I love adding some grated ginger or fresh ginger juice to my fruit. It feels like a more balanced way of eating – by pairing the fruit with greens and living probiotics, it helps balance out the blood sugar levels.

Make time: 10 minutes + component recipe | Serves: 2

¼ **pineapple**

½ **papaya**

2 **kiwifruit**

1 **mango**

1 **passionfruit**

⅓ cup **green sprouts** or **micro greens**

1 handful **mint** or **basil**, roughly torn

⅓ cup **coconut yoghurt** (see page 34)

1 **lime**

optional – 1 tsp **grated ginger**

Take a selection of fruits that you enjoy eating together and peel and cut how you like. I tend to leave them in larger pieces so I can sit and savour them slowly.

Place on plates or a shared platter and sprinkle with sprouts, herbs and ginger, if using.

Serve with coconut yoghurt and lime on the side.

Fruits are packed with vitamins and loads of antioxidants – they are wonderful nutrient-rich foods but they are packed with natural sugars, so depending on your body you might find some fruits work well for you and others don't. To work out what your body thrives on try eating single fruits by themselves and see how that works in your body. When putting together a selection of fruits, try and make sure you have some low sugar fruits in there. Berries and green apples are low sugar fruits; papaya is a medium sugar fruit but contains lots of fibre and enzymes, which help it digest easily. I find it a really excellent fruit to have around.

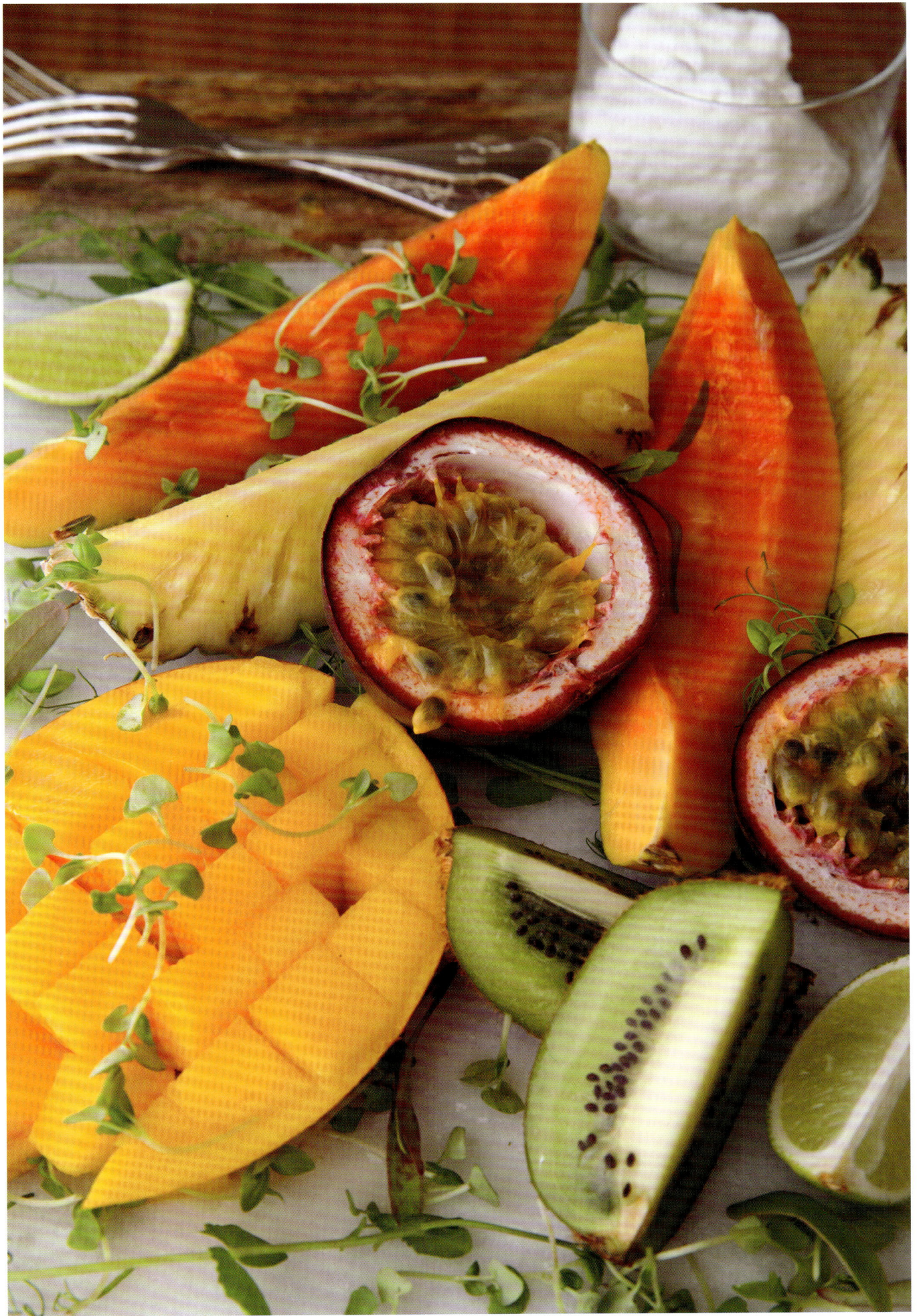

acai bowl

The perfect summer breakfast – a bowl of antioxidant-rich acai is blended with berries and banana to make a healthy sorbet topped with probiotic-filled coconut yoghurt (see page 34), raw granola and fresh fruit. A beautiful and delicious way to start the morning that the whole family will get into.

Acai – pronounced ah–sigh–EE, although I've been known to fashion my own way of saying things!

A popular breakfast dish in Brazil – acai is classed as a superfood – you get a lot of nutrition per mouthful. It is a potent source of antioxidants and lots of other goodies like omega 3, 6 and 9.

Make time: 10 minutes + component recipe | Serves: 2 | Equipment required: blender

6 tbsp **acai pulp**
(you can purchase frozen at health food stores)
or 3 tbsp **acai powder**

1 **fresh ripe banana**

70 g (2½ oz/½ cup) **frozen strawberries**

70 g (2½ oz/½ cup) **frozen blueberries**

garnish – **fresh fruit** of your choice, **home-made raw granola** and **coconut yoghurt**
(see page 34)

Blend all ingredients until very smooth. You could add a little almond milk or water to get it smooth if your blender is having difficulty with the frozen berries. You want a smooth sorbet-like texture.

You could also use fresh berries when in season; just add 100 g (3½ oz/¾ cup) ice to make it come up like a sorbet.

Pour into 2 bowls and top with your choice of fresh fruit, granola and coconut yoghurt.

chia, almond & apple bircher with activated cinnamon walnuts

We created this recipe while working on the book. Long days of shooting required some seriously good sustaining energy. This did the trick perfectly and was so enjoyable I wanted to share.

Make time: 15 minutes + component recipes | Soak time: 30 minutes | Serves: 3–4

20 g (¾ oz/¼ cup) **chia seeds**

435 ml (15¼ fl oz/1¾ cups) **almond milk** (see page 30)

2 **apples** or **pears**

3 tbsp **lemon juice**

2 tbsp **sultanas** (golden raisins)

1 tsp **cinnamon**

25 g (1 oz/¼ cup) of **caramelised walnuts** (see page 29) or crushed **dried activated almonds** (see pages 27–28)

First mix the chia seeds and almond milk in a bowl – mix well for a few minutes as the chia starts to absorb the milk to make sure there are no clumps. Leave for ½ an hour until the chia seeds have fully absorbed all the almond milk.

Grate the apples or pears and mix with some of the lemon juice to prevent it from browning.

Mix the sultanas, cinnamon and grated apple/pear with the chia seeds.

Place into bowls and sprinkle with caramelised walnuts and extra cinnamon.

If you're having a long breakfast with friends, I would recommend serving this bircher in a large bowl with additional milk, and bowls of sultanas (golden raisins), caramelised walnuts, fruits and granola so people can make their own creations.

layered citrus salad
with banana yoghurt & bee pollen

Citrus fruits make for a refreshing, immune-boosting start to the day. They are rich in vitamin C, antioxidants, phytonutrients, minerals, fibre and have a high water content, making them very hydrating. Serve these sweet and sour treats with banana yoghurt and bee pollen – considered one of nature's most complete and nourishing foods.

Make time: 15 minutes + component recipe | Serves: 2 | Equipment required: blender

2 **mandarins**, cut slices acrossways (some of the slices may break up a little but most of them should hold together nicely; use all of it)

2 peeled and segmented **oranges**

1 peeled and segmented **grapefruit** or **pomelo**

2 tsp **bee pollen**

banana yoghurt

1 large **banana**

⅓ cup **coconut yoghurt** (see page 34)

1 tsp **lime** or **lemon juice**

1 tsp **raw honey**

Peel and cut up the mandarins, oranges and grapefruit. Set aside while you make the banana yoghurt.

To make the banana yoghurt simply blend the banana with the other ingredients until smooth.

Take 2 small bowls or glasses and layer the citrus fruits with the banana yoghurt and a sprinkle of bee pollen.

If you like it sweet, or your citrus is particularly sour, drizzle with a little honey.

sprouted green lentils
with apple & ginger porridge

If you're someone who thrives on a good boost of protein in the morning, this is for you.

Sprouts are abundant in usable protein and make for an excellent breakfast. This may not sound particularly appealing but give it try! It really is rather delicious.

Make time: 10 minutes + component recipes | Marinating time: 30 minutes | Soak time: overnight | Serves: 2 |
Equipment required: food processor

90 g (3¼ oz/¾ cup) **lentil sprouts**
(red or green works well, see page 27)

4 tbsp **lime** or **lemon juice**

6 tbsp **fresh** or **dried buckwheat sprouts**
(see pages 27 and 270)

⅓ medium **avocado**, 1 **banana** or **soft pear**
(if using banana or pear – mix with 1 tbsp
of coconut oil)

pinch **sea salt**

3 cm (¼ in) **ginger**, finely grated on a microplane

1½ grated **green apples** or **pears**

185 ml (6 fl oz/¾ cup) **almond milk** (see page 30)

serving

1 **apple** or **pear**

4 **pitted dates**, sliced lengthways into thin pieces

2 tbsp **dried buckwheat sprouts** (see page 270),
activated nuts (see page 27)
or **home-made raw granola**

¼ tsp **cinnamon**

1 tsp **raw honey** (omit if you use banana as the
base, it will be too sweet)

almond milk (see page 30)

Wash the lentil sprouts well, then place 2 tablespoons of lime or lemon juice with the sprouts and mix together in a bowl – set aside for a minimum of 30 minutes. I like to prepare these the night before and leave them sitting in the refrigerator in an airtight container with the lime or lemon juice before using in the morning. It helps them break down and be even more digestible. Blend in a food processor until it reaches a chunky porridge-like texture. If you don't have any sprouted buckwheat, don't worry you can leave this out, the most important part of this recipe is the sprouted lentils.

Add the avocado and salt (my personal preference) or the banana or pear along with the ginger and remaining lemon or lime juice to the food processor and pulse until combined.

Fold in the grated apple and the almond milk.

Top with fresh slices of apple or pear, sliced dates, dried buckwheat sprouts, cinnamon and a drizzle of honey.

Serve with almond milk on the side.

strawberry chia jam
& almond butter on seeded bread

Bread with jam and butter is definitely not something that I thought I would be eating much of when I delved into the world of raw foods.

But here we have it, a fresh, fruity jam that isn't laden with boiled sugar, and beautiful almond butter that we make ourselves, all served on a raw seeded bread that's kept warm in the dehydrator.

Component recipe: **seeded bread** (see pages 38–39)

strawberry jam

Make time: 15 minutes | Makes: 1 cup | Equipment required: blender

4 tbsp **chia seeds**

250 ml (9 fl oz/1 cup) **filtered water**

125 g (4½ oz/1 cup) **frozen strawberries** (defrosted)

1 tbsp **freeze-dried strawberries**

1 tbsp **lemon juice**

1 tbsp **honey**

¼ tsp **vanilla**

Place the chia seeds in the water. Mix well so there are no clumps and put aside for approximately 10 minutes.

While the chia seeds are soaking blend all other ingredients until smooth.

Add the mixture to the chia seeds and mix together by hand.

Will store in the refrigerator for up to 1 week.

almond butter

This is surprisingly easy to make. You might not get it as smooth as a commercial one unless you have a stone grinder at home, but a good food processor will do a really good job of it.

We make larger batches of activated almonds at home and dry them in the dehydrator to keep on hand for making nut butters and flour.

Make time: 10 minutes + component recipe | Makes: 1 cup | Equipment required: food processor

240 g (2 cups) **dried activated almonds** (see pages 27–28)

¼ tsp **sea salt**

optional – **coconut oil**

Place almonds and sea salt in food processor (it needs to be a good one – otherwise it may overheat). Process for 10–12 minutes. You will need to scrape down the sides during the initial stages to get it going.

After 12 minutes the almonds will have released their oil and the butter will be ready to jar up and put in the refrigerator or a cool cupboard.

You could also use a little coconut oil to help get this moving but this does affect the flavour.

Try with other nuts like cashew or Brazil nuts – as with the milks, you can try blending combinations of nuts to make your own butter creations.

blueberry jelly jam

This recipe is similar to our strawberry jam recipe but this time we are blending the fruit and chia seeds until completely smooth to make more of a jelly.

Make time: 5 minutes | Setting time: 30 minutes | Makes: 2 cups | Equipment required: blender

465 g (3 cups) **fresh blueberries** or **frozen berries** (defrosted)

2½ tbsp **chia seeds**

6 tbsp **filtered water**

2 tbsp **raw honey**

1 tsp **lemon juice**

Make sure your berries are defrosted if using frozen. Soak the chia seeds in the filtered water for 10 minutes.

Place all the ingredients in a blender and blend for around 1½ minutes. The pectin in the blueberries will be activated by the blending and combined with the chia this will give you the jelly jam texture.

Place in the refrigerator for ½ hour to set.

Will store in the refrigerator for up to 2 weeks.

bagels with lox,
capers, dill & herb cheese

The little bird bagels are made from our favourite and very versatile raw bread recipe (see page 38). Top them with some of our favourite combinations below.

Lox with herb cheese is a surprising menu item for a raw café; the lox is a really lovely recipe (see page 57) that I have enjoyed using in many dishes at home and in the cafés. Add herb cheese, capers and dill and you have a delightful and delicate breakfast offering.

Make time: 10 minutes + component recipes | Serves: 2

2 **bagels** (see page 38)

⅔ cup **lox** (see page 57)

4 tbsp **herb cheese** (see page 44)

topping

1 tbsp **capers**

1 tbsp **dill**

freshly cracked pepper

Slice the bagels in half. If you have a dehydrator handy, warm them for 15–20 minutes before using (you could also use an oven on its lowest setting). Divide the herb cheese between the bagels; we serve our bagels open so you should be spreading it over 4 pieces. Top each one with ¼ of the lox; divide the capers and dill between the bagels.

Some lovely additions to this combination are a few slices of red onion (very thinly sliced), sliced cucumber and some fresh alfalfa sprouts or micro cress.

Finish with some cracked pepper.

bagels with avocado,
coconut bacon & tomato

As soon as the BLAT hit the menu this year it was an instant hit; our chefs now make a lot of coconut bacon each evening.

Make time: 10 minutes + component recipes | Serves: 2

2 **bagels** (see page 38)

1 **avocado**

sea salt

1 beefsteak tomato
or other large **fresh ripe tomato**

buttercrunch lettuce or other butter lettuce

¼ cup **coconut bacon** (see page 36)

freshly cracked pepper

Slice the bagels in half. If you have a dehydrator handy, warm them for 15–20 minutes before using (you could also use an oven on its lowest setting). Crush the avocado with a few pinches of sea salt in a bowl – divide between the bagels; we serve our bagels open so you should be spreading the avocado over 4 pieces. Top each one with a thick slice of ripe tomato, a few leaves of buttercrunch lettuce (you could also use a few basil leaves) and 2–3 pieces of coconut bacon.

Finish with some cracked pepper and a little sea salt.

breakfast BLAT salad

Salad isn't often seen on breakfast menus; by conditioning we tend to lean towards something sweet or bready in the morning. I encourage you to try salad dishes for breakfast – how does your mid-morning energy respond?

This salad's full of classic breakfast flavours – very similar to our BLAT bagel, minus the bagel, and with the addition of spirulina (for protein) and tomato bombs.

Make time: 10 minutes + component recipes | Serves: 4

3 large handfuls **baby English spinach**

2 large handfuls **mesclun mix**

¼ tsp **spirulina powder**

1 tsp **nutritional yeast**

5 tbsp **cold-pressed olive oil**
from the tomato bombs

2 tbsp **lemon juice**

sea salt

½ cup **coconut bacon** (see page 36)

1 cup **tomato bombs** (see page 55)

1–2 medium **avocados**, sliced into wedges

10 g (¼ oz/½ cup) **sunflower sprouts** (see page 27)
or your choice of soft green sprout or micro green

freshly cracked pepper

optional – **dried activated pumpkin seeds**
(see pages 27–28), **sunflower seeds**
or **little bird superfood salad clusters**

Place the baby English spinach and mesclun mix in a large bowl and toss with the spirulina, nutritional yeast, olive oil, lemon juice and a few pinches of sea salt.

Fold through the rest of the ingredients and serve with additional sea salt and freshly cracked pepper to taste.

Optional:
If you have dried activated sunflower or pumpkin seeds on hand you can scatter these on top, or you could use some little bird superfood salad clusters.

creamy mushrooms with
shallots & rosemary on seeded bread

Creamy mushrooms on toast are a must on any brunch menu. Our raw version is so very good that Xander, our head chef who doesn't come from a raw background, was a bit suspicious at first that it wasn't really raw ... Xander and one of his chefs Seth perfected them with some shallots and the addition of fresh chopped rosemary.

Make time: 15 minutes + component recipes | Dehydrating time: 2 hours | Serves: 3–4 | Equipment required: dehydrator

150 g (5½ oz/4 cups) **swiss brown**
or **brown button mushrooms**

½ very finely diced **shallot**

1 tbsp finely chopped **rosemary** or **thyme**

125 ml (4 fl oz/½ cup) **cold-pressed olive oil**

½ tsp **sea salt**

freshly cracked pepper (add to taste)

fresh parsley or **micro greens**

125 ml (4 fl oz/½ cup) **alfredo sauce** (see pages 49)

seeded bread (see pages 38–39)

Slice the mushrooms into thin slices and, apart from the bread and alfredo sauce, mix with the rest of the ingredients; place on a dehydrator sheet for 1½ hours at 46°C (115°F).

Mix mushrooms with alfredo sauce in a bowl and place the bowl back in the dehydrator for another ½ hour. Add more sea salt to taste if required.

Serve on our seeded bread or your favourite sprouted or essene bread.

Garnish with cracked pepper, fresh parsley or micro greens.

drinks

Liquid nutrition is a core part of the raw food philosophy. Our daily green juice packs as much greenery in one glass as you could fit on a dinner plate. Knocking back one of these runs rings around taking a multivitamin! (Buying a decent juicer is a fantastic investment – get one that crushes or presses rather than one with blades.)

Processed foods ask a lot of our digestive system, as do heavy foods and meats. If you switch part of your daily food intake to a liquid form, your body will get a bit of a break from its digestive work out, and can get busy doing other useful things (like cell rejuvenation and healing).

There are so many exciting ingredients you can add to juices and smoothies – you can have so much fun experimenting with new combinations – don't hold back! And one vital tip – don't underestimate the importance of some lemon or lime. If your special creation is tasting a little funky, add some lemon juice and hey presto: tasty creation!

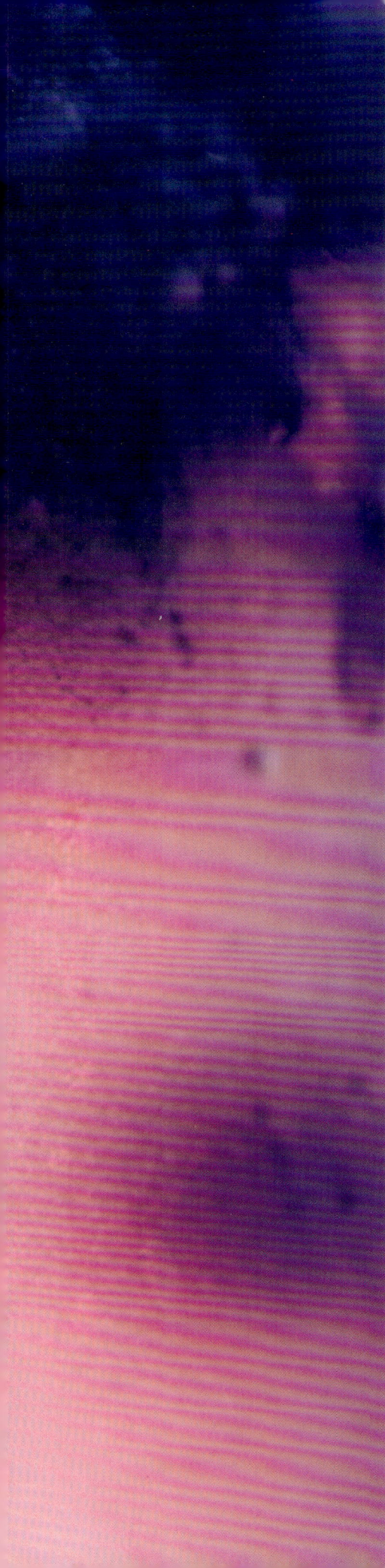

smoothies

juices

milkshakes,
nut milks & spritzers

smoothies

Smoothies, like juices, are a big part of the little bird way of enjoying goodness. Just about everyone who works at the unbakery consumes a smoothie every day – that's why they are all so lovely! Smoothies make you happy from the inside out.

They also enable you to consume a lot of good nutrition in an easily digestible and delicious form. I have heard wonderful, heart-affirming stories of people and children with health and behavioural issues finding their health through nutrient-rich smoothies. In my own health journey, green smoothies were a big part of what helped get me on an onward and upward trajectory.

I can't stress enough how beneficial a good smoothie can be, especially the green ones!

If you're new to consuming liquid greens, add more fruit to your smoothie before graduating along the green scale to recipes like the green detox. The more greens you eat the more you will crave them – feeling good is addictive!

Tip: Keeping frozen smoothie ingredients on hand is a time saver. Chop and store ripe fruit (that is just about to go past its prime) in the freezer. Do the same with your favourite seasonal fruits. If you've cut open a large pineapple or mango you can't finish, chop the rest up and freeze it. If you have an abundant garden, spend an afternoon harvesting so nothing goes to waste.

Serves: 1 for all smoothie recipes | Equipment required: blender

blackcurrant, blueberry & almond smoothie

Berries are just all-round good for you, and the more intense the colour the better. Consuming berries, which contain the antioxidant resveratrol, helps protect your cells from numerous degenerative diseases and from free radicals, giving you extra defence against disease while keeping your cells looking good!

Berries are a great base for smoothies. We love pairing them with their South American superfood cousins: acai, maqui, camu camu and baobab.

1 **frozen banana**

30 g (1 oz/¼ cup) **blackcurrants**

50 g (1¾ oz/⅓ cup) **blueberries**

1 tbsp **raw honey**

1 tbsp **lemon juice**

80 ml (2½ fl oz/⅓ cup) **almond milk** (see page 30)

1 handful **ice**

optional goodness – add 1 tsp **acai** or **maqui powder** for some extra antioxidants to the blender and ½ tsp **bee pollen** for an immune boost.

Place all the ingredients in a blender and blend until smooth.

Don't over-blend or it will warm up. Add a few cubes of ice and blend for a few seconds if this happens.

breakfast smoothie with coconut yoghurt & figs

Figs, granola, cinnamon, yoghurt and banana are a classic breakfast combination. We've crafted them into a one-stop-shop smoothie, for when you don't have time to sit and savour a meal. Figs are high in iron and folic acid, so a great choice for anyone who is pregnant.

1 frozen banana

2 dried figs

1 tsp cinnamon

1½ tbsp coconut yoghurt (see page 34)
(if you don't have any add 1 tbsp lemon juice)

1 tbsp home-made raw granola
or crushed activated walnuts (see page 27)

170 ml (5½ fl oz/⅔ cup) almond milk (see page 30)

garnish – coconut yoghurt, cinnamon and granola
or crushed activated walnuts

Place all the ingredients in a blender and blend until smooth.

Don't over-blend or it will warm up. Add a few cubes of ice and blend for a few seconds if this happens.

Top with a tablespoon of coconut yoghurt, sprinkle of cinnamon and a tablespoon of granola or the crushed walnuts.

cacao maca boost smoothie

Energise your body naturally with a cacao and maca boost. Cacao and maca work synergistically, providing you with a sustainable energy boost. The chia seeds and coconut meat make this a satisfying drink, preparing you for an action-packed day or endurance workout.

1½ tbsp cacao powder

1 tsp cacao nibs

½ tbsp maca powder

1 tsp chia seeds

1 tbsp coconut sugar or 5 pitted dates

40 g (1½ oz/¼ cup) young coconut flesh

80 ml (2½ fl oz/⅓ cup) coconut water
or filtered water

1 handful ice

optional – ½ tsp mesquite

garnish – maca powder, cacao nibs

Place all the ingredients in a blender and blend until smooth.

Don't over-blend or it will warm up. Add a few cubes of ice and blend for a few seconds if this happens.

Garnish with a fine sprinkle of maca powder and a few cacao nibs.

cacao smoothie

Another of my favourite smoothie ingredients, cacao is very high in minerals like magnesium. Those who suffer from adrenal fatigue or are sensitive to stimulants may wish to go easy on the cacao, or save it for special occasions.

1 **frozen banana**

5 **pitted dates**

1½ tbsp **cacao powder**

¼ tsp **vanilla extract**

80 ml (2½ fl oz/⅓ cup) **almond milk** (see page 30)

125 ml (4 fl oz/½ cup) **filtered water**

1 tbsp **little bird trail mix**
or 2 **brazil nuts** and ¼ tsp **cinnamon**

1 handful **ice**

garnish – 1 tbsp **little bird trail mix**
or crushed **brazil nuts**

Place banana, dates, cacao, vanilla, almond milk and filtered water in a blender with some ice and blend until smooth.

Add the trail mix and pulse.

Garnish with extra trail mix or Brazil nuts.

tropical green smoothie

Our original green smoothie, this provides a hit of green goodness in a tropical-tasting delight.

80 g (2¾ oz/½ cup) chopped **pineapple**

1 large handful **kale** or **English spinach**

1 handful **mint**

185 ml (6 fl oz/¾ cup) **coconut water**

1 tbsp **lemon juice**

1 handful **ice**

Place all the ingredients in a blender and blend until smooth.

Don't over-blend or it will warm up. Add a few cubes of ice and blend for a few seconds if this happens.

green detox smoothie

The health king of our green smoothie recipes. Handfuls of detoxifying herbs, grapefruit, kale and turmeric will leave you feeling very much alive! Wild, edible greens like dandelions are a great addition, if you can get them.

½ **grapefruit**

1 large handful **kale**

1 handful **coriander (cilantro)**

1 handful **parsley**

5 cm (2 in) piece **cucumber**

1 tbsp **lemon juice**

2 cm (¾ in) piece **fresh ginger**

2 cm (¾ in) piece **fresh turmeric**
(use ⅓ tsp turmeric powder if fresh is not available)

80 ml (2½ fl oz/⅓ cup) **filtered water**

1 handful **ice**

Chop and peel the grapefruit and wash the kale and herbs. Place all the ingredients in a blender and blend until smooth.

Don't over-blend or it will warm up. Add a few cubes of ice and blend for a few seconds if this happens.

creamy greens smoothie

Our creamy greens smoothie introduces green superfood powders. If you haven't heard of these, try a few. They are great to take on holiday when you can't get fresh greens each day. They work like a green multivitamin, keeping your health thriving and your immune system up for anything.

2 heaped tbsp **avocado**

1 handful **kale** or **English spinach**

80 g (2¾ oz/½ cup) chopped **pineapple**

1 tsp your favourite **super green powder**
or ¼ tsp **spirulina**

1 tbsp **lemon juice**

80 ml (2½ fl oz/⅓ cup) **coconut water**
or **filtered water**

1 handful **ice**

Place all the ingredients in a blender and blend until smooth.

Don't over-blend or it will warm up. Add a few cubes of ice and blend for a few seconds if this happens.

juices

Juicing is an important daily ritual for us. It's something everyone should be doing – especially vegetable juicing! Juices are healing tools that can provide people with profound health benefits in a relatively short time. Even if you are in good health, adding cold-pressed vegetable juices to your routine will often propel you to even better health.

At the unbakeries we serve cold-pressed juices made fresh each morning. Coldpressing retains more nutrients than other juicing methods as the produce isn't shredded with blades; instead it is slowly ground. This means the fruit and vegetables are exposed to less air, thereby slowing the oxidation process.

Juice is pure goodness that your body can utilise straight away; you can literally feel the goodness running through your veins. Green juices, in particular, are a great replacement for coffee in the mornings – not flavour-wise, of course – because they provide a hit of energy and a clear mind to start the day.

Organic is important! Because you are consuming more nutrient-dense fresh products, you want to use the best possible ingredients. Choosing organic means you are not risking residual chemical and pesticide consumption. It also ensures you will eat and juice seasonally. Organic produce tastes better too!

Serves: 1 for all juice recipes | Equipment required: blender, juicer

all things green juice

If it's green, you can probably juice it. Try juicing vegetables you never thought you'd drink: broccoli, snow peas (mangetout) and bok choy (pak choy).

Broccoli is a wonder food. It helps your body repair damaged tissue and regulate digestion, boosts your immune system and is an excellent source of good-for-your-bones calcium. It tastes surprisingly good in juice (use the stems as well).

½ **lemon**

1 handful **bok choy (pak choy)**

120 g (4¼ oz/2 cups) roughly chopped **broccoli** (head and stems)

2 stalks **celery**

1 handful **snow peas (mangetout)** or **shelling peas**

½ **cucumber**

1 handful **basil** or **thai basil**

3 cm (1¼ in) piece **ginger**

optional – **dandelions** or other wild **edible greens**

Peel the lemon, wash all your ingredients and chop to the right size for your juicer. When feeding the ingredients through the juicer it's a good idea to alternate between something fibrous (like the herbs and bok choy) and something juicy (like the cucumber) to help it move through easily, and use any harder pieces (like celery) to push through everything else.

carrot & turmeric with ginger & lime juice

Turmeric is a very old spice long valued for its healing properties. It is traditionally used to improve digestion, detoxify the liver and boost the immune system.

3–4 **carrots**

1 **lime**

3 cm (1¼ in) piece **fresh turmeric**

2 cm (¾ in) piece **ginger**

optional – 1 **tangelo** or **orange**

Peel the carrots, tangelo and lime; chop all the ingredients to the right size for your juicer and process.

blushing beets juice

Beetroot (beets) is well known for keeping your liver healthy, but it also contains the antioxidant betacyanin, which gives it its vibrant red colour. Consuming beetroot and its betacyanin can help reduce the risk of heart disease and stroke by relaxing the blood vessels, lowering blood pressure and helping stabilise blood sugar. Drink or eat those beets!

1 **beetroot (beets)**

½ **lemon**

½ **apple**

½ small **cucumber**

4 **fresh** or **frozen strawberries**

2 tbsp **fresh** or **frozen raspberries**

Wash and peel the beetroot and lemon. Chop the beetroot, apple, cucumber and lemon into pieces that will go through your juicer. Process the resulting juice in a blender with the strawberries and raspberries and blend until combined.

Serve with a few cubes of ice in summer if you like your drinks chilled.

pear & pineapple with ginger & rosemary juice

Rosemary might sound like an odd addition to juice but it works wonderfully with the pears and pineapple. All herbs have medicinal properties and rosemary is no exception – it can make you smarter by increasing blood flow to the brain, improving concentration. This juice makes an excellent base for an afternoon spritzer, mocktail or cocktail.

1 **lemon**

320 g (11¼ oz/2 cups) **pineapple**

1 **green pear**

3 cm (1¼ in) piece **ginger**

1 tsp **rosemary leaves**

garnish – **rosemary flowers** or **leaves**

Peel the lemon and pineapple, chop all the ingredients to the right size for your juicer and process.

Garnish with rosemary flowers or leaves in the cup.

green apple, kale, cucumber & celery with mint & parsley juice

Juicing herbs is a great way to get extra flavour and nutrition into your juices. Parsley is a particular star; it helps cleanse the blood and contains all-important iron.

Kale is our favourite when it comes to greens; it is considered one of the most nutrient-dense foods. We use it every day in our smoothies, juices and salads; it has lots of minerals and vitamins like K, A and C, along with manganese, fibre, calcium and iron. It also contains omega 3 fats!

½ **lemon**

1 **green apple**

½ **cucumber**

2 stalks **celery**

1 handful **kale**

1 handful **parsley**

1 handful **mint**

Peel the lemon, wash all your ingredients and chop to the right size for your juicer. When processing the ingredients through the juicer it's a good idea to alternate between something fibrous (like the herbs and kale) and something juicy (like the cucumber) to help it move through easily, and use any harder pieces (like apple) to push through everything else.

milkshakes, nut milks & spritzers

strawberries & cream layered shake

A beautiful looking drink that is like a dessert. You could replace the strawberries with other berries, mango, lychee or banana.

Make time: 10 minutes + component recipes | Serves: 1 | Equipment required: blender

1 large scoop **vanilla ice cream** (see page 262)

2 handfuls **ice**

½ tsp **vanilla extract**

125 ml (4 fl oz/½ cup) **almond milk** (see page 30)

50 g (1¾ oz/⅓ cup) **fresh** or **frozen strawberries** (defrosted)

¼ tsp **raw agave, raw honey** or **coconut nectar**

1 tsp **lemon juice**

garnish – fresh chopped **strawberries** and **raspberries**

Place the ice cream, ice, vanilla and 80 ml (2½ fl oz/⅓ cup) of the almond milk in the blender and blend until you get a consistency similar to a frozen slushy drink. Pour half the slushy mixture into a glass or bowl and set aside. Now place the strawberries, sweetener, remaining almond milk and lemon juice in the blender with the remaining half and blend until smooth.

Pour the strawberry mixture into a new glass and spoon in the vanilla ice cream mixture that's been set aside. Top with fresh chopped strawberries and raspberries.

iced coffee milkshake

Yummy is all we can say about this drink. It has a lot of fans! I love the taste and smell of coffee but it's not really my friend, leaving me with shaky hands and a system that's wired, then crashes. I adore this milkshake; I make it with Swiss-extracted decaffeinated cold brew, iced Teeccino® or Dandy Blend™ drink. If coffee works in moderation for you, some good organic cold brew coffee would be lovely to use here.

Make time: 10 minutes + component recipes | Serves: 1 | Equipment required: blender

1 large scoop **vanilla ice cream** (see page 262)

2 handfuls **ice**

½ tsp **vanilla extract**

125 ml (4 fl oz/½ cup) **hazelnut milk** (see page 30)

1 tbsp **chocolate sauce** (see page 249)

80 ml (2½ fl oz/⅓ cup) **cold brew coffee** or a non coffee alternative like **Teeccino®** or **Dandy Blend™**

garnish – ½ tsp **chocolate sauce**

Place the ice cream, ice, vanilla and hazelnut milk in the blender and blend until you get a consistency similar to a frozen slushy drink. Swirl the tablespoon of chocolate sauce around the inside of an empty cup or glass. Pour the slushy mixture into the glass; now pour in your coffee of choice. Use a long spoon to gently mix.

Garnish with a drizzle of chocolate sauce.

blackcurrant & jasmine iced tea

Iced tea is lovely served on a summer afternoon. It's great to have a range of non-alcoholic beverages for people to enjoy at dinners and parties that are not laden with sugar; all of our elixir drinks would make great options for this. You can make this with any other teas and berries that you enjoy.

Make time: 15 minutes | Chilling time: 2–3 hours | Serves: 2 | Equipment required: blender

3 tsp **jasmine green tea**

3 tbsp **raw honey** or **raw agave**

65 g (½ cup) **fresh** or **frozen blackberries/raspberries**

ice

garnish – **lemon wedges** and **edible flowers**

Boil a kettle, put the tea in a heatproof bowl or jug and pour 60 ml (2 fl oz/¼ cup) of cold filtered water over the tea leaves (this helps the boiling water to not burn the tea leaves, which releases a bitter flavour before the other green tea flavours are extracted from the tea). Then pour 750 ml (26 fl oz/3 cups) boiled water over the tea, add the honey and then stir until dissolved.

Carefully taste and add more honey if you like things a bit sweeter. Set the tea aside for 10 minutes then strain, cool to room temperature and then refrigerate until cold (you don't want to steam up your refrigerator). Place the iced tea in a blender with the blackberries and blend until combined. Sieve the mixture and serve over plenty of ice with lemon wedges and a few edible flowers for decoration. You can usually get little edible flowers from your rosemary and thyme plants if you have any in the backyard.

chocolate, strawberry & banana milk

Our milks are a refreshing and comforting treat, very similar to those you loved as a kid, but without the rubbish. You are never too old for a delicious glass of flavoured milk.

They're a really good treat for the kids that you can hand over knowing they won't leave them on a crazy preservative and sugar high. Instead, the milks provide kids with a treat that nourishes their bodies with plant-based protein and minerals. Our favourite milk to use for these drinks is a combination of macadamia and cashew.

Tip: If you don't have any home-made nut milk on hand, a few tablespoons of cashew butter with 170 ml (5½ fl oz/⅔ cup) filtered water will make a quick and easy base.

Make time: 5 minutes + component recipe | Serves: 1 for all milk recipes | Equipment required: blender

chocolate milk

170 ml (5½ fl oz/⅔ cup) **cashew/macadamia milk** or **almond milk** (see page 30)

1½ tbsp **cacao powder**

2 tbsp **raw agave, organic maple syrup** or **coconut nectar**

a few drops **vanilla extract**

¼ tsp **lecithin**

1 large handful **ice**

strawberry milk

170 ml (5½ fl oz/⅔ cup) **cashew/macadamia milk** or **almond milk** (see page 30)

1½ tbsp **raw agave, organic maple syrup, raw honey** or **coconut nectar**

70 g (2½ oz/½ cup) **frozen** or **fresh strawberries**

a few drops **vanilla extract**

1 tsp **lemon juice**

¼ tsp **lecithin**

1 handful **ice** (if using fresh strawberries)

banana milk

170 ml (5½ fl oz/⅔ cup) **cashew/macadamia milk** or **almond milk** (see page 30)

1½ tbsp **raw agave, organic maple syrup, raw honey** or **coconut nectar**

1 **frozen banana**

a few drops **vanilla extract**

1 tsp **lemon juice**

¼ tsp **lecithin**

1 small handful **ice**

To prepare all milks:
Place all the ingredients in a blender and blend until smooth. Don't over-blend or it will warm up; add more ice if this happens.

turmeric, orange, ginger & grapefruit spritzer

A health tonic that makes a very refreshing and enlivening afternoon spritzer without the wine.

Serves: 2 | Equipment required: juicer or blender

2 **oranges**

1 **grapefruit**

1 **lime**

3 cm (1¼ in) piece **fresh ginger**

3 cm (1¼ in) piece **fresh turmeric**
or ¼ tsp **powdered turmeric**

3 tbsp **coconut sugar** or **coconut nectar**

ice

1 bottle chilled **sparkling mineral water**

Peel all the citrus fruits and process everything other than the coconut sugar and mineral water through a juicer. Alternatively, you can place everything except the mineral water in a blender with 125 ml (4 fl oz/½ cup) of filtered water and blend until everything is liquid.

If you have used a blender you need to sieve the mixture through a very fine mesh sieve. If you have used the juicer you will need to add the coconut sugar or nectar and mix together until combined.

Place the mixture in the refrigerator to chill or serve immediately over ice.

Fill the glass approximately ⅔ with sparkling water, then slowly pour in the juice – this way you get the lovely colour gradation.

berry lemonade

A fruity, sparkling lemonade. We usually make a big batch of the lemon base and keep it chilled in the refrigerator along with a bottle of sparkling mineral water so we can make lemonade whenever the mood suits. Raspberries and strawberries can be used instead of the blueberries to make pink lemonade.

Serves: 2

125 ml (4 fl oz/½ cup) **lemon juice**

80 ml (2½ fl oz/⅓ cup) **filtered water**

4 tbsp **organic maple syrup, raw agave**
or **raw honey**

70 g (2½ oz/½ cup) **frozen blueberries**

1 **lime**, finely sliced into rounds

1 small bottle chilled **sparkling mineral water**

90 g (3¼ oz/⅔ cup) **ice**

a few **lime slices**

Place the glasses you are using in the freezer for a few hours before using for an extra frosting. For this recipe we use large glasses, around 450–500 ml (16–17 fl oz/2 cups).

Mix the lemon juice, filtered water and sweetener in a jar. Place the lid on and shake. This is your lemonade base; it will keep in the refrigerator for up to a week.

When ready to serve, place half of the frozen blueberries in the bottom of each glass and muddle with a pestle to lightly crush. Now put half of the ice in each cup with a few slices of lime. Pour half of the lemon base on top of the ice and then fill the rest of the glass with sparkling water. Stir in the glass and serve.

kelmarna gardens

organic vegies in the city

Kelmarna Gardens is a city oasis – 1.7 hectares (4.2 acres) in the heart of inner Auckland in Herne Bay, growing a huge variety of fruits and vegetables, plus chooks, cows, beehives, worm farms, composting ... all of which have been organically managed since its establishment in 1981.

The Gardens are run by The Framework Trust, an organisation providing mental health support to the community. What better place to help people regain mental balance and gain skills than a calm, lush, green wonderland?

Kelmarna is open to the public and has produce for sale. You might occasionally meet one of the gardeners, and if you do it's very likely you will be guided along to their plot and shown the amazing bounty of their efforts. It's no secret they get a commission if you buy something from their plot, but their enthusiasm is infectious nonetheless.

Apart from being a functioning garden, Kelmarna is set up as an education and preservation tool. Maintaining rare heritage fruit and vegetable varieties is one of the most valuable services that Kelmarna provides. The gardens are certified organic and run on the principles of permaculture. While it may appear to be organised chaos, everything is in its place for a reason. Species are 'zoned' next to each other if they provide benefits to each other, and if they can be most efficiently worked as a collection.

We periodically stop in at Kelmarna to see what is growing and what unusual varieties can inspire creative dishes, but even if you come away empty handed (however unlikely), it really is a wonderful place to spend a sunny afternoon.

lunch

Lunch is where our unbakeries really excel. Providing nourishing, sustaining, truly health-giving alternatives to the standard café fare has seen our business thrive.

The midday meal needs to keep us going for the rest of the day, but ideally it shouldn't send us into a slump while our system works overtime to digest it. Our lunch dishes have been carefully planned to provide lasting nutrition that is easy on the stomach.

And we frequently play with the old classics – our versions of tacos, burgers, pizzas and lasagne are all designed to evoke the same flavour profiles as their conventional counterparts, but in a healthy way. What better way to get people eating healthier than to show them that they don't have to miss out on the foods that they love?

crispy almond & hazelnut tartlets

A crispy tart shell filled with nut cheese or hummus topped with a selection of seasonal vegetables makes for a delightful lunch dish or canapé. I love how tarts package everything up so neatly into one perfect little parcel. The tart shells can be made a few days in advance, then filled just before you serve them. Following this recipe are three of our favourite fillings for you to choose from. The creamy mushrooms with shallots (see page 84) also tastes great in these.

Make time: 30 minutes | Soak time: 12 hours | Dehydrating time: 12–14 hours | Makes: 8 individual tarts |
Equipment required: blender, dehydrator, food processor, 10 cm (4 in) tart (flan) tins (or smaller canapé tins for mini versions)

60 g (2¼ oz/⅓ cup) **whole golden flax seeds**

400 g (14 oz/2½ cups) **almonds**
(soaked 12 hours)

75 g (½ cup) **hazelnuts** (soaked 6 hours)

1 tbsp **nutritional yeast**

1½ tsp **sea salt**

½ tsp **freshly cracked pepper**

3 tbsp **cold-pressed olive oil**

60 ml (2 fl oz/¼ cup) **filtered water**

Turn the whole golden flax seeds into flour in a blender. Drain the soaked nuts and rinse thoroughly.

Place all the ingredients except the olive oil and the water in the food processor – blend ingredients until thoroughly mixed, leaving some texture to the nuts. Add the olive oil and water while running. Process for a few seconds until the mixture holds together well.

Oil the individual tins with some olive oil, press the mixture evenly into the individual tart cases – you don't want the crust to be too thick – it should be around 3 mm (⅛ in). Place the bases onto a dehydrator tray and dehydrate at 46°C (115°F) for 6 hours. They should now be firm enough to remove from the tart cases – gently! Continue to dehydrate for a further 6–8 hours until completely dry and crispy.

You can store these in an airtight container lined with baking paper for a few days.

harissa chickpeas & carrots with almond hummus

Make time: 10 minutes + component recipes | Dehydrating time: 1 hour | Makes: 4 tartlet fillings |
Equipment required: dehydrator

400 g (14 oz/1 bunch) **baby carrots**

115 g (4 oz/¾ cup) **sprouted chickpeas**
(see pages 26–27)

2 handfuls **baby English spinach**

2 tbsp **sesame seeds**

1 tbsp **harissa spice mix**

½ tsp **sea salt**

2 tbsp **lemon juice**

5 tbsp **cold-pressed olive oil**

495 g (2 cups) **almond hummus** (see page 139)

garnish – **freshly cracked pepper**, 2 tbsp chopped **parsley** and 1 tbsp finely diced **preserved lemon** (see page 56)

Peel and chop the baby carrots into halves lengthways. Place the carrots, chickpeas, spinach, sesame seeds, harissa, sea salt, lemon juice and olive oil in a bowl and mix together. Place everything on a dehydrator sheet and dehydrate at 46°C (115°F) for 1 hour.

Get 4 tartlets (see recipe above) and place 2–3 tablespoons of the hummus into each.

Place a handful of the chickpea and carrot mixture on top and drizzle with some of the oil from the mixture.

Garnish with freshly cracked pepper, parsley and preserved lemon if using.

fresh fig & caramelised onion tartlets with baby rocket

Make time: 5 minutes + component recipes | Makes: 4 tartlet fillings

2 cups **herbed cheese** (see page 44)

70 g (2½ oz/1½ cups) **baby rocket (arugula)**

½ cup **caramelised onions** (see page 40)

8–10 **fresh figs**

freshly cracked pepper

garnish – **freshly cracked pepper, cold-pressed olive oil** and 1 handful **micro beetroot (beet) leaves** (optional)

Add a few tablespoons of water if needed to your herbed cheese until it is the consistency of a soft cream cheese.

Take 4 tartlet shells (see page 114) and place a small handful of rocket and ½ tablespoon of caramelised onions in the bottom of each one. Top with 2–3 tablespoons of herbed cheese. Spread the cheese until you get a flat top and can't see any rocket.

Slice the fresh figs and place on top of the cheese.

Garnish with freshly cracked pepper, a drizzle of olive oil and a few micro beet leaves (if using).

cherry tomato tartlets with basil & herbed macadamia & cashew cream

Make time: 10 minutes + component recipe | Marinating time: 30 minutes–1 hour | Makes: 4 tartlet fillings

450 g (1 lb/3 cups) **cherry tomatoes**

3 tbsp **cold-pressed olive oil**

1 tsp **balsamic** or **red wine vinegar**

¼ tsp **sea salt**

2 cups **herbed cheese** (see page 44)

micro basil or **fresh basil leaves**

garnish – **freshly cracked pepper**

Slice the tomatoes and marinate in the olive oil, vinegar and sea salt for at least 30 minutes to 1 hour.

Add a few tablespoons of filtered water if needed to your herbed cheese until it is the consistency of a soft cream cheese.

Take 4 tartlet shells (see page 114) and place 2–3 tablespoons of the cheese in each one and top with basil and the marinated tomatoes.

Garnish with freshly cracked pepper.

pad thai with coconut noodles, spicy almond & cashew sauce

This is the dish that got us on the Auckland food map, showing up in a few magazines and topping the Metro list as one of the city's favourite takeout dishes. While not a traditional pad thai, like lots of Thai food it uses an abundance of fresh vegetables and herbs, which we have paired with a spicy almond and cashew sauce. Southeast Asian flavours work especially well with raw foods.

Make time: 30 minutes + component recipes | Soak time: 2 hours | Serves: 2–3 | Equipment required: blender

pad thai sauce

3 tbsp **raw almond butter**
or 40 g (1½ oz/¼ cup) **almonds** (soaked 12 hours)

40 g (1½ oz/¼ cup) **cashews** (soaked 2 hours)

1 tbsp chopped **ginger**

1 crushed and chopped **garlic clove**

1 small deseeded and finely chopped **red chilli** (or 1–2 tsp dried red chilli flakes – depending on how hot your chillies are)

1½ tbsp **tamari**

4 tbsp **lemon** or **lime juice**

2 tbsp **coconut sugar**

pinch **sea salt**

60–125 ml (2–4 fl oz/¼–½ cup) **filtered water**

optional – 2 tbsp **tamarind water**

noodles & vegetables

80 g (2¾ oz/½ cup) **young coconut flesh**

225 g (8 oz/3 cups) finely shredded **white cabbage**

70 g (2½ oz/½ cup) halved **cherry tomatoes**

1 julienned **carrot**

½ **mango**, chopped into thin slices

50 g (1¾ oz/½ cup) julienned **snow peas** (mangetout)

10 g (¼ oz/¼ cup) **snow pea** (mangetout) **tendrils**

1 large handful **fresh coriander (cilantro)**, chopped

½ handful **thai basil**

optional – 1 tsp finely chopped **vietnamese mint**

garnish – **spiced cashews** (see page 29),
1 finely chopped **red chilli** (to taste) and
1 **lime** cut into wedges

Drain the soaked nuts and rinse thoroughly.

In a blender, combine almond butter or almonds with cashews, ginger, garlic, chilli, tamari, lemon or lime juice, coconut sugar and a pinch of sea salt. Add 60 ml (2 fl oz/¼ cup) water and blend well. You may need to add more water (add a little at a time) to get this to a consistency that is similar to mayonnaise. Make sure it is not too runny or the flavours will be watered down and the mixture won't hold on the vegetables.

Scoop and clean the young coconut flesh and slice into thin noodles.

In a large bowl, place 150 g (5½ oz/2 cups) of the finely shredded cabbage and mix with ¼ of the sauce mixture until very well combined. Very lightly fold through the rest of the vegetables, mango and coconut noodles; you don't want to coat everything with the sauce or you will lose all the beautiful colours. Throw the snow pea tendrils and herbs over the top.

Serve the rest of the pad thai sauce on the side, along with spiced cashews, finely chopped chilli (to taste) and a wedge of lime.

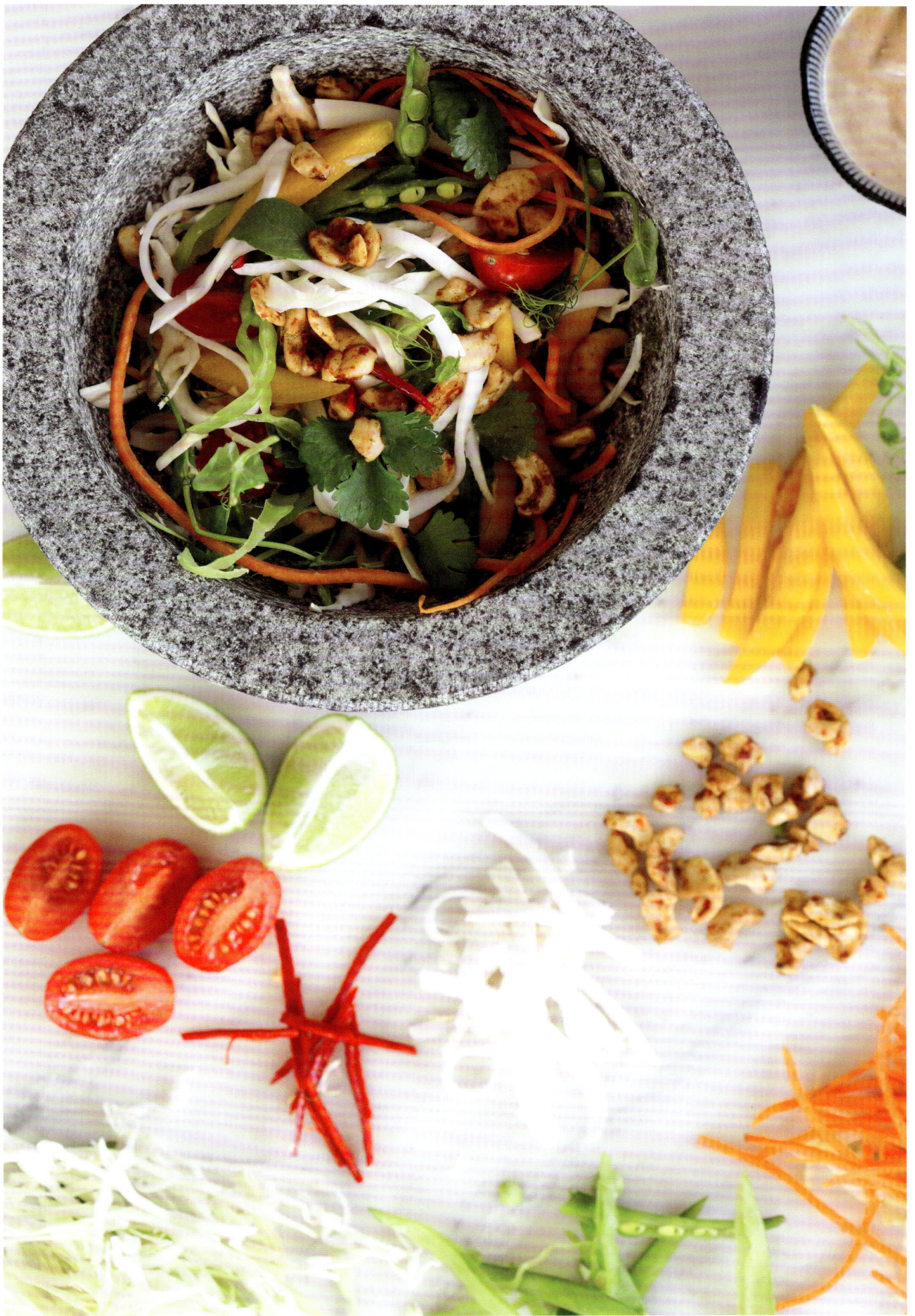

spicy thai bok choy spring rolls

This dish was originally created as a main dish for lunch or dinner, serving 4–5 spring rolls per person with a small bowl of dipping sauce on the side. It's fantastic party finger food as well – who doesn't love a spring roll! This dish has a few components that you need to prepare ahead of time but once they're made they'll store in the pantry for many weeks. The dipping sauce is deliciously moreish and can also be used to dress Asian salads.

Make time: 40 minutes + component recipe | Soak time: 2–4 hours | Dehydrating time: 12–16 hours | Makes: 16–20 small spring rolls | Equipment required: blender, dehydrator, mandoline

155 g (1 cup) **cashews** (soaked 2–4 hours)

60 ml (2 fl oz/¼ cup) **sweet soy** (see page 47)

170 g (½ packet) **kelp noodles**

6 tbsp **tamari**

4 large heads **bok choy (pak choy)**

1 medium **carrot**

1 **telegraph (long) cucumber**

230 g (2 cups) **bean sprouts**

1 handful **fresh mint**

1 handful **fresh coriander (cilantro)**

1 handful **thai basil**

dipping sauce

40 g (½ oz/¼ cup) **cashews** (soaked 2–4 hours)

125 ml (4 fl oz/½ cup) **tamari**

125 ml (4 fl oz/½ cup) **filtered water**

75 g (¼ cup) **raw agave**

½ medium **shallot**

½ medium **red chilli**

1 cm (½ in) piece **ginger**

1 medium **garlic clove**

½ tsp **toasted sesame oil**

To prepare the cashews:
Drain the soaked cashews and rinse thoroughly. Mix with the sweet soy. Dehydrate at 46°C (115°F) for 8 hours. Roughly chop and set aside.

To prepare the noodles:
Wash the kelp noodles (we use Sea Tangle brand) well in a sieve. Mix with the tamari and leave to marinate for 30 minutes until they become soft. Strain off some of the tamari and set noodles aside.

To prepare the dipping sauce:
Drain the soaked cashews and rinse thoroughly. Place all dipping sauce ingredients in a blender and process until smooth. Dipping sauce will store in the refrigerator for 3–4 days.

To prepare the bok choy rolls:
Cut the very end of the base off the bok choy and separate all the leaves – you will only use the larger outer leaves that are able to be rolled, some of the inner ones will be too small. Place the leaves you are using in a bowl. Cover with water and place inside the dehydrator for 1 hour to soften. (Alternatively you can pour hot water over the leaves and mix around until the leaves become pliable then submerge immediately in ice water. You don't want to cook them so work quickly – they should still be a vibrant green colour as that's where all the goodness and flavour is – so don't leave them in the hot water long.)

To assemble:
Julienne the carrots and cucumber finely using a mandoline. Lay out the bok choy leaves so that the base is closest to you and the inside of the leaf is facing up. Place a small amount of the carrot, cucumber and bean sprouts at the top of the base portion of the bok choy leaf. Add approximately 1 tablespoon of kelp noodles along with a couple of leaves of each herb and a sprinkle of crushed sweet soy cashews. Roll the base part of the bok choy leaf over the filling, tuck it into the rest of the leaf and roll it up tightly.

Repeat with the remaining bok choy leaves and filling ingredients.

inside-out asparagus & shiitake sushi roll

We have made a lot of great sushi in the little bird cafés – with different versions of rice and styles, including handrolls and nigiri. The inside-outside roll is a favourite; rice on the outside adds a little extra to your sushi eating experience.

Make time: 30 minutes + component recipe | Dehydrating time: 40 minutes | Makes: 4 rolls, 24 pieces | Equipment required: dehydrator, food processor, sushi mat

rice

30 g (1 oz/⅓ cup) **psyllium husk** (this helps bind it)

80 ml (2½ fl oz/⅓ cup) **filtered water**

160 g (1½ cups) diced **cauliflower**

120 g (4¼ oz/1½ cups) diced **parsnip**

55 g (2 oz/⅓ cup) **macadamia nuts**

¼ tsp **sea salt**

½ tsp **toasted sesame oil**

2 tbsp **umeboshi vinegar**

sushi

175 g (6 oz/1 bunch) washed **green** or **white asparagus**

1 tbsp **cold-pressed olive oil**

sea salt

4 **nori sheets** (there are raw brands available)

4 tbsp **balck sesame seeds**

4 tbsp **white sesame seeds**

½ tsp **toasted sesame oil**

6 medium **shiitake mushrooms**, cut into strips

½ finely chopped **red chilli**
(with or without seeds – that's up to you)

1 tsp **coconut sugar**

1 **spring onion**, finely sliced lengthways

1 handful **snow pea (mangetout) shoots**

1–2 **avocados**, sliced into wedges (8 per avocado)

garnish – **tamari** or **coconut aminos**
and **pickled ginger** (see page 56)

To prepare the rice:
Mix psyllium and water, put aside and let sit for 5 minutes. Pulse the cauliflower, parsnip, macadamia nuts and sea salt in a food processor until the texture of couscous. Place the mixture in a nut milk bag and squeeze out some of the moisture. Place in a bowl and fluff with a fork, fold through the sesame oil and vinegar.

Rub the psyllium and water mix into the rice with your fingers, until the mixture is nice and sticky and holds together well.

To prepare the fillings:
Hold each asparagus spear halfway down its length and at the thick end with your other hand – then bend it until it snaps. Don't use the thick end. (The head of the asparagus stalk is the tender tasty part – the thicker end can be very fibrous and difficult to eat). Coat the asparagus in the olive oil and a pinch of sea salt, place in a dehydrator for 30–40 minutes at 46°C (115°F) until slightly tender.

To roll the sushi:
Take a sushi mat and place it down with the slats running horizontally. Place a nori sheet shiny-side down. With wet hands, spread ¼ of rice over nori sheet. Sprinkle the sesame seeds evenly over rice. Cover with plastic wrap.

Gently turn the rice, nori & plastic over so the nori faces up – place the plastic side down against the mat.

Layer a quarter of the filling ingredients on the nori – place them approximately ⅓ of the way in from the end facing you.

Take the bottom edge of the sushi mat with your thumbs and, while pushing the sushi filling in with your fingers, start rolling it away from you. (After you've enclosed the vegetables, clamp down on the roll slightly to firm it up so the shape holds.)

Continue until you have completed the roll and it's holding firmly. Remove from the mat and plastic.

Cut into 6 pieces – clean the knife after each cut with a damp cloth. Serve with a side of tamari and pickled ginger.

smashed pea pasta
with basil & avocado pesto

If there was ever a time to go raw it's the beginning of summer, when there is an abundance of fresh sun-ripened produce around. There are many ways to use zucchini (courgette) in raw recipes, from breads and crackers (including pizza bases) to hummus – they don't have a very strong taste so you can coat them in your favourite flavour combinations.

This pasta recipe is a celebration of all things summery and green, filled with lots of fresh herbs and summer peas and folded into a herbed pesto made with avocado. Top with your choice of pine nuts, lemon zest or macadamia cheese. Works well as a main, entrée or side dish.

Make time: 15 minutes + component recipe | Serves: 4 as a main dish | Equipment required: food processor, spiraliser

4–5 small to medium **zucchini (courgettes)**; ends trimmed (can be yellow or green)

80 g (2¾ oz/½ cup) **freshly podded peas** (alternatively use snow peas (mangetout) finely chopped lengthways)

1 tbsp finely chopped **mint**

1 handful **fresh basil**, torn

1 handful **fresh parsley**, torn

1 handful **fresh rocket (arugula)**

1 handful **baby English spinach**

45 g (¼ cup) whole **green olives** – the sicilian ones have a nice grassy flavour (slice the flesh off the pip after measuring)

1 tsp **fresh lemon zest**

garnish – 40 g (1½ oz/¼ cup) **pine nuts** or **macadamia cheese** (see page 42), **freshly cracked pepper**

Start by spiralising the zucchini – these are your pasta noodles. We use the Japanese 'Benriner' horizontal spiraliser but if you don't have a vegetable spiraliser then you can use a peeler to cut the zucchini into wide strips then julienne with a knife. Set aside.

In a bowl, coat the pasta with the pesto mix (see following recipe). It should be reasonably easy to coat – if it clumps, add a little more olive oil or lemon juice to get it moving.

Gently fold through the herbs and vegetables.

Place a serving of pasta on the plate, top with pine nuts or roughly broken chunks of macadamia cheese and some freshly cracked pepper.

basil, avocado & parsley pesto

1 crushed **garlic clove**

¼ tsp **sea salt**

3 handfuls **fresh basil** and **parsley leaves**, picked and chopped (you could use just basil or a combination with rocket (arugula) instead)

1 **avocado**, flesh finely diced

5 tbsp **extra virgin cold-pressed olive oil**

1 **lemon**, juice and zest

Pound the garlic with the sea salt and the basil and parsley leaves with a pestle in a mortar, or pulse in a food processor. Fold in the avocado and crush lightly with the pestle until it combines but still has some texture. Turn out into a bowl and gently add olive oil – you need just enough to bind the sauce and get it to an oozy consistency. Finish with lemon juice and zest. Add extra sea salt to taste.

zucchini layered lasagne with baby English spinach & basil

A rustic family dish that hits all the notes a lasagne should, with lots of delicious cheese and tomato sauce coating layers of al dente pasta sheets.

Make time: 30 minutes | Soak time: 2–4 hours | Dehydrating time: 2 hours (optional) | Serves: 6 large portions | Equipment required: blender, dehydrator (optional), mandoline

cheese

275 g (9¾ oz/1¾ cups) **cashews** (soaked 2 hours or more)

1 tbsp **lemon juice**

2 tbsp **nutritional yeast**

1 **shallot**

½ tsp **sea salt**

125 ml (4 fl oz/½ cup) **filtered water**

tomato sauce

75 g (1 cup) **sundried tomatoes** (soaked 2 hours or more)

2 **pitted dates**

2 **garlic cloves**

300 g (10½ oz/2 cups) **cherry tomatoes** or regular **tomatoes**

80 g (2¾ oz/½ cup) roughly chopped **capsicum (pepper)**

1 tbsp **fresh oregano leaves**

2 tbsp **cold-pressed olive oil**

2 tbsp **apple cider vinegar**

pasta & vegies

270 g (9½ oz/6 cups) **baby English spinach**

1 handful **fresh basil**

1 tsp **cold-pressed olive oil**

¼ tsp **sea salt**

5–6 medium **zucchini (courgettes)**, cut lengthways

150 g (5½ oz/1 cup) **cherry tomatoes**, cut into three slices or use 2 large **tomatoes**

2 **red capsicums (peppers)**, sliced finely on a mandoline

garnish – **cold-pressed olive oil, freshly cracked pepper, fresh basil** and **pine nuts**

To prepare the cheese:
Drain the soaked cashews and rinse thoroughly. In a high-speed blender, blend all ingredients together, adding as little of the water as possible until a fluffy consistency is achieved.

To prepare the tomato sauce:
Drain the soaked sundried tomatoes and place all the ingredients in a blender. Blend well until the mixture is smooth.

To prepare the dish:
Toss the spinach, basil, olive oil and sea salt in a bowl and set aside.

Cut the zucchini into ribbons lengthways with a mandoline, or use a knife if you don't have a mandoline. Line the base of your dish with a layer of the zucchini strips (this is your pasta layer), overlapping them slightly. Use ⅓ of what you have per layer. Drizzle each layer with a little olive oil and a pinch of sea salt.

On top of this, put down a layer of the spinach mixture, then the cheese, then ½ of the tomatoes and capsicum and top with tomato sauce.

Repeat one more time with the layering and finish this with another layer of slightly overlapping zucchini strips.

Placing the whole dish in the refrigerator for several hours will firm it all up slightly, which will make it easier to cut into portions. In the café we dehydrate the lasagne at 46°C (115°F) for a few hours before serving to intensify the flavour.

Garnish with olive oil, black pepper, basil and pine nuts.

mexican chilli bowl with avocado, tomato salsa & iceberg slaw

Mexican flavours work incredibly well with raw food; a lot of the components are already raw like salsa, guacamole and the slaw. This Mexican chilli is the perfect antidote to a cold evening. It will warm you from the inside out leaving you feeling satisfied, while all the beautiful raw ingredients will leave you feeling refreshed.

Similar to our bird bowl (see page 170), this is a collection of recipes that work together synergistically to form the perfectly balanced fresh-yet-hearty evening meal.

chilli

Make time: 40 minutes | Soak time: 12 hours | Dehydrating time: 30 minutes | Serves: 4 |
Equipment required: blender, dehydrator, food processor

55 g (2 oz/¾ cup) finely diced **flat mushrooms**

70 g (2½ oz/½ cup) finely diced **celery**

40 g (½ oz/¼ cup) finely chopped **red onion**

1 finely chopped **red capsicum (pepper)**

3 tbsp **cold-pressed olive oil**

120 g (4½ oz/¾ cup) **almonds** (soaked 12 hours)

150 g (5½ oz/1 cup) roughly chopped **carrot**

110 g (3¾ oz/¾ cup) **sundried tomatoes** (soaked 4 hours)

1–2 **dried chipotle chillies** (soaked 4 hours)

1 **garlic clove**

125 ml (4 fl oz/½ cup) **filtered water**

2 **pitted dates**

2 medium roughly chopped **tomatoes**

2 tbsp **tamari**

1 tbsp finely chopped **fresh oregano** or 1 tsp **dried ezpazote** (mexican oregano)

1 tsp **chilli powder**

1 tbsp **cumin**

1 tbsp **apple cider vinegar**

¼ tsp **sea salt**

optional – ¼ tsp **cayenne pepper** for extra spice and/or 1–2 **dried ancho chillies** (soaked 4 hours)

Put the diced mushrooms, celery, onion and red capsicum in a bowl and coat with 3 tablespoons of olive oil and a few pinches of sea salt. Place on a dehydrator tray and dehydrate for 30 minutes (alternatively place in an oven on its lowest setting and leave the door slightly ajar). This is not essential but it will make a more traditional chilli flavour; I find dehydrating mushrooms for a short period of time really enhances their flavour.

Place the almonds and carrots in a food processor and pulse until approximately 3–4 mm (⅛–³⁄₁₆ in) sized pieces. You want it to have some texture. Place in a bowl and add the dehydrated vegetables. Set aside.

Put all the remaining ingredients in a blender and mix until smooth.

Add the wet mix to the vegetable and almond mixture and fold together until combined. Add additional sea salt to taste.

Note – this chilli, like a lot of dishes with dry spices in them, will taste better if you let it sit for a few hours. I love eating the chilli for leftovers lunch the next day.

little bird guacamole

Make time: 10 minutes | Makes: 2 cups

2 **avocados**

1 crushed **garlic clove**

juice 1 **lemon** (add to taste)

pinch **sea salt** (add to taste)

175 g (6 oz/1 cup) finely diced **cucumber**

2 tsp finely chopped **coriander (cilantro)**

Place the avocado, garlic, lemon and sea salt into a bowl and crush with a fork until mostly smooth. Fold in the cucumber and then the coriander.

bowl assembly

Serves: 4

⅛ **white cabbage**

⅛ **red cabbage**
or half an **iceberg lettuce**
(this is instead of both cabbages)

salsa (see page 132)

guacamole (see recipe above)

1 handful **coriander (cilantro)**

1 **lime**, cut into wedges

corn chips (see page 50)

optional – **sour cream** (see page 46)

To assemble the bowls:
Finely shred the cabbage or iceberg lettuce on a mandoline or with a knife. Don't worry if you only have one type of cabbage – the two colours are more for colour than flavour (white cabbage has a softer, sweeter flavour so if you choose to use just one, this is the preferable variety).

Place a few handfuls of the slaw in the bottom of the bowl with about ½–¾ cup of the chilli mixture followed by salsa, guacamole and sour cream (if using).

Top with coriander and serve with wedges of lime and a side of chips.

mexican tacos with chimichurri & salsa

Our raw tacos are a real favourite with our customers. Recently we took them off the menu in the café for the first time since opening, but we received such an outcry from our customers, we won't be taking them off again.

In this dish we are making a traditional-style taco with our exceptional soft corn tacos (see page 50) but you could also use a collard leaf as the taco shell if you don't have time or access to a dehydrator to make the soft taco shells.

chimichurri

This Mexican salsa verde is so moreish and delicious you will want to make extra to keep around. Use it here and in other Mexican dishes but don't feel restricted; by using it as a dressing on many salads you can transform a plain plate of green leafy vegetables into a delicious, dynamic tasting meal.

Make time: 15 minutes | Makes: 1 cup | Equipment required: food processor

1 very large handful **flat-leaf (italian) parsley**

1 very large handful **coriander (cilantro)**

1 crushed and chopped **garlic clove**

1 finely chopped **green chilli**

½ tsp **cumin powder**

½ tsp **sea salt**

½ finely chopped **red onion**

40 g (1½ oz/¼ cup) **pickled jalapenos**

60 ml (2 fl oz/¼ cup) **red wine vinegar**

80 ml (2½ fl oz/⅓ cup) and 2 tbsp **cold-pressed olive oil**

Wash and roughly chop the parsley and coriander – you can use some of the softer stems as well, not just the leaves. Blend the parsley and coriander in a food processor until they are well chopped.

Add the garlic, green chilli, cumin powder, sea salt, red onion and jalapenos, and blend until combined, leaving no large chunks. Add the vinegar and, while the food processor is running, add the oil in a slow drizzle.

Chimichurri keeps in the refrigerator for around 1 week but will lose some of its vibrant colour after a few days.

salsa

Make time: 15 minutes | Makes: 2½ cups

3 firm **ripe tomatoes**
or 375 g (13 oz/2½ cups) mixed **cherry tomatoes**, diced into approximately 5 mm (¼ in) pieces

1 **red** or **yellow capsicum (pepper)**, diced into approximately 5 mm (¼ in) pieces

1 very finely diced **shallot** or ¼ **red onion**

2 crushed or finely chopped **garlic cloves**

1 small handful **coriander (cilantro)**, chopped

1 tbsp **apple cider vinegar**

1 tbsp **cold-pressed olive oil**

1 tbsp **lime juice**

¾ tsp **cumin**

¾ tsp **sea salt**

finely minced **jalapeno**
or **chipotle chilli** (add to taste)

Mix all the ingredients in a bowl, adding more jalapeno and sea salt if needed. You can serve it straight away but if you have the time it's nice to let it sit for 1–2 hours for the flavours to develop.

assembly

Makes: 12 tacos

¼ **white** or **red cabbage**

1 squeeze **lime juice**

pinch **sea salt**

12 **tacos** (see page 50) or use 12 **collard leaves**

½ batch **raw chilli recipe** (see page 130)

guacamole (see page 131)

1 small handful **coriander (cilantro) leaves**

optional – **sour cream** (see page 46)

garnish – 2 **limes** cut into wedges

To assemble the tacos:
Finely shred the cabbage on a mandoline or with a knife. Squeeze a little lime juice and a pinch of sea salt on it and set aside.

Place the taco shell or collard leaf down on a plate and layer with the cabbage followed by the raw chilli, salsa, chimichurri, guacamole, sour cream if using and lastly some fresh coriander. Serve with fresh lime wedges.

pizza with tomato sauce, herbed cheese, olives & rocket pesto

This pizza was a hit when we put it on the menu at our Summer Street unbakery. The simple, traditional flavours balance perfectly to create an exceptional pizza experience.

Make time: 20 minutes + component recipes | Makes: 4 single serve pizzas |
Equipment required: food processor or pestle and mortar, mandoline

2 medium **zucchini (courgettes)**

125 g (4½ oz/¾ cup) **cherry tomatoes**

75 g (½ cup) **olives**

4 **pizza bases** (see page 38)

½ cup **tomato sauce** (see page 54)

4 tsp **pine nuts**

¾ cup **herbed cheese** (see page 44)

2 handfuls **rocket (arugula)**

1 handful **basil** or **micro basil**

60 g (2¼ oz/¼ cup) **pesto** (see following recipe)

Slice the zucchini into fine ribbons lengthways on a mandoline. Chop the cherry tomatoes and olives in half.

Take 4 pizza bases (if you're getting them from the refrigerator put in the dehydrator for ½ an hour to warm up).

Place 2–3 tablespoons of tomato sauce on each pizza and spread evenly. Place the zucchini slices across the pizza as shown in the picture. Top with cherry tomato halves, olives and pine nuts and 4–5 dollops of herbed cheese.

Place the rocket and basil in a bowl with the pesto and lightly mix until coated – top each pizza with a quarter of the rocket and pesto mixture.

basil & rocket pesto

Makes: ⅔ cup

1 **garlic clove**

sea salt

3 handfuls **fresh rocket (arugula)** and **basil** leaves picked and chopped (you could use parsley instead)

80 g (2¾ oz/½ cup) **pine nuts** or **macadamia nuts**

extra virgin cold-pressed olive oil

optional – ½ tsp **nutritional yeast** or 2 tbsp of **cashew parmesan** (see page 45), **lemon juice**

Pound the garlic in a pestle and mortar with a little pinch of sea salt and the rocket and basil leaves (alternatively pulse in a food processor). Add the pine nuts to the mixture and pound again. Turn out into a bowl and gently add olive oil – you need just enough to bind the sauce and get it to an oozy consistency.

Season to taste. Pour in some more oil if needed and add nutritional yeast or cheese if using. You can add a squeeze of lemon juice at the end to give it a little zest but it's not essential.

spaghetti with walnut & mushroom meatballs

Raw pasta is a dish where zucchini (courgette) out-does itself – the texture is perfectly al dente and it maintains a good background status, enabling our delicious Italian meatballs and tomato sauce to show off.

Zucchini are low in calories and high in vitamin C and fibre, making them an excellent food to eat a lot of. They help keep your digestive system healthy and functional.

Make time: 45 minutes + component recipes | Soak time: 4–6 hours | Dehydrating time: 4–5 hours | Serves: 4 | Equipment required: blender, dehydrator, food processor, spiraliser

walnut & mushroom meatballs

150 g (5½ oz/1¼ cups) **walnuts** (soaked 4–6 hours)

75 g (½ cup) **sunflower seeds** (soaked 4–6 hours)

60 g (2¼ oz/⅓ cup) **whole golden flax seeds**

4–5 medium **portobello mushrooms**

1 medium **carrot**

2 stalks **celery**

½ **onion**

2 crushed and finely chopped **garlic cloves**

2 pinches **sea salt**

½ tsp **freshly cracked pepper**

1 tsp finely chopped **thyme**

1 tsp finely chopped **sage**

60 ml (2 fl oz/¼ cup) **filtered water**

3 tbsp **tamari** or **nama shoyu**

1 tbsp **dijon** or **wholegrain mustard**

4 tbsp **cold-pressed olive oil**

Drain the soaked walnuts and sunflower seeds and rinse thoroughly. Blend in a food processor into a coarse couscous-like texture.

Grind the flax seeds into a flour in a high-speed blender or spice mill.

Finely dice the mushrooms, carrot, celery and onion – you could use a food processor to do this, just make sure you keep enough texture so the vegetables don't become mushy.

Mix the walnuts and sunflower seeds with the flax flour, vegetables, garlic, sea salt, pepper and the herbs and combine until evenly mixed. Now add the water, tamari, mustard and olive oil to the mixture, being careful not to over-mix it. You want the mixture to just come together, over working it will cause the flax to become too gummy.

Shape into meatballs, approximately 20 x 3–4 cm (1¼–1½ in) each. Place in dehydrator at 46°C (115°F) until mostly dry, 4–5 hours. You want them moist but with a nice crust.

zucchini pasta

5–6 medium **zucchini (courgettes)**

220 g (7¾ oz/1½ cups) **cherry tomatoes**

2 cups **tomato sauce** (see page 54)

3 handfuls **rocket (arugula)**

2 large handfuls **parsley**, finely chopped

½ cup **cashew parmesan** (see page 45)

pinch **sea salt**

freshly cracked pepper

optional – 4 tbsp **organic red wine**

Take the ends off the zucchini and spiralise into noodles using a spiraliser (alternatively you can use a peeler to make thin ribbons). Chop the cherry tomatoes into halves.

Take the tomato sauce and add red wine (if using). Otherwise add 3–4 tablespoons of filtered water to loosen the mixture up if needed.

Mix the zucchini noodles with the tomato sauce and lightly fold through the rocket, cherry tomatoes and parsley.

Divide the mixture between 4 bowls and top with 3–4 meatballs and sprinkle with parmesan. Add sea salt and pepper to taste.

portobello burger with almond hummus

Like any good burger, this portobello mushroom version is a little messy and saucy. There's no pattie in the mix, with the meaty mushrooms standing in as buns! If you do want to add a pattie, the falafels (see page 198) or the meatballs (see page 136) work well. And any of our cultured nut cheeses (see page 42) would be a great addition.

Make time: 20 minutes + component recipes | Dehydrating time: 3 hours | Serves: 4 | Equipment required: dehydrator

8 large **portobello mushrooms**

60 ml (2 fl oz/¼ cup) **cold-pressed olive oil**

2 tsp **toasted sesame oil**

1 tsp **rice wine vinegar**

2 tsp **tamari**

sea salt

2 tbsp **white sesame seeds**

freshly cracked pepper

½ cup **tomato sauce** (see page 54)

2 tsp **apple cider vinegar**

½ tsp **coconut sugar**

¼ tsp **smoked paprika**

pinch **cayenne pepper**

¼ medium finely shredded **red cabbage**

2 tbsp chopped **parsley**

2 tsp **lemon juice**

1 large peeled and grated **beetroot (beets)**

almond hummus (see following recipe)

1 large **beefsteak tomato** or other large tomato, sliced into thick rounds

1–2 large **avocados**, cut into wedges

2 handfuls **alfalfa sprouts**

4 **lettuce leaves** (iceberg or buttercrunch)

Remove the stems from the mushrooms, place in a bowl with the olive oil, toasted sesame oil, rice wine vinegar, tamari and a pinch of sea salt. Mix until thoroughly coated.

Place the mushrooms with the stem side up on a dehydrator sheet and pour over any juices from the mushroom mixture; dehydrate for 2 hours at 46°C (115°F).

Remove from the dehydrator (the flesh should be soft). With a spoon, gently scrape out ⅓ –½ of the flesh from each mushroom, leaving the outer part intact. If you love a bold mushroom flavour you can omit this step – depending on how thick your mushrooms are. The portobello flavour can dominate over the other flavours if the mushrooms are too thick.

Place back in the dehydrator for 1 hour, stem side down and sprinkle the tops with sesame seeds and freshly cracked pepper.

Mix the tomato sauce with 1 teaspoon of apple cider vinegar, the coconut sugar, smoked paprika and cayenne (add cayenne to taste) until combined.

To prepare the vegetables, mix the cabbage with parsley, a pinch of sea salt and the lemon juice. Separately mix the beetroot with the remaining apple cider vinegar and a pinch of sea salt. Set both aside to marinate for 5–10 minutes.

Take the mushrooms out of the dehydrator. Take 4 of the mushrooms and place stem side up – now you get to build your burgers. Place a small handful of cabbage then beetroot on the mushrooms followed by 2–3 tablespoons of the hummus and tomato slices. Top the tomato with a tablespoon of the paprika tomato sauce and then 2–3 avocado wedges, alfalfa and iceberg.

Finish with your portobello mushroom sesame bun top.

almond hummus

Make time: 10 minutes | Soaking time: 12 hours | Makes: 2½ cups | Equipment required: food processor

420 g (4¼ oz/¾ cup) **almonds** (soaked 12 hours)

2 medium peeled and roughly chopped **zucchini** (courgettes)

135 g (4¾ oz/½ cup) **raw tahini** (or a good organic tahini)

3 tbsp **cold-pressed olive oil**

80 ml (2½ fl oz/⅓ cup) **lemon juice**

1 tsp **sea salt**

1 tsp **cumin**

1 large crushed and finely chopped **garlic clove**

¼ tsp **chilli powder** or a pinch **cayenne pepper**

Drain the soaked almonds and rinse thoroughly (you could use cashews or macadamia nuts here as well). Put all the ingredients in a food processor and run until smooth, wiping the sides down as you go.

You want a thick hummus for the burgers. You can add a little water to make it more fluid if you're using it as a dip.

thai herbed mushroom larb with lemongrass in cos cups & buckwheat crunch

This is one of those recipes that people look at then flick the page. A long ingredient list can seem a bit overwhelming, but this recipe is worth it! None of the steps are technical, it's just a lot of simple prep work.

Larb is a Laotian and Thai dish packed with fresh herbs, notably lemongrass. You will often see it served in iceberg or cos (romaine) lettuce cups, as we're doing here. Fish sauce is an integral part of Asian cuisine, so Xander created this vegan alternative for us to use instead. Serve as a canapé or main dish.

Make time: 50 minutes + component recipes | Dehydrating time: 4–5 hours | Makes: 18–20 individual cos (romaine) cups | Equipment required: dehydrator

150 g (5½ oz/4 cups) **swiss brown button mushrooms**

1 tbsp freshly minced **lemongrass**

3 tbsp finely chopped and deseeded **red chilli flesh**

30 g (1 oz/¼ cup) finely diced **shallot**

1 minced and chopped **garlic clove**

pinch **sea salt**

80 ml (2½ fl oz/⅓ cup) **cold-pressed olive oil**

3 tbsp **tamari**

1 **spring onion (scallion)**

200 g (7 oz/2 cups) **red cabbage**

1 **telegraph (long) cucumber**

1 handful **thai basil leaves**

1 handful **coriander (cilantro) leaves**

1 handful **mint leaves**

½ tsp **kaffir lime powder**
(you can use 2 fresh leaves very finely minced)

230 g (2 cups) **bean sprouts**

2 tbsp **sweet soy** (see page 47)

60 ml (2 fl oz/¼ cup) **fish sauce**
(see following recipe)

60 ml (2 fl oz/¼ cup) **lime juice**

3–4 heads **baby cos (romaine) lettuce**

garnish – **dehydrated sprouted buckwheat** (see page 270), 1 handful **micro coriander (cilantro)** or **fresh coriander (cilantro) leaves** and **sweet soy** (see page 47) to taste

Dice the mushrooms and place in a mixing bowl with the lemongrass, 1 teaspoon of the freshly chopped chilli, 1 tablespoon of the finely chopped shallot, garlic, pinch of sea salt, olive oil and tamari. Mix well.

Place the mushrooms including the juices on a dehydrator sheet and dehydrate at 46°C (115°F) for 1 hour or until the mushroom juices start to release. Put mushrooms and their juices into a mixing bowl. Leave the mixture to marinate for ½ hour and strain, reserving the juice for the fish sauce (see following recipe). The fish sauce takes 3–4 hours to dehydrate (make this before moving onto the next steps).

Finely slice the spring onion (bias cut) and red cabbage then place in iced water for 1 hour.

Cut the cucumber in half, (skin on), seed and slice thinly on an angle and set aside.

To assemble:
Strain the water off the cabbage and spring onions. Put the mushrooms in a bowl with the rest of the ingredients, except for the baby cos. Mix well. Taste and season with fish sauce (see following recipe) and lime juice if needed.

To finish, take the outer leaves from the baby cos. Rinse and dry (the smaller inner leaves will be too difficult to work with; you can just eat these while you're working). Lay the leaves out on a plate, taking approximately 3 tablespoons of your mushroom filling and placing it in each of the cos leaf cups.

Garnish with a sprinkle of crunchy buckwheat, micro coriander and sweet soy to taste.

vegan fish sauce

1 shallot

2 tbsp spring onion (scallion)

1 tbsp fresh red chilli

½ nori sheet

1 tbsp capers

reserved juices (from the larb mushrooms preparation)

2 tbsp rice wine vinegar

80 ml (2½ fl oz/⅓ cup) tamari

125 ml (4 fl oz/½ cup) filtered water

1 tbsp dried wakame pieces

1 tsp white miso or chickpea miso

1 minced garlic clove

2½ tbsp coconut sugar

optional – 1 tsp porcini mushroom powder

Finely chop the shallot, spring onion and chilli. Chop the nori and capers into small pieces.

Take your reserved mushroom juices and combine in a bowl with all the other ingredients – mix well, put a cover over the bowl (you could use a plate as a lid) and dehydrate for 3–4 hours at 46°C (115°F). Strain through a sieve and throw away the solids. Will last in the refrigerator for 3–4 days.

herbed 'chicken' sandwich
with watercress & cucumber

The onion and zucchini flat bread (see page 40) is an excellent base for sandwiches. Here, the zucchini (courgette) and onion work perfectly with the flavours of the 'chicken'.

Not exactly your typical raw-sounding dish! It can be hard to name a raw dish in a way that will evoke the right flavours. This is what we ended up calling it in the café after much deliberation. The 'chicken' itself works well in wraps, as a canapé with witlof (chicory) boats and as a side to a simple salad.

Make time: 30 minutes + component recipes | Soak time: 4–6 hours | Makes: 4 | Equipment required: food processor

chicken filling

½ cup **cashew aioli** (see page 46)

80 g (2¾ oz/½ cup) **cashews** (soaked 2–4 hours)

120 g (4¼ oz/¾ cup) **sunflower seeds** (soaked 4–6 hours)

½ **cucumber**, peel first if the skin is tough

½ **small red onion**

½ **apple**

1 **celery stalk**

3 tbsp **capers**

1 tsp **wholegrain mustard**

2 tbsp chopped **fresh dill** or **tarragon**

½ tsp **sea salt** (add to taste)

optional – 2 tbsp finely chopped **cornichons** or **gherkins (pickles)**

sandwich

8 pieces **onion and zucchini bread** (see page 40)

60 g (2¼ oz/2 cups) loosely packed **watercress**

½ sliced **cucumber**

1 small **buttercrunch lettuce** or other butter lettuce

optional – **alfalfa sprouts**

To prepare the chicken filling:
Make the aioli recipe (see page 46).

Drain the soaked cashews and sunflower seeds and rinse thoroughly. Blend in a food processor until finely chopped – there should still be some texture to the mixture.

Very finely dice the cucumber, onion, apple, celery, capers and cornichons (if using).

Mix the vegetables together with the cashews and sunflower seeds. Fold through the aioli and remaining ingredients.

Will keep in the refrigerator for 2 days.

To prepare the sandwich:
Take 4 pieces of the bread. Fill each with watercress, ¼ of the chicken mixture, sliced cucumber, a handful of sprouts if using and a few leaves of lettuce.

Place the lid on the sandwiches, chop into halves and serve straight away.

moroccan wraps

I created this light and flavourful wrap as a base for quick and easy lunches using leftover vegetables. Of course if you want to make it a little fancier, you can go to town, layering Moroccan-flavoured vegetables with raw falafels (see page 198), tzatziki, hummus and tabouleh.

This recipe is for the wrap itself, not the filling.

Make time: 30 minutes | Dehydrating time: overnight | Makes: 6 wraps | Equipment required: blender, dehydrator

90 g (3¼ oz/½ cup) **whole golden flax seed**

4 medium roughly chopped **carrots**

1 roughly chopped **red capsicum (pepper)**

8 **cherry tomatoes** or 1 large **tomato**

¼ tsp **dried chilli flakes** (add to taste)

3 tsp **harrisa spice mix**

20 g (¾ oz/¼ cup) **psyllium**

435 ml (15¼ fl oz/1¾ cups) **filtered water** (extra as needed)

2 tbsp **lemon juice**

1 tsp **cumin seeds**

⅓ tsp **sea salt**

Process the flax seeds into flour in your blender or grinder (see page 38).

Blend all the ingredients in a high-speed blender until very smooth, adding more water as you need. If you end up making the mixture too liquid just add in a little more psyllium or flax seed powder to thicken it up. The consistency should be that of pancake mixture.

Spread wrap batter evenly onto 2 dehydrator sheets approximately 4 mm (³⁄₁₆ in) thick. Dehydrate at 41°C (106°F) for about 4 hours, or until the wrap is firm enough for you to peel it away from the sheets. If they tear easily then you will need to keep dehydrating until they're more pliable to work with.

Next take one of the mesh sheet trays from the dehydrator and flip your dehydrator sheet (with the wrap on it) upside down onto the mesh sheet beneath, then carefully peel back the dehydrator sheets. Place back in the dehydrator and continue dehydrating for another 1½ hours or until completely dry but not crisp in any areas.

The finished wrap should be firm but still flexible; you don't want it too dry around the edges and cracking. That said, if you do get a little cracking around the edges you can tidy them up with a knife or pizza wheel when you cut the wraps up.

Once they are ready, take them out of the dehydrator and with a knife or a pizza wheel cut each sheet into thirds so you end up with 3 wraps per sheet. If you want to create large wraps just cut into halves.

We generally don't use the wraps straight away so will store them in an airtight container in the refrigerator. Placing them in the refrigerator helps get rid of some of the brittleness from over-drying, which often happens around the edges.

Will keep in the refrigerator for 1 week.

north valley farms

growing up green

The gardens at North Valley Farms hold a special place in our hearts. As the unbakery's popularity started to build in the early days, Jason and Tracy were the first growers with whom we established a direct supply relationship.

Jason and Tracy have chosen the country life 'up north' for their little family. Their first son John tears around the property with bare feet and a permanent smile. There is lots of open space and plenty of land, but the growing all happens 'indoors', in big, stretched polytunnel grow houses.

We met Jason via the Whangarei Growers' Market, the Big Daddy of growers' markets in New Zealand. Founded in 1998 to foster small and medium growers and provide consumers with fresh alternatives, it was the first of its kind in the country and remains the biggest. There is a vast range of produce available throughout the year, and the market guarantees its customers that all produce is grown and processed by stallholders.

It was on the recommendation of the market organiser that we approached Jason and his stall, which we had noticed quickly sold out each week. Jason is big on organics, and also on education, having taught horticulture at tertiary level.

His business now is polytunnels (which he builds and sells) and growing within them. It takes know-how to successfully convert to a growing regime inside polytunnels, but the results are incredible, both in terms of quality and volume.

For our weekly deliveries, we managed to tap into a network of friends and family who were already commuting between Whangarei and Auckland, meaning we could avoid adding to our carbon footprint while still getting the best veg produced in this country.

salads

Ok, so this is what everyone thinks of when you say 'raw foods', right? Salad? 'So, you guys just eat salad all the time?'

Well, yes, kinda, actually we do usually eat at least one type of salad a day. Because greens are very good for you. And because salads the way we make them are damn tasty.

The great thing about a salad is that you can eat it any time of the day, and it will always make you feel good.

wild rice & peach salad with rosemary, onion bread & caramelised walnuts

When peaches are plump and perfect in the middle of summer, it's hard to find a more delicious fruit. After you've gorged yourself on them at the beginning of the season, you'll want to find new ways to enjoy them while the season lasts. They work especially well in salads; not overly sweet, they have an almost savoury tartness.

In this dish, we have marinated peaches and paired them with nutty wild rice and spicy rocket (arugula), all wrapped in a light herbed dressing.

Prep time: 1–2 days activating rice | Make time: 40 minutes + component recipes | Serves: 4 as a starter or 2 as a main | Equipment required: dehydrator (optional)

salad

100 g (3½ oz/⅔ cup) **sprouted wild rice**
(65 g (⅓ cup) raw wild rice soaked 1–2 days will make around ⅔ cup (see pages 26–27))

3–4 sliced **fresh peaches**
(nectarines or apricots would also work)

½ finely diced **shallot**

½ tsp finely chopped **fresh rosemary**

pinch **sea salt**

1 tbsp **cold-pressed olive oil**

freshly cracked pepper

2 handfuls **rocket (arugula)**

1 handful **frisée**

1 small **butter lettuce**

2 tbsp **picked parsley** or **chervil**

⅓ cup **caramelised walnuts** (see page 29)

optional – **cashew parmesan** (see page 45) or **fresh herbed cheese** (see page 44) and **onion bread** (see pages 40)

dressing

3 tbsp **cold-pressed olive oil**

2 tbsp **balsamic vinegar**

1 tbsp **apple cider vinegar**

1 tsp **organic maple syrup** or **raw honey**

1 tbsp finely diced **shallot**

½ tsp finely crushed **garlic**

1 tsp finely chopped **oregano**

pinch **sea salt**

To prepare the wild rice:
This needs to be prepared 1–2 days ahead if you are sprouting.

Place wild rice in a bowl and submerge it in at least 250–500 ml (9–17 fl oz/1–2 cups) water.

Soak for 1–2 days, changing the water twice daily and rinsing well. You'll know it's ready when some of the rice has opened up and softened. It will still be chewy.

Once it has bloomed, rinse it well in fresh water. Let it dry a little before using.

To prepare the salad:
Place the peaches in a bowl with the shallot, rosemary, pinch of sea salt, olive oil and cracked pepper. You want to marinate and warm them lightly – we do this by placing them in the dehydrator at 46°C (115°F) for a ½ hour. Alternatively you could place them in an oven on its lowest setting until warmed.

Meanwhile, in a small bowl whisk together all ingredients for the dressing. Set aside.

Place the wild rice, rocket, frisée, butter lettuce, peaches and herbs in a large bowl, pour over the dressing and toss to combine. Toss in the caramelised walnuts just before serving and crumb over the cheese if you're using.

Serve with an optional side of onion bread (see page 40)

Sprouting wild rice is actually called 'blooming' (it doesn't technically sprout but rather blooms and becomes soft and chewy). We love using wild rice in its bloomed or sprouted form – it is packed with nutritive value, it contains protein, B vitamins and dietary fibre and is really sustaining.

summer salad with baby kale, balsamic berries & caramelised hazelnuts

Incorporating more raw food into your meals should happen naturally over summer, when fresh produce is plentiful and the weather is warm. There is no better time to eat fresh baby greens and shoots – they are always so much sweeter and more delicate in spring and early summer, as they grow quickly in lush, moist soils.

Fresh berries are another summer highlight. Blackberries work particularly well in this salad; they are plump and their tartness is lovely with cheese and caramelised nuts.

Make time: 20 minutes + component recipes | Serves: 4 | Equipment required: mandoline

2 **lettuces** (buttercrunch if available)

2 small **red radishes**

170 g (4 cups) **baby kale**

3 tbsp **dill leaves**

4 tbsp **chervil** or **flat-leaf (italian) parsley leaves**

20 g (¾ oz/⅓ cup) **snow pea (mangetout) shoots**

150 g (5½ oz/1 cup) **strawberries**

135 g (4¾ oz/1 cup) **blackberries**

80 g (2¾ oz/½ cup) **blueberries**

1 tsp **balsamic vinegar**

pinch **sea salt**

½ cup **macadamia feta** (see page 44)

freshly cracked pepper

½ cup **caramelised hazelnuts** (see page 29)

80 ml (2½ fl oz/⅓ cup) **balsamic dressing** (see page 49)

Cut the bottom of the lettuces and gently pull off the leaves. Carefully wash and dry. Slice the radishes finely on a mandoline and place in a bowl with the lettuce, kale, herbs and snow pea shoots (keep the herbs whole by picking the leaves off the stems).

Slice the strawberries and blackberries lengthways – around 2 mm (1/16 in) thick. Toss them in a bowl with the blueberries and balsamic vinegar.

Fold the berries and a pinch of sea salt into the salad mix and top with macadamia feta, cracked pepper and caramelised hazelnuts. Serve with the balsamic dressing on the side.

kale salad with feta, walnuts, preserved lemon & onion bread

A simple kale salad is a surprisingly enjoyable and satisfying meal. Once you learn the trick to making kale delicious, you will look at this crazy-good-for-you green leaf with new respect.

Finely chopping the kale then massaging it with a few pinches of sea salt until it changes to a more vibrant green colour creates a softer leaf with an enhanced flavour.

Make time: 10 minutes + component recipes | Serves: 4

2 bunches **curly kale** (approximately 16 leaves)

pinches **sea salt**

4 tbsp **cold-pressed olive oil**

2 tbsp freshly squeezed **lemon juice**

¾ cup of **macadamia feta** (see page 44)

2 tbsp finely chopped **preserved lemon** (see page 56)

1 small very finely diced **shallot**

2 tbsp chopped **parsley**

garnish – your favourite **sprouts** or **micro greens**, 4 slices **onion and zucchini bread** (see page 40)

Remove the centre ribs from the kale then wash and dry it. Finely shred by placing a bunch of leaves together in a stack – roll them up and finely slice.

Place the kale in a large bowl and add 2 pinches of sea salt, the olive oil and lemon juice – massage it until it changes to a more vibrant green colour and the leaves are soft.

Take your macadamia feta and rehydrate it to make a more ricotta-style cheese – do this by putting it in a bowl with a few tablespoons of filtered water and mix to soften. It should become fluffy and moist and have a ricotta texture; add more water as needed to achieve this.

Add the preserved lemon, shallot and parsley to the kale and combine.

Divide between the 4 plates or serve in 1 large bowl – top with the rehydrated macadamia feta, sprouts or micro greens and serve with a side of onion and zucchini bread (see page 40).

The best way to describe the massaging is tender rubbing between your fingers and thumb ... I know this all sounds a bit ridiculous but really just try it, the proof is in the soft, tender kale you are going to fall in love with.

wedge salad with caesar dressing, paprika pumpkin seeds & cherry tomatoes

Wedge salads are a fantastic way to add texture and fun to your salad experience. I always loved going to our local Japanese yakitori bar and being given a wedge of dressed cabbage to start with – it's so refreshing and much better for you than a bowl of bread. And somehow things just taste better when you can use your hands.

If you don't have all the ingredients in this recipe, feel free to improvise. If you have Mexican leftovers, for example, you could top your lettuces wedges with salsa, guacamole, chimichurri and corn chips to create a Mexican version.

Make time: 15 minutes + component recipes | Serves: 4

40 g (1½ oz/⅓ cup) **paprika pumpkin seeds** (see page 28)

⅓ cup **coconut bacon** (see page 36)

¼ cup **cashew parmesan** (see page 45)

caesar dressing (see page 48)

1 **iceberg lettuce**

3–4 **baby cos (romaine) lettuces**

150 g (5½ oz/1 cup) halved **cherry tomatoes**

1 large handful **flat-leaf (italian) parsley**, chopped

Make sure you have the dressing and other additional recipes made first; the rest is just assembling the salad.

Remove the base and limp outer eaves from the iceberg and cos lettuces. Cut the lettuce heads into four wedges along the centre axis (if you have a large lettuce you might want to cut into smaller wedges). Gently rinse each wedge and pat dry.

Divide the lettuce wedges amongst 4 plates and pour the caesar dressing over them. Divide the rest of the ingredients between the plates and scatter over the dressed wedges.

waldorf salad with soft leaf lettuce, kraut, activated walnuts & creamy dressing

A delicate and pretty salad with some lovely autumnal vegetables. We cleverly use sauerkraut here instead of vinegar in the dressing. We serve this salad as a starter or a side dish. If serving it as a main I'd include the avocado option and a side of either seeded bread or our onion and zucchini flat bread (see page 40).

Make time: 15 minutes + component recipes | Serves: 4 | Equipment required: mandoline

½ cup **cashew aioli** (see page 46)

½ tsp **wholegrain mustard**

1 tsp **raw honey**

2 tbsp **cold-pressed olive oil**

2 tbsp **lemon juice**

75 g (½ cup) **sauerkraut** (see page 58) (if using store-bought get a plain white cabbage one)

1 large **fennel bulb**, finely sliced on a mandoline

2 stalks **celery**, finely sliced diagonally

⅓ small **celeriac bulb**, shaved into fine pieces (you could use a vegetable peeler)

2 **granny smith apples**, finely sliced into thin strips on mandoline

pinch **sea salt** (add to taste)

180 g (1½ cups) **dried activated walnuts** (see pages 27–28)

2–3 tbsp **filtered water**

2 **soft leaf lettuces**, leaves picked and washed

3 tbsp **fresh dill leaves**

1 small handful **parsley leaves**

3 tbsp freshly chopped **chives**

optional – 1 **avocado**, diced into rough pieces

Place the cashew aioli in a medium bowl with the mustard, honey, olive oil and lemon juice. Mix together until combined. Depending how thick your aioli is you might need to add some water. You want to achieve the consistency of a fluid mayonnaise (I usually add a few tablespoons).

Add the sauerkraut, half of the fennel, half of the celery, half of the celeriac and half of the apple to the dressing and gently fold through. Add any additional sea salt to taste; if the sauerkraut is very salty you will not need to add any.

Place the rest of the ingredients in a large salad bowl and gently fold through with the already dressed vegetables and apple.

watermelon & pomegranate tabouleh with macadamia feta & thyme crisp

A visually spectacular dish that is full of juicy summer vegetables and fruits. It's a very hydrating salad as the cucumber and watermelon are comprised of around 90 percent water. I find in the summer months that eating water-rich fruits and vegetables is the best way to keep hydrated in the heat.

Pomegranate can be used in sweet and savoury recipes. It is a versatile fruit that you should be incorporating into your diet when in season. It's considered a superfood – its little jewel seeds are juicy sweet morsels of goodness, containing an abundance of vitamins, minerals and phytonutrients that keep your heart healthy and your skin glowing.

The macadamia feta and thyme crisps are really optional here. The salad is perfect as it is and can be enjoyed without them.

Make time: 20 minutes + component recipes | Serves: 4

540 g (1 lb/3 cups) **watermelon**, diced into 2 cm (¾ in) cubes

150 g (5½ oz/1 cup) **cherry tomatoes**, cut into quarters

350 g (12 oz/2 cups) **cucumber**, diced into 2 cm (¾ in) cubes

¾ cup **fresh pomegranate seeds** (approximately 1 pomegranate)

sea salt (add to taste)

2 tbsp **fresh lemon juice**

1 tsp **red wine vinegar**

4 tbsp **cold-pressed olive oil**

3 very large handfuls **flat-leaf (italian) parsley**, finely chopped

1 large handful **mint**, finely chopped

freshly cracked pepper

¾ cup **macadamia feta cheese** (see page 44)

4 **thyme crisps** (see following recipe)

Place the watermelon, tomato, cucumber and pomegranate seeds in a large bowl; lightly toss with a few pinches of sea salt, lemon juice, vinegar and olive oil. Fold through the herbs and serve on a plate or in a large bowl. Season with freshly cracked pepper and more sea salt to taste if needed.

Serve with macadamia feta and a thyme crisp on the side.

thyme crisp

Make time: 30 minutes | Soak time: 4–6 hours | Dehydrating time: 2 days | Makes: 24 crisps, 3 x 18 cm (1¼ x 7 in) |
Equipment required: blender, dehydrator, food processor

60 g (2¼ oz/⅓ cup) **golden flax seeds**

275 g (6 oz/2 cups) **hazelnuts** (soaked 4–6 hours)

3 tbsp **cold-pressed olive oil**

1½ tsp **nutritional yeast**

½ tsp **sea salt** (add to taste)

1 tbsp **freshly cracked black pepper**

1 tbsp finely chopped **thyme**

125 ml (4 fl oz/½ cup) **filtered water**

optional – ¼ tsp **freshly cracked white pepper**

Make the flax seeds into a flour in your blender or grinder.

Drain the soaked hazelnuts and rinse thoroughly. In a food processor, blend into the consistency of chunky couscous. Make sure it is not too fine or the crisps will not have a nice consistency. Place in a bowl with the rest of the ingredients and mix by hand until well combined. If the mixture is not coming together, add a few more tablespoons of water as needed.

Spread the mixture out evenly onto dehydrator sheets 36 x 36 cm (14¼ x 14¼ in). Place a clean dehydrator sheet or piece of baking paper on top and roll with a rolling pin on top of that (otherwise the roller will stick to the mixture). The resulting spread should measure 4 mm (³⁄₁₆ in) high. Score the mixture into 3 cm (1¼ in) wide and 18 cm (7 in) long crisps and dehydrate at 46°C (115°F) for 24 hours, then flip and put on mesh sheets. Dehydrate at 41°C (106°F) for another 24 hours.

Store in an airtight container. They are delicious as a snack or served with our cultured cheese as a starter.

ultimate raw goodness salad

While it looks like a salad from your local health food store in the 1980s, or a random collection of everything in the refrigerator, this nutritional powerhouse is carefully thought out. It contains many of my favourite health-building essentials: sprouts, sea vegetables, greens, beetroot (beets), wild rice, apple cider vinegar, something fermented and the essential avocado.

The recipe has three parts: first we have all the vegetables and sprouts to prepare, followed by a marinade for the sprouted chickpeas and sunflower seeds, then our green goodness dressing.

I have recommended you use 4 different types of salad greens: radicchio, witlof (chicory), baby cos (romaine) and a mesclun mix (which in itself is a range of different greens). However you can use whatever salad greens are available; just make sure one of them has a bitter element to aid digestion so you will get more out of the rest of the meal as well.

Prep time: 1–2 days activating rice | Make time: 20 minutes + component recipes | Soak time: 6 hours | Serves: 4 |
Equipment required: blender, mandoline, spiraliser

75 g (½ cup) **sprouted wild rice** (see pages 26–27) (soaked 1–2 days, will make around 1 cup)

1 large **carrot**

3–4 **small beetroots (beets)**, in various colours (when available)

1 handful **parsley**, roughly chopped

1 tbsp finely chopped **tarragon**

30 g (1 oz/½ cup) **alfalfa sprouts**

20 g (¾ oz/1 cup) **sunflower sprouts**

1 handful **pea shoots**

1 head **radicchio**, cut into eighths

1–2 **witlof (chicory)**, end cut off and leaves separated

2 **baby cos (romaine) lettuces**, cut into quarters

3 handfuls **mesclun mix**

1 tbsp **korengo** or **wakame**

miso marinated chickpeas and sunflower seeds (see following recipe)

optional – ¼ cup **micro greens**

green goodness dressing (see following recipe)

To prepare the wild rice:
This needs to be prepared 1–2 days ahead if you are sprouting.

Place wild rice in a bowl and submerge it in at least 250–500 ml (9–17 fl oz/1–2 cups) water.

Soak for 1–2 days, changing the water twice daily and rinsing well. You'll know it's ready when some of the rice has opened up and softened. It will still be chewy.

Once it has bloomed, rinse it well in fresh water. Let it dry a little before using.

If your rice doesn't bloom (it may not be true wild rice or old) or if you prefer it softer, you can place the sprouted rice in a pot or bowl and pour boiling water over it and leave for 2–3 minutes then drain to create a very lightly cooked version.

To prepare the salad:
Spiralise the carrot or shred into ribbons using a peeler. Peel and finely slice the beetroot on a mandoline.

Toss all the vegetables together in a bowl leaving some of the sprouts, herbs and micro greens to garnish. Lightly fold through the miso marinated chickpeas and sunflower seeds, including the marinade itself.

Top with sprouts, herbs and micro greens set aside for the garnish and serve with dollops of green goodness dressing.

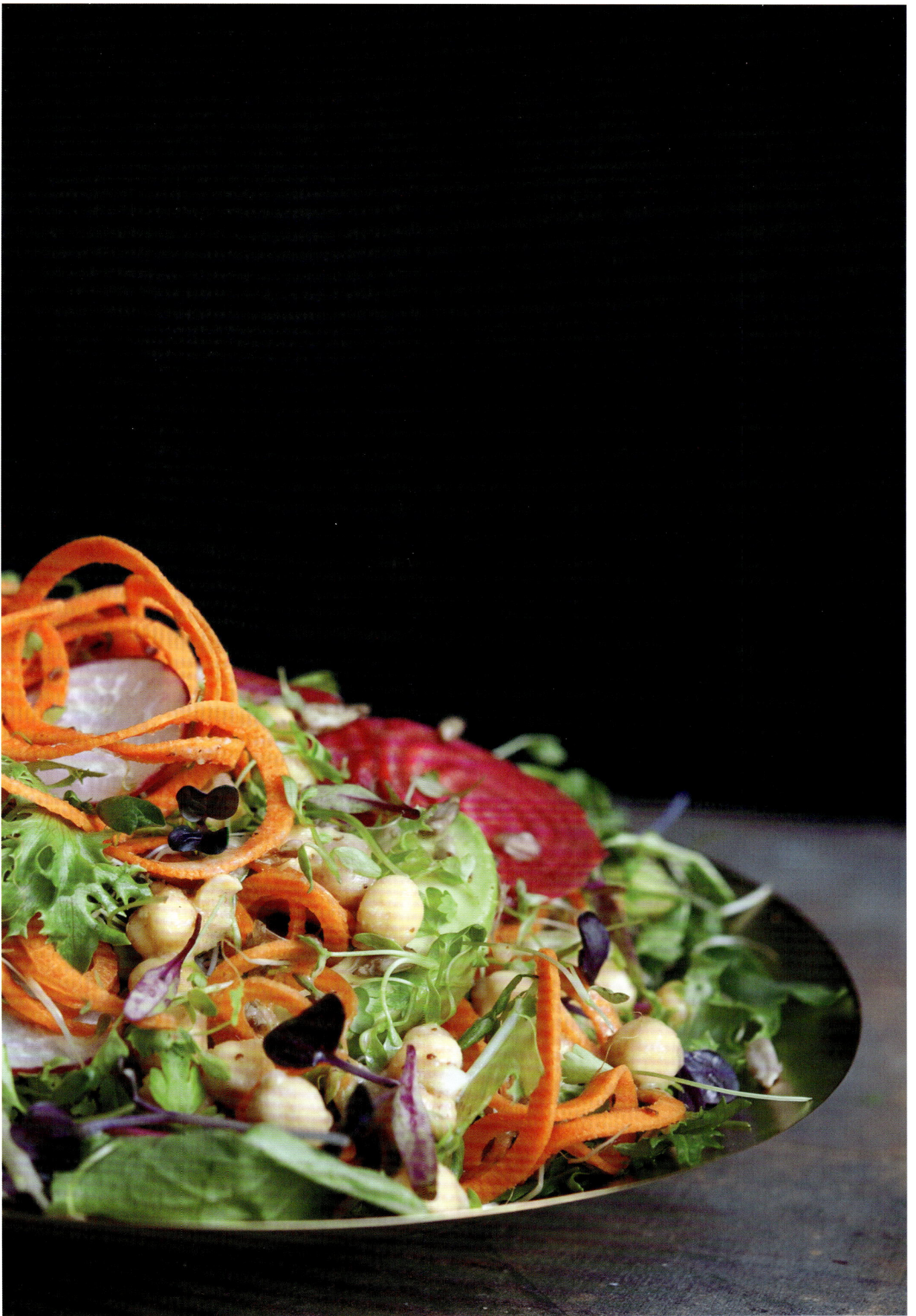

miso & mustard marinade
for sprouted chickpeas & sunflower seeds

A quick and easy marinade dressing that will leave your sprouts, nuts and seeds tasting extra nutty and delicious for salads.

Soak time: overnight | Makes: 2 cups

55 g (2 oz/⅓ cup) **sunflower seeds**
(soaked overnight)

115 g (4 oz/¾ cup) **sprouted chickpeas**
(see pages 26–27)

marinade

1 tbsp **white miso**

2 tbsp finely diced **shallot**

2 tsp **wholegrain mustard**

3 tbsp **apple cider vinegar**

juice ½ **lemon**

2 tbsp **tahini**
or **cold-pressed olive oil** (if you don't have tahini)

60 ml (2 fl oz/¼ cup) **filtered water**

pinch **sea salt** (add to taste)

optional – 3 drops **toasted sesame oil**
if using olive oil

Drain the soaked sunflower seeds and rinse thoroughly, set aside. Mix all the marinade ingredients into a bowl. Add the sprouted chickpeas and sunflower seeds to the marinade – you can use immediately but the chickpeas will increase their digestibility within a few hours of marinating and will keep 2–3 days in the refrigerator.

green goodness dressing

This dressing is thick in consistency similar to mayonnaise. You can use it like an aioli in any other dish. The idea here is to place dollops of the dressing on the salad and dip the wedges of cos (romaine) and leaves of witlof (chicory) into the dressing to mop up all the flavours; a little like a wedge salad.

Soak time: 2–4 hours | Makes: 1¼ cups | Equipment required: blender

3 tbsp **cashews** (soaked 2–4 hours)

1 medium **avocado**

2 tbsp **cold-pressed olive oil**

juice ½ **lemon**

3 tbsp **apple cider vinegar**

3 tbsp chopped **parsley**

175 g (6 oz/1 cup) chopped and
skin removed **cucumber**

1 large or 2 small **garlic cloves**

½ tsp **sea salt**

garnish – 1 tsp chopped **tarragon**,
1 tsp chopped **chives** and
1 tsp finely diced **shallot**

optional – pinch **volcanic sea salt**

Drain the soaked cashews and rinse thoroughly. Place all ingredients in a blender except the garnish and blend until completely smooth. Add 60 ml (2 fl oz/¼ cup) of water if required, it will depend on the water content of your cucumber. The finished texture should be the consistency of a light aioli. Lightly fold in the garnish ingredients.

Add more lemon juice, salt and vinegar to taste.

bird bowl

Nothing is more little bird than our bird bowl; it's great for the person who loves to try a bit of everything. It's the café's most popular dish and always follows this basic formula: a kale salad base, a handful of mesclun mix, an avocado half, some sauerkraut (see page 58) and sprouts, and a selection of three flavourful salads. The beauty of eating like this is that you never get bored, switching components as you please.

Serve your bird bowl with a slice of caramelised onion and zucchini flat bread (see page 40).

Make time: component recipes | Makes: each salad below makes around 2 cups

beetroot noodle salad

110 g (3¾ oz/2 cups) spiralised beetroot (beets)

3 tbsp apple cider vinegar

1 tbsp cold-pressed olive oil

½ tsp chopped rosemary

½ tsp chopped thyme

pinch sea salt

Mix all ingredients together and leave to marinate for 30 minutes. Store in the refrigerator.

brussels sprouts with sprouted lentils

100 g (3½ oz/1⅔ cups) shredded brussels sprouts

50 g (1¾ oz/⅓ cup) sprouted green lentils (see page 270)

1 tbsp finely minced shallot

3 tbsp preserved lemon dressing (see page 49)

pinch sea salt

Mix all ingredients together – massaging gently to break down the brussels sprouts.

kale and cucumber salad

200 g (7 oz/3 cups) finely chopped kale

3 tbsp lemon juice

1 tsp cold-pressed olive oil

pinch sea salt

90 g (3¼ oz/½ cup) diced cucumber

Place the kale in a bowl with the lemon juice, olive oil and sea salt. Massage for a couple minutes then fold in the cucumber.

moroccan carrots

155 g (1 cup) shredded or julienned carrots

½ tsp ras el hanout

pinch sea salt

Use a mandoline or knife to slice the carrots.

Mix all ingredients. We only use a small amount of this per portion, approximately 2 tablespoons per bowl.

sesame slaw

40 g (1½ oz/½ cup) finely shredded **red cabbage**

40 g (1½ oz/½ cup) finely shredded **white cabbage**

30 g (1 oz/⅓ cup) finely julienned **carrot**

35 g (1¼ oz/⅓ cup) finely chopped **snow peas (mangetout)**

30 g (1 oz/⅓ cup) finely julienned **red capsicum (pepper)**

2 tbsp thinly sliced **spring onion (scallion)**

1 tsp **toasted sesame oil**

2 tbsp **rice wine vinegar**

pinch **sea salt** (add to taste)

garnish – 1 tbsp **white sesame seeds**

Mix everything in a bowl except the sesame seeds and toss until all the vegetables are coated in the oil and vinegar. Garnish with white sesame seeds.

spinach & mushroom salad

40 g (1½ oz/1 cup) **swiss brown mushrooms**

¼ **garlic clove**

5 tbsp **cold-pressed olive oil**

½ tsp chopped **thyme**

1 tbsp minced **shallot**

sea salt

freshly cracked pepper

135 g (4¾ oz/3 cups) **baby English spinach**

3 tbsp **red wine vinaigrette** (see page 48)

40 g (1½ oz/¼ cup) **sunflower seeds**, dried and activated (see pages 27–28)

Slice the mushrooms into thin slices. Crush the garlic and mix with the mushrooms, 3 tablespoons of olive oil, the thyme, minced shallot, a pinch of sea salt and some freshly cracked pepper. Dehydrate for 1 hour at 46°C (115°F).

Mix the spinach with the remaining 2 tablespoons of olive oil and sea salt. Dehydrate at 46°C (115°F) for 15 minutes until lightly wilted. Mix the spinach and mushrooms together with the red wine vinaigrette and garnish with sunflower seeds.

broccolini & almond salad

8 pieces **broccolini**

1 tbsp **cold-pressed olive oil**

2 pinches **sea salt**

3 tbsp lightly crushed **dried activated almonds** (see pages 27–28)

45 g (⅓ cup) halved **cherry tomatoes**

2 tbsp **preserved lemon dressing** (see page 49)

Cut the broccolini in half lengthways. Mix with olive oil and pinch of sea salt and dehydrate for a ½ hour at 46°C (115°F). Mix the lightly wilted broccolini with the activated almonds, tomatoes, preserved lemon dressing and a pinch of sea salt.

avocado with tahini

½ **avocado** per person

tahini dressing (see page 49)

black sesame seeds

pinch **sea salt**

Slice avocado in half and remove stone. With a table knife cut a grid into the flesh of the avocado. Salt the avocado, drizzle with tahini dressing and sprinkle black sesame seeds on top.

cucumber, watercress & sea vegetables with japanese sesame dressing

The addition of wild rice and kale to this Japanese-inspired salad make this a nutritional dream of a salad. Nutrient rich, it should refresh and energise. I try to eat some sea vegetables every day. Another of nature's powerhouse foods, sea vegetables provide you with all fifty-six essential elements for human health.

Many minerals we require are not present in our food in the right quantities because our soils have been depleted by over-intensive farming and chemical use. But sea vegies have them in abundance! Start by adding things like nori and sprinkle wakame on salads. You can also mix your salt with kelp granules – our salt jar at home when I was growing up always consisted of half kelp, half sea salt to ensure we got good amounts of natural bio-available iodine and other minerals in our diets.

Prep time: 1–2 days activating rice | Make time: 20 minutes | Serves: 4 | Equipment required: mandoline

100 g (3½ oz/⅔ cup) **sprouted wild rice**
(65 g (⅓ cup) raw wild rice soaked 1–2 days will make around ⅔ cup (see pages 26–27))

1 **cucumber**

1 tsp **toasted sesame oil**

50 ml (⅕ cup) **lime juice**

1 tsp **organic maple syrup**

55 g (2 oz/¼ cup) **white miso**

2 tbsp **mirin (rice wine)**

sea salt

4 tbsp **filtered water**

35 g (¼ oz/⅓ cup) **dried seaweeds**
(wakame and korengo work well here)

1 bunch **kale** (around 16 leaves)
or other similar leafy green

2 tbsp **cold-pressed olive oil**

1 tbsp **lemon juice**

3 handfuls **watercress**

1 small handful **mitsuba leaves** (japanese wild parsley) or other similar herb, torn

2 tsp **black sesame seeds**

2 tsp **white sesame seeds**

1 large **avocado**, cut into 8 wedges

optional – **pickled ginger** (see page 56)

To prepare the wild rice:
This needs to be prepared 1–2 days prior if you're sprouting.

Place wild rice in a bowl and submerge it with at least 250–500 ml (9–17 fl oz/1–2 cups) water. Soak for 1–2 days, changing the water twice daily and rinsing well. You'll know it's ready when some of the rice has soften and opened up or 'bloomed' (it will still be chewy). Rinse well in fresh water, and let it dry a bit before using.

To prepare the cucumber:
Fill a bowl with cold water with ice, set aside. Peel the cucumbers then slice lengthways on a mandoline into long strips about 2–3 mm (¹⁄₁₆–⅛ in) in) thick – don't use the middle part with the seeds. Slice the long strips into 1.5 x 6 cm (⅝ x 2½ in) rectangular pieces. Place the strips in the ice water for 10 minutes until they are tightly curled. Place in the salad at the last minute when all the other ingredients are ready.

For the dressing:
Place the sesame oil, lime juice, maple syrup, white miso, mirin, a few pinches of sea salt and 2 tablespoons of water in a bowl and whisk vigorously together until combined.

Put the seaweeds in a cup with an additional 2 tablespoons of water to allow them to rehydrate. Place the kale and seaweeds in a large bowl and add a few pinches of sea salt, olive oil and lemon juice – massage until the kale changes to a more vibrant green colour and the leaves are soft; the sea vegetables should soften as well.

Add the watercress, wild rice, mitsuba, cucumber and sesame seeds to the bowl and lightly toss. Fold through the dressing. Serve with wedges of avocado and pickled ginger.

sprouted falafel salad with garlic tahini dressing

This salad is nourishing and sustaining enough for a winter dinner. The sprouted falafels are full of protein and very satisfying, especially when paired with our tahini garlic dressing (see page 49). Use this recipe as a guide. Ideally you will include some avocado, herbs and a few bitter leafy greens – the rest is up to the seasons.

Bitter greens, like radicchio and mustard greens, are often found in a good mesclun mix. If you're new to bitter greens you should start slowly, adding small amounts to your salads until you start to enjoy the taste. The bitterness promotes bile salts, which aid digestion and stimulate enzyme production, so they're important in helping you get the most nutrition from your meal.

Make time: 20 minutes + component recipes | Serves: 4

1 small head **radicchio**

½ medium **cucumber**

½ **red** or **yellow capsicum (pepper)**

¼ **red onion**

5–6 handfuls **mesclun mix** or any leaf lettuces

150 g (5½ oz/1 cup) halved **cherry tomatoes**

1 roughly diced **avocado**

25 g (1 oz/¼ cup) **dried activated sunflower seeds** (see pages 26–28)

1 handful **parsley leaves**

pinch **sea salt**

16 **falafels** (see page 198)

freshly cracked pepper

125 ml (4 fl oz/½ cup) **tahini dressing** (see page 49)

Remove the radicchio leaves and wash. Tear into small pieces.

Slice the cucumber into half moons. Finely julienne the capsicum and very finely slice the red onion.

Place the vegetables, sunflower seeds and parsley together in a large mixing bowl with a pinch of sea salt and fold together.

Top each serving with four falafels and freshly cracked pepper. Serve with tahini dressing on the side.

green papaya salad with green beans, lime, chilli & kaffir spiced cashews

Originating from Laos, green papaya salad is a mainstay of the Laotian dinner table. It's also a hugely popular in neighbouring Thailand and Cambodia. Many cultures have raw dishes as a part of their diets – raw food is definitely not a new thing.

Our green papaya salad needs little altering from the traditional recipe – we use additional lime juice as a replacement for fish sauce, add extra herbs because we love them, and top it with a handful of our spicy cashews.

Make time: 20 minutes + component recipe | Marinating time: 30 minutes | Serves: 2
Equipment required: blender, mandoline (optional)

dressing

3 tbsp **coconut sugar**

1 tbsp **tamari**

juice 2 **limes**

¼ **fresh red chilli**

2 **garlic cloves**

1 tsp **tamarind water**

salad

1 **green papaya**
(you can find these at most asian supermarkets)

1 handful **snow peas (mangetout)**

1 handful **green beans**

125 g (4½ oz/¾ cup) halved **cherry tomatoes**

1 small handful picked **coriander (cilantro) leaves**

1 small handful picked **thai basil leaves**

70 g (2½ oz/½ cup) crushed **spiced cashews**
(see page 29)

optional – 1 handful **bean sprouts** and 1 **carrot**

garnish – **coriander (cilantro) leaves, thai basil leaves, thinly sliced fresh chilli, spiced cashews** (see page 29) and **lime wedges**

To prepare the dressing:
Blend all ingredients in a high-speed blender for 15 seconds.

To prepare the salad:
Peel the papaya and shred it on a mandoline or with a shredding hand peeler.

Pour the dressing over the grated green papaya and leave to marinate for a ½ hour while getting the remaining ingredients ready.

Chop the snow peas into long thin strips. Cut the green beans lengthways. This can be a bit tricky – using a sharp knife will make it easier.

If you're using carrots, shred these the same way as the papaya.

Toss everything together until combined.

Garnish with coriander leaves, thai basil leaves, fresh chilli, a handful of spiced cashews and a lime wedge.

Pizza
8 7 6 5 4 3 2 1

Phil Matheson

mushroom whisperer

Mushrooms are one of nature's wonder foods, and so uniquely beautiful in their myriad varieties. Their health benefits are amazing and incredibly diverse.

They can be used to support hormonal balance and increase immunity, fight pathogens, reduce stress, improve sleep quality, boost energy, support vital organs, help balance blood sugar levels, improve memory and concentration, protect the nervous system ... we could go on.

When you also consider their savoury, nutty flavours and meaty texture, it's easy to see why they are a big part of raw cuisine. We first met Phil from Out of the Dark Mushrooms at the Clevedon Farmers' Market, selling beautiful mushrooms in little brown paper bags (he also has a stall at the Parnell Farmers' Market). Phil likes a good chat (and he always has a story) and he quickly sold us on the quality of his offerings. It wasn't long before he was personally delivering mushrooms to the unbakeries each week.

Phil's growing house is very cool; racks of mushroom apartments (well, special logs) are regularly misted with a water blaster ... not your typical produce growing operation. There is, of course, more to growing a great mushroom than that, but we leave the mushroom whispering to Phil and his team. We're just happy to reap the rewards for our daily meals.

Iceland

Quorn™ and Lentil Cottage Pie
with Crunchy Potato Topping

HOLLY BELL

SERVES 4

70 MINS

This is a cottage pie with a difference. It's one for vegetarians – with Quorn™ mince and lentils replacing beef – but it is guaranteed to please meat eaters too. Crunchy diced potatoes, flavoured with fresh thyme, are a speedy alternative to the usual mash.

INGREDIENTS

3 tablespoons olive oil
1 onion, peeled and finely chopped, or use frozen diced onions
1 carrot, peeled and diced
1 celery stick, including leaves, finely chopped
300g Quorn™ mince, frozen
1 teaspoon freshly ground black pepper
2 tablespoons fresh thyme leaves
1 x 400g can of chopped tomatoes
2 tablespoons tomato purée
1 teaspoon Marmite®
50g dried red lentils
1 vegetable stock cube
750g potatoes, peeled and diced into 2cm cubes
(about 8 medium potatoes)

COOKING INSTRUCTIONS

1. Heat 1 tablespoon of the oil in a large saucepan and sweat the onion, carrot and celery for 5 minutes over a medium heat until soft.

2. Add the mince, fry for 2 minutes, then add the black pepper, 1 tablespoon of the fresh thyme, tomatoes, tomato purée, Marmite®, lentils and stock, made from adding the stock cube to 500ml boiling water.

3. Turn the hob down to low and leave to simmer, uncovered, for 30 minutes.

4. Preheat the oven to 200°C/Fan 180°C/Gas Mark 5

5. Parboil the potatoes for 5 minutes, drain and toss them in the remaining oil and thyme.

6. Pour the Quorn™ and lentil mixture into a casserole dish about 27 x 20 x 5cm and arrange the potatoes on top.

7. Bake for 25 minutes until the potatoes are golden and a knife will pass through them easily.

#PowerofFrozen

Iceland Food TV

C31 24 16

dinner

Dinner can be tricky for those trying to 'go raw'. It's the time of day we are most used to sitting down to a hearty, cooked meal. Luckily, you can ease yourself into a raw dinner with our secrets: use the dehydrator to warm a meal before eating, make a broth for that bowl of veg or try warming the plates.

It actually doesn't take that long to get used to a raw dinner, and with the flavours on offer in the following recipes you really shouldn't have any trouble at all.

In the evenings our bodies are winding down, getting ready for the regeneration that happens when we sleep. Eating a light dinner means you are not handing your digestive system a bunch of homework to do after it has just left school. Try eating a little more at lunch and a little less at dinner, and see how this makes you feel over the course of a few weeks.

dinner party cheese platter

It's lovely to start an evening with a bountiful platter of seasonal fruit and vegetable musings served with cheeses and crackers for people to nibble at their pleasure while they share great conversation.

Our favourite cheese boards have some fresh seasonal vegetables, marinated fruits, a small selection of our activated spiced nuts and our favourite thing – nut cheese. All served with a beautiful array of raw crackers, breads and some fresh herbed salsas.

The recipes that follow are some ideas for you to build your ideal platter from. You will want to mix them up with caramelised nuts (see page 29), cheeses (see pages 42–45), breads (see pages 38–40) and crackers (see page 52) to create your own bountiful seasonal platter.

quick nut cheese

This is a quick nut cheese recipe that we make if we don't have time to make the cultured cheese (see page 42). It doesn't have the probiotic goodness of our cultured cheese but still tastes great. To add an extra bit of panache to it we roll the rounds in some ingredients that pair well with cheese, like crushed peppercorns, smoked paprika, finely chopped herbs or chopped olives.

Make time: 20 minutes | Soak time: 2–4 hours | Setting time: 3–4 hours | Makes: 2 rounds | Equipment required: food processor

155 g (1 cup) **macadamia nuts** (soaked 2–4 hours)

155 g (1 cup) **cashews** (soaked 2–4 hours)

1 tbsp finely diced **shallot**

1 tsp **nutritional yeast**
(available from organic and health food stores)

1 tbsp **cold-pressed olive oil**

¼ tsp **sea salt** or **himalayan crystal salt**

1 tsp **lemon juice**

Drain the soaked nuts and rinse thoroughly. Place all the ingredients except the lemon juice in a food processor and blend until smooth (this will take around 5 minutes, stopping every now and then to scrape down the sides). If the mixture is too thick, add very small amounts of filtered water – just enough to get it smooth while still remaining thick (a bit like cream cheese).

Add lemon juice and pulse until combined. Taste to check it has a suitably cheese flavour. Add more sea salt, yeast and lemon juice to taste and pulse briefly if needed.

Shape mixture into rounds by spooning and pressing into a 9 cm (3½ in) cookie-cutting ring, then loosen ring with a knife and remove (this part is a bit fiddly as the mixture is quite sticky; you could refrigerate the mixture first to make it easier to work with).

Place cheeses in refrigerator on a piece of baking paper to firm up for approximately 3–4 hours.

black olive tapenade

Tapenade is a classic cheese board condiment for good reason – it works perfectly with cheese and is delicious.

Makes: ½ cup | Equipment required: food processor

75 g (½ cup) **raw bojita** or pitted **kalamata olives**

1 tbsp **capers**

1 **garlic clove**

3 tbsp **extra virgin cold-pressed olive oil**

3 tbsp **fresh parsley leaves**

optional – **lemon zest**

Thoroughly rinse olives in cool water and pat dry. Put all ingredients in a food processor and pulse into a fine salsa texture.

walnut & fig log

This log looks great on a cheese board, and figs and walnuts are a delicious pairing. I have gone for a peppery finish to balance the cinnamon and the sweetness of the figs.

Makes: 1 log, 12 cm (4½ in) x 3 cm (1¼ in) | Equipment required: food processor

90 g (3¼ oz/½ cup) roughly chopped **figs**, with stems removed

40 g (1½ oz/¼ cup) roughly chopped **pitted dates**

¼ tsp **cinnamon** and extra for dusting

¼ tsp **freshly ground white pepper** (or use black pepper)

65 g (¾ cup) **dried activated walnuts** (see pages 27–28)

Blend figs, dates, cinnamon and pepper in a food processor until finely diced. Add the walnuts and pulse until they are well incorporated but still have some texture to them.

Shape into a log, dust with cinnamon and wrap in baking paper.

Store in the refrigerator for 1–2 months.

blackcurrant, blueberry & juniper berry preserve

The juniper berries give this preserve a peppery, aniseed flavour.

Makes: 1 cup | Equipment required: blender

100 g (3½ oz/⅔ cup) **fresh** or **frozen organic blueberries** (defrosted)

2 tbsp **raw honey** or **pitted dates** (add to taste)

2 tbsp **lemon juice**

35 g (1¼ oz/¼ cup) **frozen organic blackcurrants** (defrosted or use fresh if available)

½ tsp roughly crushed **whole dried juniper berries**

Blend the blueberries with the raw honey and lemon juice in a high-speed blender until smooth. Add the blackcurrants and crushed juniper berries and stir until well combined.

Will keep for 2–3 days in the refrigerator.

walnut & kale pesto

Two superfoods come together in this delicious pesto. You could also try the basil and rocket pesto recipe (see page 134).

Makes: 1½ cups | Equipment required: food processor

½ roughly chopped **bunch kale** (around 8 leaves), stems removed

65 g (¾ cup) **dried activated walnuts** (see pages 27–28)

1 very large handful **flat-leaf (italian) parsley**, chopped

2 crushed and finely chopped **garlic cloves**

1 tbsp **nutritional yeast**

3 tbsp **lemon juice**

½ tsp **sea salt**

80 ml (2½ fl oz/⅓ cup) **cold-pressed olive oil**

freshly cracked **pepper**

Put the kale in a food processor and process until fine. Place all the other ingredients in the food processer except the olive oil and pulse together until you get a chunky salsa texture – add the olive oil gradually while the motor is running until combined.

Add sea salt, pepper and more lemon juice to taste.

winter spice marinated tamarillos

Tamarillos, also known as tree tomatoes, are more tart than sweet, making them an excellent cheese board addition.

If you don't have tamarillos, pears also work in this recipe – you may need to add liquid when marinating to ensure they are well covered.

Makes: 1 cup | Equipment required: dehydrator

6–8 **tamarillos**

250 ml (9 fl oz/1 cup) **red wine**

90 g (3¼ oz/¼ cup) **raw honey**

2 **cinnamon sticks**

2 **star anise flowers**

2 **cloves**

1 **vanilla bean**, sliced in half

3 sprigs **thyme**

pinch **sea salt**

lemon zest
(use a vegetable peeler to get several large pieces)

Peel the tamarillos with a knife or soft fruits peeler. Set aside.

In large bowl, combine all other ingredients and stir until honey dissolves.

Place tamarillos in the bowl, making sure they are all well covered. Cover and leave to marinate on the bench overnight. Alternatively, place in a dehydrator for 6–8 hours to intensify the flavour.

Cut the marinated tamarillos in half, place on a dehydrator sheet and pour the marinade syrup overtop – dehydrate for a further 10–12 hours.

olive & basil zucchini cannelloni bites

Light and full of flavour, these bite-sized Italian canapés are always a hit at events. Anytime I need to make a quick plate to take to a party, this is my go-to recipe.

Make time: 20 minutes + component recipe | Makes: 20 bite-sized canapés | Equipment required: mandoline

2 medium **zucchini (courgettes)**

1 tbsp **cold-pressed olive oil**

pinch **sea salt**

40 **fresh basil leaves**

¾ cup **macadamia and cashew cultured nut cheese** (see page 42)

10 halved **cherry tomatoes**

20 **pitted olives** (dried or fresh)

20 **bamboo skewers**

Using a mandoline, cut the zucchini lengthways into thin strips approximately 2.5–3 mm (⅛ in) thick. Brush the slices with olive oil and sprinkle lightly with sea salt. Set aside until ready to use.

Assembly:
Place zucchini slices on a flat work surface. Put 1 basil leaf along the end nearest to where you are going to roll up from.

Layer with 1 teaspoon of the cheese and 1 cherry tomato, take the end of the zucchini and wrap it over the filling. Roll into a circular shape as in the image.

Sit on a plate with the basil leaf side at the bottom, place another basil leaf and 1 olive on top and thread a bamboo skewer through the cannelloni.

Makes approximately 20 bite-sized cannelloni.

mediterranean dolmas
with cashew tzatziki

Dolmas are a brilliant party food. In Turkey, 'dolma' refers to something that is stuffed; in Greece it refers to stuffed vine leaves. This recipe uses grape vine leaves and replaces the traditional rice with parsnip and cauli rice, which is mixed with herbs, capers and preserved lemons.

The fresh flavours of Mediterranean food work really well in raw cuisine; this dish is a particular favourite. The tzatziki is a wonderful accompaniment to many dishes and can be enjoyed as a dip.

Make time: 30 minutes + component recipe | Serves: 4 | Equipment required: food processor

1 jar **grape vine leaves**

90 g (3¼ oz/1 cup) peeled and chopped **parsnip**
or **jerusalem artichoke** (when in season)

90 g (3¼ oz/¾ cup) chopped **cauliflower**

1½ tbsp freshly squeezed **lemon juice**

2 tbsp **cold-pressed olive oil**
and more for coating the dolma

90 g (3¼ oz/½ cup) peeled and seeded **cucumber**,
in small cubes

½ crushed and chopped **garlic clove**

3 tbsp finely chopped **capers**

2 tbsp finely chopped **preserved lemon**
(see page 56), optional – if you don't have
preserved lemons, add the zest of ½ lemon
and an extra tbsp of lemon juice

3 tbsp **pine nuts** or chopped **macadamia nuts**

1 finely chopped **shallot**

3 tbsp **currants** or **bilberries**
(you can get bilberries at persian food stores)

6 pitted and chopped **olives** of your favourite kind

1 tbsp finely chopped **dill** (add to taste)

5 tbsp finely chopped **parsley**

1 large handful **fresh mint leaves**, finely chopped

pinch **sea salt**

freshly ground black pepper

The grape vine leaf wraps:
You can get these from speciality Mediterranean food stores or Persian food stores (check the label to make sure it is a simple brine of vinegar, sea salt and water; you don't want any numbers or unnatural preservatives on the ingredient list).

Alternatively, you could make your own by preserving fresh grape vine leaves in a sea salt and water brine. Or soak overnight in some olive oil, apple cider vinegar and lemon juice.

If either of these 2 options are not available, use one of nature's other wraps like a collard leaf, English spinach or even the top leafy part of a bok choy (pak choy).

To prepare the filling:
In a food processor, pulse the parsnip and cauliflower pieces to achieve the texture of large rice grains.

Put the mixture in a nut milk bag or muslin cloth and squeeze out some of the moisture, leaving it with a light and fluffy texture.

Transfer the mixture to a bowl and pour the lemon juice over, mixing with a wooden spoon to preserve the colour. Then mix in 2 tablespoons of olive oil and gently stir in the rest of the ingredients. Season with sea salt and pepper.

Rinse the grape leaves and pat dry. Put around 1½ tablespoons of the filling into the centre of each leaf and fold. The stem end gets folded up first, followed by the sides, after which you are ready to roll tightly.

Coat the rolled dolmas with some olive oil, they will keep in the refrigerator for several days.

Never feel limited by what we suggest in our recipes, they are a guide. Use any edible green leaf that you have in the garden that doesn't taste too strong.

cashew yoghurt tzatziki sauce

Tzatziki is often served in Greek and Persian cuisine. It is traditionally made with strained yoghurt and a mix of garlic, sea salt, cucumber and herbs. Here we use cashews instead of yoghurt, but the rest remains the same, creating a versatile sauce that you can use to embellish many dishes.

Soak time: 2–4 hours | Makes: 1½ cups | Equipment required: blender

155 g (1 cup) **cashews** (soaked 2–4 hours)

60 ml (2 fl oz/¼ cup) **filtered water** (add more as needed)

80 ml (2½ fl oz/⅓ cup) **lemon juice**

½ tsp **sea salt**

1 crushed **garlic clove**

2 tbsp chopped **dill**

90 g (3¼ oz/½ cup) finely diced **cucumber**

Drain the soaked cashews and rinse thoroughly. Place all the ingredients except the dill and the cucumber in a blender – blend until creamy and smooth. Now fold through the dill and cucumber.

Leave to rest for a ½ hour before serving for the flavours of the cucumber and dill to develop in the sauce. Add more salt to taste.

Keep in the refrigerator in an airtight container up to 5 days.

stuffed zucchini flowers with herbed macadamia cheese & summer succotash

An elegant summer dish that will impress. Stuffed zucchini (courgette) flowers are great as a canapé or as an accompaniment to a cheese board. Here we serve them for dinner; the richness of the herbed cheese works well with the freshness of a summer succotash.

Zucchini flowers are abundant in spring and summer. You can easily grow your own, or find them at your local farmers' market or specialist produce store.

Make time: 30 minutes + component recipe | Marinating time: 30 minutes | Serves: 4

12 **zucchini (courgette) flowers**

¾ cup **macadamia herbed cheese** (see page 44)

optional – 40 g (1½ oz/¼ cup) **pine nuts**

succotash

50 g (1¾ oz/½ cup) finely diced **zucchini (courgette)**

80 g (2¾ oz/½ cup) finely diced **red capsicum (pepper)**

100 g (3½ oz/½ cup) fresh **sweetcorn kernels**

55 g (2 oz/¼ cup) very finely diced **red onion**

50 g (1¾ oz/¼ cup) quartered **cherry tomatoes**

2 tbsp finely chopped **basil**

2 tbsp **sherry vinegar**

2 tbsp **cold-pressed olive oil**

1 tsp **sea salt**

1 tbsp **lemon juice**

garnish – **pine nuts** (if using) and **freshly cracked pepper**

Make the succotash by mixing all ingredients together. Leave to marinate for a ½ hour.

Fill each flower with 1 tablespoon of herbed cheese; twist the tips of the petals to secure the filling.

Spread ¼ cup of the succotash across the plate and top with 3 stuffed zucchini flowers per dish. Finish with a teaspoon of pine nuts scattered across the dish (if using) and some freshly cracked pepper.

tom kha with kelp noodles & thai herbs

A tomato-based soup from Thailand with an abundance of beautiful Thai ingredients like lemongrass, kaffir lime and chilli. This delicious broth soup is filled with kelp noodles and a vegetable herb stack that transforms a soup into a beautiful main meal event.

Make time: 30–40 minutes | Dehydrating time: 1½ hours | Serves: 6 |
Equipment required: blender, dehydrator, mandoline

broth

300 g (10½ oz/2 cups) **cherry tomatoes**

5 cm (2 in) piece **lemongrass**
(measure from the base)

2 cm (¾ in) piece of **ginger**

1 medium chopped **shallot**

3 large smashed **garlic cloves**

120 g (4¼ oz/¾ cup) **coconut meat**

500 ml (17 fl oz/2 cups) **coconut water**

625 ml (21½ fl oz/2½ cups) **filtered water**

80 ml (2½ fl oz/⅓ cup) **tamari**

1 **red thai chilli** (add more or less to taste)

1 cm (½ in) piece **fresh turmeric**

2 tbsp **light raw honey** or **coconut sugar**

1 **kaffir lime leaf**

pinch **sea salt** (add to taste)

noodles & vegies

340 g (1 pack) **kelp noodles**

80 ml (2½ fl oz/⅓ cup) and 3 tbsp **tamari**

2 tsp **toasted sesame oil**

60 g (2¼ oz/½ cup) thinly sliced **spring onion**
(scallion)

2 medium **carrots**

80 ml (2½ fl oz/⅓ cup) **cold-pressed olive oil**

½ finely crushed **garlic clove**

sea salt

2 **limes**

¼ head **white cabbage**

110 g (3¾ oz/3 cups) **button mushrooms**

230 g (2 cups) **bean sprouts**

220 g (7¾ oz/1½ cups) halved **cherry tomatoes**

1 handful **coriander** (cilantro) leaves

1 handful **thai basil leaves**

garnish – **lime wedges, extra herbs** and
micro coriander (cilantro)

To prepare the broth:
Blend all ingredients on high in blender for approximately 2 minutes, strain, adjust consistency with water until the consistency of a broth (not a thick sauce) and add sea salt to taste.

Put in the dehydrator to keep warm before serving.

To prepare the kelp noodles:
Rinse kelp noodles well under running water. Place in a mixing bowl with 80 ml (2½ fl oz/⅓ cup) of tamari. Mix thoroughly and set aside for 10 minutes. Strain tamari, add toasted sesame oil and 30 g (1 oz/¼ cup) of finely sliced spring onion.

To prepare the carrots:
Julienne carrots on the mandoline. Mix with 2 tablespoons of olive oil, ½ of finely crushed garlic clove and a pinch of sea salt. Place on a dehydrator sheet and dehydrate at 46°C (115°F) for 40 minutes. Finish with the juice of 1 lime.

To prepare the cabbage:
Shred cabbage very finely on the mandoline or by hand, season with a few pinches of sea salt and 1 tablespoon of olive oil. Place on a dehydrator sheet and dehydrate at 46°C (115°F) for 40 minutes.

To prepare the mushrooms:
Cut the mushrooms into quarters and place in a mixing bowl with 60 ml (2 fl oz/¼ cup) olive oil and ½ teaspoon sea salt. Mix well and place on a dehydrator sheet and dehydrate at 46°C (115°F) for 1½ hours. When finished add 3 tablespoons of tamari and remaining spring onion.

To finish:
Place the prepared kelp noodles, carrots, cabbage and mushrooms in a large mixing bowl with the remaining vegetables and herbs.

To plate, pour 310 ml (10¾ fl oz/1¼ cups) of broth into each bowl. Stack approximately 2 cups of the vegetable kelp noodle mixture in the broth.

Garnish with a lime wedge, extra herbs and micro coriander if you have available.

middle eastern feast

Middle Eastern cuisine has a rich cultural history dating back to 500–300 BC. With its foundations in beautiful ingredients like dates, figs, pistachio nuts and pomegranates, you know it's going to be good, and the ingredients lend themselves well to many raw dishes. The wonderfully pungent herbs and spices add so much flavour to many simple vegetable dishes.

While there are many benefits to living in a young country like New Zealand, a rich history of cuisine is not one of them. It's crazy to think that most countries and cuisines have their roots in food preparations thousands of years old. I love tasting new foods and learning about the influences in each one – it's like a walk through history with your taste buds.

This is our raw take on some Middle Eastern classics; it is a range of dishes that can be shared with friends and family.

smoked paprika tomatoes

Make time: 10 minutes | Marinating time: 1 hour

280 g (10 oz/2 cups) **vine tomatoes** (small or medium)

½ very finely diced **shallot**

¼ tsp **smoked paprika**

½ tsp **sumac**

1 tbsp very finely chopped **thyme**

1 tsp **sesame seeds**

½ tsp **freshly cracked pepper**

¼ tsp **chilli powder**

3 tbsp **cold-pressed olive oil**

¼ tsp **sea salt**

If you're using small tomatoes, cut them into quarters; dice larger tomatoes into approximately 2 cm (¾ in) sized pieces. The idea is that this makes a chunky salsa-style dish.

Place all the ingredients in a bowl and mix well. Leave to marinate for 1 hour before eating.

cauliflower couscous

A versatile dish that makes a good accompaniment to many meals. We often use this as a component in our bird bowls.

Make time: 10 minutes + component recipe | Equipment required: food processor

⅓ head **cauliflower**

½ tsp **sea salt**

1 very large handful **mint**, finely chopped

2 large handfuls **parsley**, finely chopped

1 large handful **coriander (cilantro)**, finely chopped

2 tbsp **lemon juice**

2 tbsp **cold-pressed olive oil**

2 tbsp diced **preserved lemon** (see page 56)

optional – 2 tbsp finely chopped **pistachio nuts** and 2 tbsp **currants** or **barberries**

Process the cauliflower and sea salt in a food processor until a couscous-like consistency.

Place the cauliflower mixture in a nut milk bag or cloth and squeeze out any moisture.

Put the cauliflower in a bowl along with all the other ingredients and fluff with a fork. Add a small amount of pistachio nuts and currants if you are using at the end and fold through the mixture.

harissa spiced vegetables

An excellent main that also works as a starter; serve with a bowl of tzatziki for dipping – delicious! We layer the vegetables in lettuce cups alongside other Middle Eastern goodies.

Make time: 15 minutes | Dehydrating time: 1½ hours | Equipment required: dehydrator

185 g (6½ oz/1½ cups) **cauliflower florets**

200 g (7 oz/½ bunch) **baby carrots**
or 3 **regular carrots**, peeled and cut into halves

1–2 **red** or **yellow capsicums (peppers)**

2 tbsp **lemon juice**

3 tbsp **cold-pressed olive oil**

1 tbsp **harissa spice**

30 g (1 oz/¼ cup) **dried activated almonds**
(see pages 27–28), ground into coarse flour in your
food processor or blender

⅓ tsp **sea salt**

¼ tsp **freshly cracked pepper**

Place all the ingredients in a bowl and mix until all the vegetables are coated in the spice and almond flour.

Spread onto a dehydrator sheet and dry at 46°C (115°F) for 1½ hours.

falafel

Xander came up with this falafel recipe in a stroke of genius one day after trying a few nut-based versions that didn't quite hit the mark. These falafels use sprouted chickpeas, which are a great source of protein. Because they are sprouted they are full of extra goodness and much easier for you to digest.

Make time: 15 minutes + component recipe | Soak time: 4–6 hours | Dehydrating time: 4–6 hours |
Makes: 30–35 falafel | Equipment required: dehydrator, food processor

290 g (10¼ oz/2 cups) **sunflower seeds**
(soaked 4–6 hours)

600 g (1 lb 5 oz/4 cups) **sprouted chickpeas**
(see pages 26–27)

1 crushed and chopped **garlic clove**

155 g (1 cup) diced **onion**

1 large handful **parsley**, chopped

1 large handful **coriander (cilantro)**, chopped

3 tbsp **cold-pressed olive oil**

1½ tbsp **cumin**

1 tsp **chilli powder**

80 ml (2½ fl oz/⅓ cup) **lemon juice**

1 tbsp **nutritional yeast**

2 tbsp **tamari**

Drain the soaked sunflower seeds and rinse thoroughly. Place the sprouted chickpeas and sunflower seeds in a food processor and blend until chunky; the mixture should hold together when you roll them into balls.

Add all other ingredients and pulse until combined.

Roll into approximately 3 cm (¼ in) wide balls (this mixture will make around 30–35 falafel). Place in a dehydrator at 46°C (115°F) for 4–6 hours. Alternatively you can dry these in a low-temperature oven.

feast assembly

Serves: 6–8

2 **iceberg lettuces**

90 g (3¼ oz/1 bunch) **fresh coriander (cilantro) leaves**, washed and picked

preserved lemons (see page 56)

cashew yoghurt tzatziki (see page 191)

almond hummus (see page 139)

Wash and remove the old outer leaves from the lettuce. Take the base of the lettuce and peel off the leaves, keeping them intact so you can use them as cups for your Middle Eastern goodness.

Place all your prepared dishes into serving bowls and platters. Serve with a stack of lettuce cups.

Encourage your dinner guests to create their own falafel kebab creations – tasting all the different components first then choosing their favourites to layer inside the lettuce cups. Fold in the sides of the lettuce leaves to create a fully enclosed wrap.

Putting the saucy components in the middle layers makes for an easier/tidier eating experience!

beetroot, balsamic & macadamia cheese ravioli with basil oil

A classic raw dinner party dish. Our version uses marinated beetroot (beets), herbed macadamia and cashew cheese with basil oil. Serve with a side of salad greens.

Make time: 30 minutes + component recipes | Marinating time: 2 hours | Serves: 4 | Equipment required: mandoline

1–2 large **beetroots (beets)**
(we used organic red beetroot; you could use any colour you have available)

¼ tsp **sea salt**

50 ml (⅕ cup) **balsamic vinegar**

1 finely crushed **garlic clove**

60 ml (2 fl oz/¼ cup) **basil oil** (see page 57) or **cold-pressed olive oil**

1 cup **herbed macadamia cheese** (see page 44)

garnish – 80 g (2¾ oz/2 cups) **mesclun salad leaves**, 3 tbsp chopped **basil** and **chives, freshly cracked pepper, basil oil** or **cold-pressed olive oil** and **aged balsamic vinegar**

Using a mandoline, finely slice the beetroot into thin rounds (make sure these are paper-thin otherwise the texture will be difficult to work with, but not so thin that they break). Marinate in a bowl with the sea salt, balsamic, garlic and basil oil (or olive oil) for around 2 hours, making sure you have some basil oil left over for garnish.

Lay the sliced beetroot out individually; place approximately 1 small tablespoon of the herbed macadamia cheese filling in the centre of each piece and place another beetroot piece over top, pressing around the sides to seal.

Place 4–5 pieces of ravioli on a plate, garnish with a side of mesclun mixed with the finely sliced chives and basil and top the dish with cracked pepper. Drizzle with the reserved basil oil and aged balsamic vinegar.

mushroom risotto
with watercress, chive oil & micro greens

This creamy risotto is great comfort food. You will be surprised at just how delicious and satisfying a raw dish can be. Parsnips are abundant most of the year in New Zealand but are at their sweetest during the cooler months, when their starches are converted into sugar. Parsnip works surprisingly well as a 'rice' base for many dishes and its slight smoky flavour pairs perfectly with mushrooms.

Make time: 45 minutes + component recipes | Dehydrating time: 2 hours | Serves: 4 |
Equipment required: dehydrator, mandoline

190 g (6¾ oz/5 cups) quartered **swiss brown mushrooms**

80 ml (2½ fl oz/⅓ cup) and 3 tbsp **cold-pressed olive oil**

2 tsp **sea salt**

1 tsp finely chopped **thyme**

1 tsp **rosemary**

55 g (2 oz/½ cup) finely diced **shallot**

freshly cracked pepper

3 tbsp **sherry vinegar** or 2 tbsp **red wine vinegar**

250 ml (9 fl oz/1 cup) **alfredo sauce** (see page 47)

6 medium peeled **parsnips**

3 tbsp finely chopped **chives**

filtered water (add as needed)

garnish – 4 handfuls **watercress** or **baby cress**, **chive oil** (see page 57) and **freshly cracked pepper**

Place the mushrooms in a bowl with 80 ml (2½ fl oz/⅓ cup) of olive oil, 1 teaspoon of sea salt, thyme, rosemary, shallot and ½ a teaspoon of freshly cracked pepper.

Place on a dehydrator sheet and dehydrate at 46°C (115°F) for 1½ hours. When finished, put into a mixing bowl and add the sherry vinegar.

At this point, if you want a more mushroomy flavour, mix the alfredo sauce with the mushrooms and place in the dehydrator for another ½ hour for the flavour to develop. Otherwise if you want a more creamy flavour add the alfredo in at the end stage.

Julienne the parsnips on a mandoline or by hand, then cut into rice-sized pieces. Mix with 3 tablespoons of olive oil and 1 teaspoon of sea salt. Place on a dehydrator sheet and dry at 46°C (115°F) for ½ an hour.

To finish:
Combine the parsnip rice, mushrooms, chives and alfredo sauce if not added earlier. Add a small amount of water if you want a looser consistency, and season with sea salt and pepper.

Serve with a handful of watercress, a drizzle of chive oil and freshly cracked pepper.

INGREDIENTS

3 tablespoons olive oil
1 onion, peeled and finely chopped, or use frozen diced onions
1 carrot, peeled and diced
1 celery stick, including leaves, finely chopped
300g Quorn™ mince, frozen
1 teaspoon freshly ground black pepper
2 tablespoons fresh thyme leaves
1 x 400g can of chopped tomatoes
2 tablespoons tomato purée
1 teaspoon Marmite®
50g dried red lentils
1 vegetable stock cube
750g potatoes, peeled and diced into 2cm cubes
(about 8 medium potatoes)

COOKING INSTRUCTIONS

1. Heat 1 tablespoon of the oil in a large saucepan and sweat the onion, carrot and celery for 5 minutes over a medium heat until soft.

2. Add the mince, fry for 2 minutes, then add the black pepper, 1 tablespoon of the fresh thyme, tomatoes, tomato purée, Marmite®, lentils and stock, made from adding the stock cube to 500ml boiling water.

3. Turn the hob down to low and leave to simmer, uncovered, for 30 minutes.

4. Preheat the oven to 200°C/Fan 180°C/Gas Mark 5

5. Parboil the potatoes for 5 minutes, drain and toss them in the remaining oil and thyme.

6. Pour the Quorn™ and lentil mixture into a casserole dish about 27 x 20 x 5cm and arrange the potatoes on top.

7. Bake for 25 minutes until the potatoes are golden and a knife will pass through them easily.

#PowerofFrozen

Iceland Food TV

C31 24 16

Iceland

Easy Mid-Week Suppers

Quorn™ and Lentil Cottage Pie
with Crunchy Potato Topping

HOLLY BELL

SERVES 4

70 MINS

This is a cottage pie with a difference. It's one for vegetarians – with Quorn™ mince and lentils replacing beef – but it is guaranteed to please meat eaters too. Crunchy diced potatoes, flavoured with fresh thyme, are a speedy alternative to the usual mash.

shiitake dumplings in a kombu & sesame broth

Make time: 15 minutes | Dehydrating time: 2–4 hours | Serves: 4–6 |
Equipment required: dehydrator, food processor, mandoline

1 large **chinese cabbage** (wong bok), separate out
1 wilted leaf and finely julienne (green part only)

3–4 **fresh shiitake mushrooms**

2 tbsp **tamari**

1 tsp **toasted sesame oil**

310 g (11 oz/2 cups) **cashews**

1 finely chopped **red chilli**

2 finely chopped **spring onions (scallions)**

1 cm (½ in) finely chopped **ginger**

pinch **sea salt**

1 large handful **coriander (cilantro)**, finely
chopped

1 handful very finely julienned
and diced **snow peas (mangetout)**

1 peeled, very finely julienned (pref use a
mandoline) and diced **carrot**

1 tbsp **umeboshi vinegar** or **brown rice vinegar**

30 g (1 oz/1 bunch) **chives**

garnish – **finely chopped chives** and
black sesame seeds

Cut off the base of the cabbage and carefully pull off the large leaves. You just want to use the top part of the cabbage that doesn't contain the hard white stem.

Place leaves in a large bowl covered in filtered water and place in the dehydrator at 46°C (115°F) for 1–2 hours; alternatively cover with warm water until slightly wilted. Then pat dry with a tea (dish) towel.

Finely slice the shiitake mushrooms; mix with the tamari and sesame oil, place in dehydrator at 46°C (115°F) for 1 hour.

Mix the cashews in a food processor with the chilli, spring onions, ginger, sea salt and coriander and pulse until you achieve a coarse but formed texture.

Dice the dehydrated mushrooms and fold through the cashew mixture with any of the leftover marinade.

Put the snow peas, cabbage and carrot in a separate bowl and toss with the umeboshi vinegar.

Fold the vegetables through the cashew mixture.

Take a cabbage leaf – pat dry, fill the centre with 3 heaped tablespoons of the cashew and vegetable mixture. Gather up the four edges of the cabbage and pull upwards, pinch at the point just above the mixture and then twist until you create a money bag shape. Place a tie around the twisted part of the dumpling with a strand of chive.

Place three or four dumplings in a bowl and surround with 50 ml (⅕ cup) of broth (see following recipe). Garnish with finely chopped chives and black sesame seeds. Add more tamari to taste.

kombu & sesame broth

Makes: 1¼ cups

1 **fresh** or **dried shitake mushroom**

1 stick **kombu**

375 ml (13 fl oz/1½ cups) **filtered water**

3 tbsp **tamari**

½ tsp **toasted sesame oil**

Finely slice the shiitake and place in a small pot with the kombu and water. Place in a dehydrator at 46°C (115°F) for 2–4 hours. Discard the kombu and shiitake. Add tamari and sesame oil. Serve while still warm from the dehydrator.

wild mushroom plate with truffled parsnip pasta & caramelised shallots

Fresh truffles are not commonly available in New Zealand, so we use good organic truffle oil and some porcini powder to create a similar earthy flavour. Use fresh truffles if you are lucky enough to have access to them!

This dish should satisfy any cravings you have for a creamy mushroom pasta experience.

Make time: 20 minutes + component recipe | Soak time: 2–4 hours | Dehydrating time: 2–3 hours | Serves: 4 |
Equipment required: blender, dehydrator, spiraliser

80 g (2¾ oz/½ cup) **caramelised shallots** (see page 36)

120 g (4¼ oz/3 cups) **wild mixed mushrooms**

70 g (2½ oz/1 cup) **crimini mushrooms**

2 tbsp chopped **thyme**

1 tbsp chopped **rosemary**

freshly cracked **pepper**

½ tsp **sea salt**

80 ml (2½ fl oz/⅓ cup) **cold-pressed olive oil**

6–7 **parsnips** (small or medium)

optional – 1 litre (35 fl oz/4 cups) **organic chardonnay**

garnish – a few handfuls **baby rocket (arugula) leaves**

sauce

120 g (4½ oz/¾ cup) **cashews** (soaked 2–4 hours)

75 g (½ cup) **macadamia nuts** (soaked 2–4 hours)

1 tsp **porcini powder** (a gourmet supermarket will stock this)

185 ml (6 fl oz/¾ cup) **filtered water** or for a richer creamy sauce use **macadamia milk** (more as needed)

¾ crushed **garlic clove**

¼ **shallot**

3–4 tbsp **truffle oil** (depending on how strong yours is)

pinch **sea salt**

freshly cracked **pepper**

optional – 2 tbsp **organic chardonnay**

Make sure you have the caramelised shallots ready.

To prepare the mushrooms:
If you have any large mushrooms in your mixture, remove the stems and chop finely. The mixture we use has a combination of enoki, woodear, black trumpet and straw. Thinly slice the crimini mushrooms (approximately 2–3 mm (1/16–⅛ in) thick). Place the mushrooms in a bowl with the herbs, freshly cracked pepper, sea salt, olive oil and the wine – if using – and combine. Place everything on a dehydrator tray and dehydrate at 41°C (106°F) for 2–3 hours; the mushrooms shouldn't be overly dried out but some of them will have dried ends.

Peel the parsnip and spiralise – if you have blade size options on your spiraliser, use the medium or large setting. Place in a bowl with a few pinches of sea salt.

To prepare the sauce:
Place all the ingredients in a high-speed blender – blend until creamy and smooth. There should be no texture to it and it should be like a thick but still fluid cream. Add extra sea salt, pepper and truffle oil to taste.

Place the parsnip, half of the mushroom mixture and the sauce in a bowl and mix together.

Divide the mixture between four plates and top with the remaining mushrooms, caramelised shallots, a drizzle of truffle oil and freshly cracked pepper and sea salt to taste.

Serve with a small side of fresh baby rocket leaves.

dessert

You've been waiting for this section, right? We still get a kick out of greeting a first-time customer who has come to us after hearing we offer gluten-free, dairy-free desserts.

They tell us they have allergies and ask which of the items they can eat. The look on their faces when we say 'everything' makes all the hard work that goes into making these treats so worth it.

What's more, these goodies are raw, organic and don't contain highly-refined sugars. They're actually good for you.

Desserts take people to their happy place, and we know exactly what it is like to be denied that because of stupid allergies. Rejoice! Dessert is back on the menu!

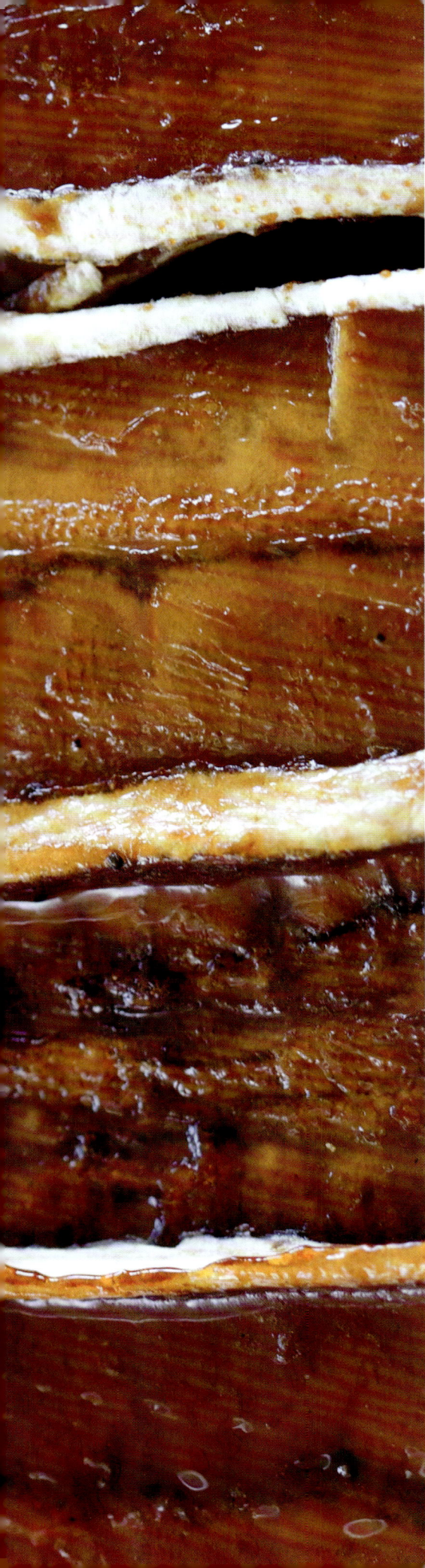

apricot & ginger torte

I love making this torte when Otago apricot season hits. Their brilliant orange colour and flavours are stunning.

Make time: 50 minutes + component recipes | Soak time: 2–4 hours | Dehydrating time: 5–6 hours |
Setting time: 6–8 hours/overnight | Serves: 12–16 | Equipment required: blender, dehydrator (optional), food processor

base

120 g (4¼ oz/1 cup) **dried activated almonds**
(see pages 27–28)

210 g (7½ oz/1¼ cups) **pitted dates**

65 g (¾ cup) **desiccated (shredded) coconut**
(ground into a flour in your food processor)

¼ tsp **vanilla bean**

¼ tsp **sea salt**

1½ tbsp **dried ginger**

2 tbsp melted **cold-pressed coconut oil**
(see page 270)

cream filling

235 g (8½ oz/1½ cups) **cashews** (soaked 2–4 hours)

80 g (2¾ oz/½ cup) **young coconut flesh** (these are
the white coconuts, don't use the ones with the
brown husk. If you can't get young coconut you
can use another 80 g (2¾ oz/½ cup) cashews.)

80 ml (2½ fl oz/⅓ cup) **almond milk** (see page 30)
or just use filtered water

60 ml (2 fl oz/¼ cup) **filtered water**

60 ml (2 fl oz/¼ cup) **lemon juice**

100 g (3½ oz/⅓ cup) **raw agave**, **organic maple
syrup, coconut nectar** or **raw honey**

pinch **sea salt**

¼ tsp **vanilla bean**

1 tbsp **vanilla extract**

185 ml (6 fl oz/¾ cup) melted **cold-pressed
coconut oil** (see page 270)

10–12 **fresh apricots**
or other fruit like figs, peaches or pears

ginger syrup

100 g (3½ oz/½ cup) **coconut sugar**

3 tbsp **ginger juice**

80 ml (2½ fl oz/⅓ cup) **filtered water**

To prepare the base:
Blend almonds and dates together in a food processor
until almost a couscous-like texture. Add the remaining
ingredients and pulse a few times until combined. The
mixture should hold together well. Add 1–2 teaspoons of
water if the mixture is too dry and crumbly.

Line a 22 cm (8½ in) tart (flan) tin (with a removable base)
with plastic wrap, press the mixture firmly into the tin. It will
need to be approximately 4–5 mm (³⁄₁₆–¼ in) thick on the
bottom and up the sides of the tin to maintain the structure.
For individual tortes use mini tart cases.

Place torte base in the refrigerator while you make the filling.

To prepare the cashew and vanilla coconut cream filling:
Blend all the ingredients except the coconut oil and fruit in
a high-speed blender – being careful not to let it heat up.
Blend until really smooth – like the texture of a silky cream.

Slowly pour in the coconut oil with the blender going until
completely combined into the mixture.

This torte has a soft cream; if you want it to set more firmly
add another 60 ml (2 fl oz/¼ cup) of coconut oil.

Pour into the torte base and leave to set for approximately
1 hour in the refrigerator.

To prepare the syrup:
There are several ways to make ginger juice. One is with
a juicer. Another is in a food processor – put fresh ginger
chopped into pieces in a food processor until pulp-like then
strain the mixture with a sieve, nut milk bag or muslin cloth.

Place all the ingredients in a bowl and mix well. If you have
a dehydrator place in here at 46°C (115°F) for 5–6 hours until
it forms a syrupy consistency; if you don't have a dehydrator
you could try placing in the oven on the lowest setting – this
will keep in the refrigerator for around 1 week.

To finish:
Top the cream in the torte base with fresh apricot halves,
pressing lightly into the mixture. Cover the torte with plastic
wrap and leave to set for another 6–8 hours or overnight in
the refrigerator. When ready to serve, remove from tin and
remove plastic wrap, then pour ginger syrup over the torte.

berry tartlets with a cacao base & cashew cream filling

This dessert closely resembles a traditional French custard tart, apart from the chocolate crust. The custard is more delicate in flavour and softer in texture than our other creams, and works best in individual servings so the tart doesn't need to be cut into slices.

Top with your choice of seasonal fruits; berries and cherries work exceptionally well with chocolate and custard cream.

Make time: 40 minutes + component recipes | Soak time: 2 hours | Setting time: 6 hours | Makes: 6 tarts |
Equipment required: blender, food processor

base

120 g (4¼ oz/1 cup) **dried activated almonds** (see pages 27–28)

80 g (2¾ oz/½ cup) **cashews**

210 g (7½ oz/1¼ cups) **pitted dates**

2 tbsp **cacao nibs**

¼ tsp **vanilla bean powder** or **vanilla extract**

3 tbsp **cacao powder**

1 tbsp melted **cacao butter**

vanilla custard cream

235 g (8½ oz/1½ cups) **cashews** (soak 2 hours)

250 ml (9 fl oz/1 cup) **almond milk** (see page 30)

¼ cup **sweetener** (organic maple syrup, raw agave, coconut crystals, raw honey) or **dates**

1 tsp **vanilla extract**

½ tsp **vanilla bean powder** or seeds of 1 **vanilla bean**

pinch **salt**

80 ml (2½ fl oz/⅓ cup) melted **cold-pressed coconut oil** (see page 270)

optional – ¼ tsp **lecithin**

topping

440 g (15½ oz/2 cups) **fresh berries** or **cherries**, pitted and cut in halves

To prepare the base:
In a food processor, blend nuts until almost couscous-like – leave them with a bit of texture.

Add the dates and blend until well combined and until the mixture is slightly sticky. Add the remaining ingredients and pulse a few times until combined. The mixture should hold together well.

Line 6, 10 cm (4 in) French fluted tart (flan) tins with plastic wrap. Press the mixture firmly into each tart tin – it will need to be approximately 3–4 mm (⅛–³⁄₁₆ in) thick on the bottom and up the sides of the tins to maintain the structure.

Place the tart base in the refrigerator while you make the filling.

To prepare the cream filling:
Drain the soaked cashews and rinse thoroughly. Place all ingredients in a high-speed blender except the coconut oil – process until very smooth. Slowly add the oil into the blender while the motor is running until well combined.

Pour the filling between the six tarts and top with fresh berries or cherries.

blackberry & apple crumble cake

A homely-style cake that leaves you feeling happy inside, like you just finished off a family meal with one of Nan's perfect apple and blackberry pies.

Make time: 30 minutes + component recipes | Serves: 12–16 | Equipment required: food processor, mandoline

crumble/base

130 g (1½ cups) **dried activated walnuts** (see pages 27–28)

180 g (1½ cups) **dried activated almonds** (see pages 27–28)

245 g (1½ cups) **pitted dates**

1 tsp **cinnamon**

¼ tsp **ground nutmeg**

pinch **sea salt**

½ tsp **vanilla bean powder**

filling

8 medium-sized **apples** (granny smith or braeburn are best)

90 g (3¼ oz/½ cup) packed **pitted medjool dates**

45 g (¼ cup) **sultanas (golden raisins)** or **currants**

¼ tsp **ground nutmeg**

2 tsp **cinnamon**

1 tbsp **vanilla extract**

pinch **sea salt**

1 **lemon**, zest and juice

260 g (9¼ oz/2 cups) **fresh blackberries**

To prepare the crumble/base:
In a food processor, combine all crumble/base ingredients until they start to stick together – you want it to have some chunks so it maintains lots of texture to bite on. Press half of the mixture into the base of a 20 cm (8 in) round cake tin.

To prepare the filling:
Peel and core all apples.

Chop 2 of the apples into rough chunks. In a food processor, pulse the chopped apples with the dates, currants, nutmeg, cinnamon, vanilla, sea salt and lemon until combined and there is some stickiness to the mixture. Set aside.

Chop the remaining apples into thin slices – approximately 2 mm (¹⁄₁₆ in) thick on a mandoline or by hand.

Lightly mix the apple slices and the spiced apple mixture together in a bowl.

To finish:
Layer half the sliced apple on the base of the cake and then the blackberries. Layer the rest of the apple on top of the blackberries and press down on top to ensure that everything sits flat.

Top with the remaining crumble mixture, sprinkling it over the top of the filling like you would a crumble, then press down lightly on the mixture. You want it to come together but not be firmly pressed or totally uniform so it still has that lovely, crumbly, varied texture to it.

Enjoy with a little almond cream or coconut cashew cream (see page 218).

queen peach melba drizzled in raspberry coulis with coconut cashew cream

The Peach Melba was invented in the 1890s by the very famous French chef Escoffier at the Savoy Hotel in London to honour the Australian soprano, Nellie Melba. It is a very simple dessert that consists of peaches, raspberry coulis and vanilla cream. Our version is created in honour of Escoffier and the queen peach (a New Zealand breed); when at their best, queen peaches are fruit perfection and require no tampering.

Make time: 20 minutes | Serves: 4 | Equipment required: blender

4 ripe **queen peaches** or other **yellow peaches**

1 tbsp **lemon juice**

1 tbsp **light raw agave** or **organic maple syrup**

½ tsp **vanilla extract**

40 g (1½ oz/⅓ cup) **fresh raspberries**

raspberry coulis

90 g (3¼ oz/¾ cup) **fresh** or **frozen raspberries** (defrosted)

3 tbsp **light raw agave** or **organic maple syrup**

1 tbsp **lemon juice**

1 tsp **vanilla extract**

You want to select perfectly ripe queen peaches; the flesh should be sweet and soft, not too dissimilar to a poached peach (which is what the original peach melba was made with).

Peel the peach with a soft fruits peeler or very sharp knife; delicately remove the pit with a small paring knife from the top end where the stem is attached if you want to keep it whole, otherwise cut into halves and remove the pit.

Coat the peaches with the lemon juice, agave/maple syrup and vanilla and set aside. If your peaches are not as ripe as you would like, you can dehydrate them for 1 hour to intensify the flavour and lightly soften them.

Make the coulis by placing everything in a high-speed blender and blend until smooth.

Place a peach in each bowl and pour over ¼ of the raspberry coulis mixture.

Top each serving with 3 tablespoons of coconut cashew cream (see recipe below) and fresh raspberries.

basic coconut cashew cream

We don't generally consider our foods to be substitutes, but once you start making custards and creams from nuts and coconuts, you won't feel as though you are missing out on creamy treats.

Make time: 10 minutes | Soak time: 2–4 hours | Setting time: 1–2 hours | Makes: 2 cups | Equipment required: blender

155 g (1 cup) **cashews** (soaked 2–4 hours)

160 g (1 cup) **young coconut flesh**

2 tbsp **raw agave** or **organic maple syrup**

½ tsp **vanilla bean powder** or ½ tsp **vanilla extract**

2 tbsp melted **cold-pressed coconut oil** (see page 270)

optional – ½ tsp **lecithin**

Drain the soaked cashews and rinse thoroughly. Blend the cashews and coconut flesh until smooth (add a little filtered water or coconut water to get things moving if you need it, but keep it to a minimum).

With the blender running, pour in the remaining ingredients, blend until smooth. Add more sweetener to taste.

Refrigerate for 1–2 hours before serving. Will keep for 2–3 days in the refrigerator.

hazelnut mousse cups
with caramelised hazelnuts

Rich, chocolatey and good for you. This is a delicious way to get some goodness into you while treating yourself to dessert. It's also really quick to put together.

Make time: 10 minutes + component recipes | Setting time: 2 hours | Serves: 4–6 | Equipment required: food processor

2 large **ripe avocados**

185 ml (6 fl oz/¾ cup) **hazelnut milk** (see page 30)

80 g (2¾ oz/¾ cup) and 1 tbsp **cacao powder**

175 g (6 oz/½ cup) **organic maple syrup, coconut nectar** or **raw agave**

1 tsp **vanilla extract**

2 pinches **sea salt**

2 tbsp melted **cold-pressed coconut oil** (see page 270)

2 tbsp melted **cacao butter**

optional – **caramelised hazelnuts** (see page 29) and **chocolate sticks** (see page 249)

Place all ingredients except the coconut oil and cacao butter in a food processor. Process until very smooth. Add coconut oil and cacao butter while the food processor is running until completely combined into the mixture.

Pour into individual cups and refrigerate for 2 hours (the mousse will not achieve the desired taste until well chilled).

If you want to speed up the setting process place in the freezer for 20 minutes.

To make this simple mousse a more sophisticated desert, you can top with crushed activated hazelnuts or caramelised hazelnuts and chocolate flakes made from grating the chocolate sticks.

Hazelnuts contain vitamins, minerals, protein, fibre and healthy fats. They also contain phytochemicals, including proanthocyanidins, quercetin and kaempferol. These flavonoids may support brain health, improve circulation and reduce symptoms associated with allergies.

Avocado contains many nutrients that you need in your diet; it is full of healthy fats like oleic acid, which can actually help reduce cholesterol. Avocado contains more potassium than bananas, something that is essential for muscle growth and organ function. Avocado also contains vitamins C and E, antioxidants that keep the immune system strong and your skin beautiful.

mango & coconut sticky rice served in a banana leaf with coconut cream

When we go to Thailand I eat this traditional treat nearly every day. I absolutely love the subtle flavours that the pandan and banana leaf wrapping impart – and the fact that your dessert comes in the most biodegradable packaging there is.

Instead of sticky rice, we mix cauliflower and coconut with a little psyllium, then top with fresh mango, coconut cream and coconut sugar syrup.

Make time: 20 minutes + component recipe | Dehydrating time: 3 hours | Serves: 2 |
Equipment required: blender, dehydrator, food processor

sticky rice

185 g (6½ oz/1½ cups) roughly chopped **cauliflower**

55 g (2 oz/⅓ cup) **young coconut flesh**

3 tsp **birch xylitol** or **coconut nectar**

1 tsp **psyllium husk**

½ tsp **vanilla extract**

optional – 2 drops **jasmine essential oil**

Blend cauliflower in a food processor until texture of rice. Put in a nut milk bag and squeeze out the excess moisture. Discard the liquid.

Place cauliflower back in the food processor with the remaining ingredients and pulse until combined. It should retain the texture of rice.

coconut cream

250 ml (9 fl oz/1 cup) **coconut milk** (see page 32)

40 g (1½ oz/¼ cup) **young coconut flesh**

Blend the ingredients in a high-speed blender until smooth. Sieve the milk if needed.

lime coconut sugar syrup

50 g (1¾ oz/¼ cup) **coconut sugar**

60 ml (2 fl oz/¼ cup) **filtered water**

60 ml (2 fl oz/¼ cup) **lime juice**

Mix all ingredients together by hand and place in the dehydrator to reduce at 46°C (115°F) for 3 hours.

to serve

1 large **banana leaf**

1 **mango**

1 **lime**

Cut 2 approximately 20 x 20 cm (8 x 8 in) squares out of the banana leaf. Place half the coconut rice mixture into the centre of the leaf and shape into a rectangle; top with half a mango sliced into long pieces.

At this stage you could squeeze a little lime over the mango and wrap the parcels up and store in the refrigerator until you wish to serve them.

Pour ¼ cup coconut cream over each serving and sprinkle with a tablespoon of the lime coconut sugar syrup.

Serve with more coconut cream, wedges of lime and lime coconut sugar syrup on the side. Our ginger syrup (see page 212) would be a lovely option to use instead of the lime coconut sugar syrup.

shrewsbury cookies
with chia raspberry jam

Growing up in New Zealand, shrewsbury cookies were a kids' favourite. Unable to eat gluten or dairy, I really felt I was missing out, although I did manage to sneak quite a few on the sly ...

These, I have to say, taste even better. The chia raspberry jam, in particular, is a revelation; it's so fruity and flavourful without the insane quantities of boiled sugar in regular jam.

Make time: 30 minutes + component recipe | Chill time: 30 minutes | Makes: 24 |
Equipment required: blender, dehydrator (optional), food processor

75 g (¾ cup) **gluten-free rolled (porridge) oats**

65 g (¾ cup) **desiccated (shredded) coconut**

90 g (3¼ oz/¾ cup) **dried activated almond** (see pages 27–28)

pinch **sea salt**

270 g (9½ oz/1½ cups) **pitted medjool dates**

225 g (8 oz/⅔ cup) **raw chia raspberry jam** (see following page)

Using a food processor, separately blend oats, coconut and almond into coarse flours – leaving ¼ of the oat flour to the side for rolling out the mixture. Put all the remaining oat, almond and coconut flour back in the food processor together, add sea salt and dates. Process until mixture comes together but still retains a small amount of texture – see picture for the best guide to what it should look like.

When you can squeeze a bit of the mix in your hand and it sticks easily, it's ready. If you find that it's too crumbly, blend for another minute or add a few more dates.

Divide the mixture in half. Lightly dust a dry surface with some of the oat flour. Roll one half of the mixture out until it's about 5–6 mm (¼ in) thick. Cut it into 6 cm (2½ in) circles or squares with a cookie cutter. Repeat with the other half, take a small circle or heart cutter to cut out the centre of the second half of the cookies. Transfer all of the cookies – the ones with and without cut-outs – into the refrigerator and let them chill for 30 minutes.

Repeat with the scraps left over from the first round until all the mixture is used up and you have enough to make around 20 cookies.

Spread a dollop of chia raspberry jam into the centre of each cookie that doesn't have a cut-out, and then top it with a cookie that does. Repeat until you've used up all of the dough.

Store cookies in the refrigerator until you're ready to enjoy them.

If you have a dehydrator you can place them in there on a mesh sheet for 4–6 hours at 41°C (106°F) to create a slightly more crispy biscuit exterior.

They are delicious either way.

chia raspberry jam

250 g (9 oz/2 cups) **fresh** or **frozen raspberries**

3–4 **pitted medjool dates** (add to taste)

4 tbsp **chia seeds**

Blend the raspberries and dates in a high-speed blender until smooth.

Transfer the mixture to a bowl. Stir in 2 tablespoons of chia seeds and sit for a few minutes, then stir again and a few minutes after that.

Let jam thicken in the refrigerator for a few hours before using, and add more chia seeds as needed.

superfood maca & cacao cookies

These are mini chocolate cookies that have a superfood kick. Maca is an everyday superfood from Peru that is used in many preparations from baking to making beer (it is a root vegetable that grows at high altitudes). It's thought to nourish and balance the body's delicate endocrine system, helping it cope with stress. It also naturally energises the body and can aid in reproductive function, helping to balance hormones and increase fertility.

These are feel-good chocolate cookies that are a perfect little power-up or sweet treat snack. If you don't enjoy maca or don't have any around, you can leave it out completely or replace it with another superfood like acai or maqui for a resveratrol hit.

Making time: 20 minutes + component recipes | Dehydrating time: 12 hours | Makes: 24 small cookies | Equipment required: dehydrator, food processor

120 g (4¼ oz/1 cup) **dried activated almonds** (see pages 27–28)

45 g (½ cup) **desiccated (shredded) coconut**

2 tbsp **chia seeds**

55 g (2 oz/½ cup) **cacao powder**

¼ tsp **sea salt**

65 g (⅓ cup) **coconut sugar**

2½ tbsp **maca powder**

85 g (3 oz/½ cup) **pitted dates**

1 tsp **vanilla extract**

¼ cup **almond butter** (see page 78)

2 tbsp melted **cold-pressed coconut oil** (see page 270)

60 ml (2 fl oz/¼ cup) **filtered water**

optional – 2 tbsp **cacao nibs**

garnish – 24 **dried activated almonds**

Make the almonds into a fine flour in a food processor or blender and set aside. Now make the desiccated coconut and chia seeds into flour; you can do this by placing them together in a food processor and blending until fine. Add to the almond flour along with the rest of the dry ingredients (cacao, salt, coconut sugar, maca) and lightly mix together.

Blend the dates in a food processor or blender until almost making a paste. A little texture is good – the mixture should be nice and sticky.

In a bowl mix the dates, vanilla, almond butter and melted coconut oil, stir until combined. It will be a thick sticky mixture.

Pour the sticky wet mixture into the dry one. With your hands, rub the dry and wet mixture together (like you would rub butter if you were making scones).

Now add the water and mix with a fork until thoroughly combined. Fold in cacao nibs if using.

Leave for 5 minutes for the dry mixture to soak up the water. The ideal mixture should be easy to shape – not too wet or sticky. Add some more chia seed and coconut flour if the mixture is too wet.

Take spoonfuls of the mixture (approximately the size of a small walnut) and roll into balls; you should get approximately 24 cookies from the mixture. Place on a dehydrator sheet and press down lightly with the back of a fork. Press in an activated almond on top of each cookie.

Dry in a dehydrator at 46°C (115°F) for 12 hours.

Will keep for a few days in an airtight container in the pantry or several weeks in the refrigerator.

blackberry & strawberry coconut ice

Coconut ice is a Kiwi bake sale classic. Traditionally it has a very high sugar content, red food colouring (which is the one we want to avoid the most) and dairy. This is a more healthful and flavourful version that can be enjoyed without overdosing on sugar. Instead of red food colouring, we use freeze-dried berries, which add a delicious summery flavour that kids love.

Make time: 20 minutes | Setting time: 45 minutes | Makes: approximately 20 pieces, each 3 cm (1¼ in) square

6 tbsp melted **coconut butter** – this is different to coconut oil and has a paste-like consistency (see tip)

90 g (3¼ oz/1 cup) **desiccated (shredded) organic coconut**

3 tbsp **light raw agave** or **light coconut nectar** (you could use a light-coloured honey but it will impart a stronger flavour)

60 ml (2 fl oz/¼ cup) melted **cold-pressed coconut oil** (see page 270)

1 tsp **vanilla extract**

pinch **sea salt**

5 g (⅛ oz/¼ cup) **freeze-dried strawberries** or **raspberries**, crushed so about half is powder

optional – ½ tsp **rosewater**

Stir all the ingredients, except the freeze-dried berries and optional rosewater, in a bowl until well combined.

Divide mixture between two bowls. Add berries to one of the bowls and mix until beautifully pink. Mix the rosewater, if using, into the same bowl.

Line a small rectangular container or tin, approximately 15 x 12 cm (6 x 4½ in), with plastic food wrap; spoon in a 1 cm- (½ in-) deep layer of white mixture, then place in the freezer for 15 minutes until slightly firm. Spread the pink mixture on top and freeze for 30–40 minutes until completely firm.

Cut into 3 cm- (1¼ in-) square pieces and store in the refrigerator in an airtight container for several weeks.

Tip: You can make coconut butter if you have a high-speed blender or small handheld blender, by blending desiccated (shredded) coconut on high until it forms a paste. The best way to melt cacao butter or coconut oil is in a bowl over another bowl filled with hot water. The pot should be on the bench, not on the stovetop, or your oil won't be raw any more.

chocolate, goji & coconut bark

A versatile recipe that can easily be personalised; like little chocolate pizzas, each household member can add their favourite toppings. We've used macadamia nuts, coconut and goji berries in this bark recipe. Use your imagination, but be sure to include something crunchy and something a bit chewy.

Make time: 20 minutes | Setting time: 1 hour

60 ml (2 fl oz/¼ cup) melted **cacao butter** (see page 270)

125 ml (4 fl oz/½ cup) melted **cold-pressed coconut oil** (see page 270)

75 g (¼ cup) **raw agave** or **organic maple syrup**

80 g (2¾ oz/¾ cup) **cacao powder**

small pinch **sea salt**

1 tsp **vanilla extract**

45 g (⅓ cup) lightly chopped **macadamia nuts**

20 g (¾ oz/⅓ cup) **coconut chips**

2 tbsp **goji berries**

optional – ½ tsp **cinnamon**

Melt the cacao butter and coconut oil (see page 270).

Add the agave, cacao powder, sea salt, vanilla and cinnamon (if using).

Stir gently until the mixture is well combined, at least 10 minutes. You want the temperature to stay around 41°C (106°F) to ensure a smooth and consistent chocolate that doesn't separate. Keeping the bowl with the chocolate in it over another bowl filled with hot water will help you maintain the temperature.

The coconut oil in the mixture prevents us tempering it like a traditional chocolate but there are still benefits from reducing the temperature before using.

To do this place some ice in a bowl of water and make a cooling version of the double boiler.

Remove the bowl of chocolate mixture from the double boiler and place in the iced water. Stir continuously to reduce the temperature evenly. Do this for approximately 1–2 minutes until the chocolate is around body temperature. (You can test this by placing some on your chin just under your lip, the chocolate should not feel warm or cold.)

Take a baking tray (that fits in your freezer) and line with baking paper. Pour over the chocolate mixture and sprinkle with the macadamia nuts, coconut chips and goji berries.

Place in the freezer for 1 hour or until set firmly, then cut or break into large pieces of bark. The coconut oil means it will melt if left at a moderate room temperature so store it in an airtight container to keep it at its best.

chocolate logs

We married in Bali a few years ago, the perfect place for lovers of raw food to enjoy their wedding without having to make all the food. Bali is a raw food mecca, and the quality and variety gets better every year. Our chocolate log recipe is inspired by the delicious logs from Bali Buda, an organic store on the island.

The logs are an excellent energy boost of sustaining energy; we even have one of New Zealand's competitive athletes using them for races.

This recipe makes a large batch, but the logs will last a few months in the refrigerator in an airtight container and are so good I'm sure you will get through them. If you're unbaking for just one or two people, you could halve the recipe.

Make time: 35 minutes | Makes: 30 logs | Equipment required: food processor

310 g (11 oz/2 cups) **cashews**

55 g (2 oz/½ cup) **cacao powder** and extra for dusting

175 g (6 oz/1 cup) **cacao nibs**

¼ tsp **sea salt**

320 g (11¼ oz/2 cups) **pitted dates**

1 tbsp **raw honey**

80 ml (2½ fl oz/⅓ cup) and 3 tbsp melted **cold-pressed coconut oil** (see page 270)

1 tbsp **vanilla extract**

Blend the cashews in a food processor into a chunky flour so there are still pieces that are a similar size to cacao nibs in there. Place the cashews and all of the other dry ingredients together in a bowl and lightly mix.

Blend the dates in a food processor with the honey, coconut oil and vanilla until combined and until the dates are sticky but not forming a paste. Now fold this mixture into the dry mix bowl until everything is really well combined. You should be able to form a log shape that holds together; if it is too crumbly place some of the mixture back into the food processor and blend until sticky, then fold back into the rest of the mix.

Shape and roll into 30 logs, about 50 g (1¾ oz) each, dusting with cacao before placing in the refrigerator to set.

Store in the refrigerator in an airtight container for up to 2 months.

cacao & hazelnut tart

Chocolate and hazelnut is a classic combination that should be celebrated. This tart is similar in texture to a traditional chocolate tart with a beautiful buttery texture that melts in your mouth.

Make time: 40 minutes + component recipes | Soak time: 2–4 hours | Setting time: 6 hours | Serves: 12–16 | Equipment required: blender, food processor

base

120 g (4¼ oz/1 cup) **dried activated almonds** (see pages 27–28)

55 g (2 oz/½ cup) **dried activated hazelnuts** (see pages 27–28)

210 g (7½ oz/1¼ cups) **pitted dates**

¼ tsp **vanilla bean powder** or **vanilla extract**

3 tbsp **cacao powder**

1 tbsp melted **cacao butter** (see page 270)

hazelnut and cacao filling

205 g (7¼ oz/1⅓ cups) **cashews** (soaked 2–4 hours)

185 ml (6 fl oz/¾ cup) **hazelnut milk**
or use almond milk (see page 30) if you don't have any available

175 g (6 oz/½ cup) **organic maple syrup**

pinch **sea salt**

1 tbsp **vanilla extract**

80 ml (2½ fl oz/⅓ cup) melted **coconut oil** (see page 270)

60 ml (2 fl oz/¼ cup) melted **cacao butter** (see page 270)

40 g (1½ oz/⅓ cup) **cacao powder**

topping

cacao powder

optional – **dried activated hazelnuts** (see pages 27–28)

To prepare the base:
In a food processor, blend nuts until almost like couscous – leave them with a bit of texture.

Add the dates and blend until well combined and until the mixture is slightly sticky. Then add the remaining ingredients and pulse a few times until combined. The mixture should hold together well.

Line a 22 cm (8½ in) French fluted tart (flan) tin with plastic wrap or for individual tarts use mini tart cases. Press mixture firmly into the tart tin – it will need to be approximately 4–5 mm (³⁄₁₆–¼ in) thick on the bottom and up the sides of the tin to maintain the structure.

Place the tart base into the refrigerator while you make the filling.

To prepare the hazelnut and cacao filling:
Drain the soaked cashews and rinse thoroughly. Blend all the ingredients except the coconut oil, cacao butter and cacao powder in a high-speed blender – be careful not to let it heat up. Make sure you blend until completely smooth – like the texture of a silky cream.

Slowly pour in the coconut oil and cacao butter with the blender going until completely combined into the mixture. Lastly, add the cacao powder and blend until completely incorporated.

Pour into the prepared base(s) and leave to set in the refrigerator for approximately 6 hours.

To finish:
Dust with a fine layer of sieved cacao powder and some dried activated hazelnuts.

blueberry crumble slice

Our blueberry crumble slice was created by our beautiful pastry princess Rejina. She has truly shone in our pastry kitchen, creating all sorts of beautiful cakes and treats for people who have previously had to go without. It's so rewarding seeing how thrilled people are when they bite into our delicious treats free from refined flours, sugar, dairy and gluten.

This is one of our nut-free treats using sprouted buckwheat, gluten-free rolled (porridge) oats and coconut for the base, and topped with a summery blend of blueberries and apples.

Make time: 50 minutes + component recipes | Dehydrating time: 12 hours | Setting time: 1–2 hours | Makes: 12 large slices | Equipment required: blender, dehydrator, food processor

base

65 g (¾ cup) **desiccated (shredded) coconut**

95 g (3¼ oz/1 cup) **gluten-free rolled (porridge) oats** or regular if gluten is not an issue for you

70 g (2½ oz/½ cup) **sprouted dehydrated buckwheat** (see pages 26–28 and 270)

245 g (1½ cups) **pitted dates**

40 g (1½ oz/¼ cup) **dried currants**

¼ tsp **sea salt**

60 ml (2 fl oz/¼ cup) melted **cold-pressed coconut oil** (see page 270)

125 ml (4 fl oz/½ cup) **filtered water** or enough to make the mixture bind together

blueberry filling

250 g (9 oz/2 cups) **frozen blueberries** (defrosted)

½ roughly chopped **green apple**

2 tbsp **raw honey**

2 tbsp **lemon juice**

1 tsp **vanilla extract**

2 tbsp **irish moss paste** (see page 33)

pinch **sea salt**

optional – 8 g (¼ cup) **freeze-dried blackcurrants/ blueberries**

To prepare the base:
Place the desiccated coconut in the food processor and blend into a flour. Add the oats, buckwheat and dates and blend into a couscous-like texture. Add the remaining ingredients and pulse until combined. The mixture should hold together well.

Add up to 125 ml (4 fl oz/½ cup) of water if the mixture is too dry and crumbly.

Line a 20 cm (8 in) slice (slab) tin with baking paper and press the mixture into the tin – it will need to be around 4–5 mm (³⁄₁₆–¼ in) thick to maintain the structure.

Place the base in the refrigerator while you make the filling.

To prepare the filling:
Blend all the ingredients in a high-speed blender – be careful not to let it heat up. Blend until it's really smooth.

Pour the filling over the prepared base.

crumble

75 g (½ cup) **dried currants**

160 g (1 cup) **pitted dates**

50 g (1¾ oz/⅓ cup) **sprouted dehydrated buckwheat** (see pages 26–28 and 270)

65 g (¾ cup) **desiccated (shredded) coconut**

75 g (¾ cup) **gluten-free rolled (porridge) oats**

1 tsp **lemon zest**

125 ml (4 fl oz/½ cup) **cold-pressed coconut oil** (see page 270)

2 tbsp **coconut sugar**

1 tsp **vanilla extract**

pinch **sea salt**

optional – 20 g (¾ oz/⅓ cup) **freeze-dried blueberries** or **blackcurrants**, 60 ml (2 fl oz/¼ cup) **ginger juice** (see page 270)

To prepare the crumble:
Place all ingredients in a food processor and pulse until combined into a sticky mixture.

Crumble the mixture on top of the slice filling and place in the dehydrator at 46°C (115°F) for 12 hours.

Remove and put in the refrigerator to set for 1–2 hours. Then cut it into 12 pieces.

Will keep in the refrigerator in an airtight container for up to 1 week.

banana & caramel brownie

Totally moreish this rich, sweet, chocolaty treat will satisfy any caramel fans. There are a few steps in this recipe for the caramel and the caramelised bananas that are more fiddly, but the base itself is quick to make and is delicious on its own without the caramel or caramelised bananas. If you wanted to make a variation without them you could add some freeze-dried raspberries for a berry brownie and serve with a scoop of vanilla ice cream (see page 262).

Make time: 1 hour | Dehydrating time: 6 hours | Setting time: 4–6 hours | Makes: 15 squares |
Equipment required: dehydrator, food processor

caramelised bananas (optional)

3 **ripe bananas** (not over-ripe)

3 tbsp **lemon juice**

50 g (1¾ oz/¼ cup) **coconut sugar** to sprinkle

caramel

50 g (1¾ oz/½ cup) **pecans**

220 g (7¾ oz/1⅓ cups) **pitted dates**

1 tsp **vanilla extract**

175 g (6 oz/½ cup) **organic maple syrup/raw agave/coconut crystals/raw honey**

base

490 g (3¼ cups) **brazil nuts**

135 g (4¾ oz/1¼ cups) **cacao powder**

pinch **sea salt**

320 g (11¼ oz/2 cups) **pitted dates**

1½ **avocados**

2 tsp **vanilla extract**

Firstly caramelise the bananas – these are optional so if you don't have a dehydrator don't worry about using them.

To prepare the bananas:
Slice bananas horizontally to get 5 mm (¼ in) slices. You will get 4 to 6 slices per banana. Place the slices on a dehydrator sheet and drizzle with lemon juice, then sprinkle with coconut sugar. Dehydrate for 6 hours at 46°C (115°F).

To prepare the caramel:
Make the pecans into a flour in your food processor, set aside. Process the dates and vanilla extract until they form a paste. Scrape the dates from the sides as you go.

Add sweetener and blend until you get a lighter coloured mixture. Add the pecan flour and blend until combined. Set aside while you make the base.

To prepare the base:
In the food processor, blend Brazil nuts into a coarse flour – there should still be some nut chunks. Place in a bowl and mix with the cacao powder and sea salt. Set aside. Using the food processor, blend the dates into approximately 5 mm (¼ in) chunks; add the avocado and vanilla and blend again until there are no chunks of avocado to be seen. Lastly, add the Brazil nut and cacao mixture and pulse until combined – be careful not to over-mix, you want it to be just coming together to retain some of the texture from the Brazil nuts.

Assembly:
Line a 20 cm (8 in) slice (slab) tin with plastic wrap. Press ¾ of the base mixture into tin – you want to make lengthways indentations, creating lines like waves so that the caramel can be set in between the 'waves'.

Fill the indentations with the caramel using a spoon or piping bag. Cover with the remaining base mixture – making sure you can't see any of the caramel. Layer the caramelised bananas on top (if using), pressing them lightly into the mixture. Cover with plastic wrap and refrigerate 4–6 hours.

Remove from the refrigerator and cut into approximately 15 square slices. This will keep for 1 week in an airtight container in the refrigerator.

ginger slice

Our original ginger slice for the cafés tasted amazing but was a bit temperamental and rather fiddly to construct. After some experimenting in the kitchen, Carter came up with this brilliant version that doesn't require a dehydrator to make and is just as delicious.

Make time: 50 minutes + component recipe | Setting time: 5–6 hours | Makes: 1 large slice, cut into 20 small squares | Equipment required: blender, food processor

base

155 g (1 cup) **cashews**

120 g (4¼ oz/1 cup) **dried activated almonds** (see pages 27–28)

90 g (3¼ oz/1 cup) **desiccated (shredded) coconut**

160 g (1 cup) **pitted dates**

2 tsp **vanilla extract**

2 pinches **sea salt**

1 tsp **lemon zest**

ginger topping

250 ml (9 fl oz/1 cup) melted **cold-pressed coconut oil** (see page 270)

190 g (6¼ oz/2 cups) **gluten-free rolled (porridge) oats**

185 ml (6 fl oz/¾ cup) **ginger juice** (see page 270)

150 g (5½ oz/¾ cup) **coconut sugar**

3 tbsp **raw agave**

90 g (3¼ oz/¼ cup) **organic maple syrup**

1 tbsp **vanilla extract**

pinch **sea salt**

235 g (8½ oz/1½ cups) **cashews**

55 g (2 oz/½ cup) **ginger powder**

To prepare the base:
Separately blend the cashews, almonds and desiccated coconut into flours using your food processor. Flours should be the consistency of breadcrumbs. We do them separately because they all take different amounts of time to break down. Put all the 'flours' back in the food processor together with the dates, vanilla extract, sea salt and lemon zest until combined. The mixture should stick together – if it doesn't, blend a little longer or add a few more dates.

Line a 26 x 20 cm (10½ x 8 in) baking tin with plastic wrap and firmly press the base mixture evenly into the tin until it's uniformly 1 cm (½ in) thick. (We put plastic wrap on the bottom because once the slice has been refrigerated and set, it is a lot easier to get out.)

To prepare the topping:
Melt the coconut oil and set aside. Blend the oats into a flour in your food processor and set aside.

In a high-speed blender, blend oat flour, ginger juice, 50 g (1¾ oz/¼ cup) coconut sugar, raw agave, maple syrup, vanilla extract and sea salt until smooth.

Blend the cashews, melted coconut oil and ginger powder in the food processor until smooth.

With the food processor running, take the blended oat and ginger mixture and place into the food processor with the cashew and coconut oil mixture and blend until combined. Do not over-process as the oil may separate.

Fold in 4 tablespoons of the remaining coconut sugar by hand.

Pour the mixture over the base and sprinkle with remaining coconut sugar.

Leave to set in the refrigerator for 5–6 hours. Once set, cut into 5 x 4 cm (2 x 1½ in) squares.

Store in the refrigerator with layers of baking paper in between so they don't stick together.

mango & pineapple mousse cake (nut free)

This delicious, soft mousse cake is free of nuts so caters for people with nut allergies. It is fresh and light in consistency and best to make when mangoes are perfectly ripe and in season. Our favourite mangoes are the delicious ones from Kensington in Australia. They are available in stores in the early summer months and are so juicy and sweet they are hard to resist.

Make time: 40 minutes + component recipe | Setting time: overnight (refrigerator) or 2–3 hours (freezer) |
Serves: 12–14 | Equipment required: blender, food processor

base

45 g (½ cup) **desiccated (shredded) coconut**

105 g (¾ cup) **sprouted dehydrated buckwheat**
(see pages 26–28 and 270)

75 g (¾ cup) **gluten-free rolled (porridge) oats**

135 g (4¾ oz/¾ cup) **pitted dates**

45 g (¼ cup) **sultanas (golden raisins)**

2 tbsp melted **cold-pressed coconut oil**
(see page 270)

mango mousse

600 g (1 lb 5 oz/3¼ cups) chopped **fresh
ripe mango**

120 g (4¼ oz/¾ cup) chopped **fresh ripe pineapple**

100–150 g (3½–5½ oz/⅓–½ cup) **raw agave**
or **birch xylitol** (the amount depends on how
sweet your fruit is)

125 ml (4 fl oz/½ cup) **fresh lemon juice**

juice 1 **lime**

pinch **sea salt**

½ tsp **vanilla extract**

250 ml (9 fl oz/1 cup) melted **cold-pressed
coconut oil** (see page 270)

2 tbsp melted **cacao butter**

1 tsp **lecithin**

To prepare the base:
In a food processor blend the coconut into flour. Add the buckwheat and oats and, again, process into flour. Add the dates and sultanas and blend to a fine couscous-like consistency. Lastly add the melted coconut oil and pulse for 15 seconds.

Line a 20 cm (8 in) cake tin with plastic wrap and firmly press the base evenly into the tin. You can put the base in the refrigerator whilst doing the next step.

To prepare the mousse:
In a high-speed blender, blend the mango, pineapple, agave, lemon juice, lime juice, sea salt and vanilla until smooth. Lastly add the coconut oil, cacao butter and lecithin and blend for 10–15 seconds (no more than 20 seconds or it will over-process).

To make:
Pour the mango mousse filling on top of the base. Cover with plastic wrap and either put in the refrigerator overnight or the freezer for 2–3 hours to set.

The cake is best served straight from the refrigerator as it's easier to cut. We often serve it with slices of fresh mango and coconut yoghurt (see page 34).

Will store for 4–5 days in the refrigerator or for a few weeks in the freezer.

blueberry cheesecake

Our cheesecakes at the unbakery are probably one of the things that made us most popular in the beginning – a way to someone's food heart is often entered with an amazing dessert experience, which this cheesecake truly delivers.

People often come back after trying one of our tarts or cakes to ask if it was really free of cream or butter. They simply can't imagine how we create such creamy desserts without dairy. The secret is cashews and coconuts, and even if you don't have problems with dairy products, it's nice to try something new. Made from nuts and dates, the simple base will surprise you at how close it tastes to a regular biscuit base.

Make time: 40 minutes + component recipes | Soak time: 2–4 hours | Setting time: overnight | Serves: 16 | Equipment required: blender, food processor

base

65 g (¾ cup) **desiccated (shredded) coconut**

120 g (4¼ oz/1 cup) **dried activated almonds** (see pages 27–28)

50 g (1¾ oz/⅓ cup) **cashews**

210 g (7½ oz/1¼ cups) **pitted dates**

¼ tsp **vanilla bean powder**

¼ tsp **sea salt**

2 tbsp melted **cold-pressed coconut oil** (see page 270)

filling

195 g (1¼ cups) **cashews** (soaked 2–4 hours)

320 g (11¼ oz/2 cups) **young coconut flesh** (if you can't get young coconut you can use another 235 g (8½ oz/1½ cups) of cashews)

125 ml (4 fl oz/½ cup) **almond milk** (see page 30) or just use filtered water

80 ml (2½ fl oz/⅓ cup) **filtered water**

3½ tbsp **lemon juice**

90 g (3¼ oz/¼ cup) **raw honey**

pinch **sea salt**

¼ tsp **vanilla bean powder**

1 tbsp **vanilla extract**

250 ml (9 fl oz/1 cup) melted **cold-pressed coconut oil** (see page 270)

390 g (13¾ oz/2½ cups) **fresh** or **frozen blueberries** (defrosted)

To prepare the base:
Blend the desiccated coconut in the food processor until it becomes a 'coconut flour'.

Blend the nuts and dates together in a food processor until almost a couscous-like texture. Add the remaining ingredients and pulse a few times until combined. The mixture should hold together well.

Add 1–2 teaspoons of water if the mixture is too dry and crumbly.

Line a 20 cm (8 in) cake tin with plastic wrap. Press the mixture into the base of the tin evenly and firmly.

Place the cheesecake base into the refrigerator while you make the filling.

To prepare the filling:
Drain the soaked cashews and rinse thoroughly. Blend all the ingredients except the coconut oil and berries in a high-speed blender – be careful not to let it heat up. Blend until it's really smooth.

Slowly pour in the coconut oil with the blender going until completely combined into the mixture.

Divide the mixture into two halves. Add the blueberries to one half of the mixture. Blend and mix until well combined, then pour the blueberry mixture into the cake tin.

Now pour the cream half of the mixture over the base blueberry mix and with a teaspoon, swirl them together until you get a nice marbling effect. Be careful not to get carried away otherwise you will end up with an entirely purple cake and no white cream to seen.

Cover the cake with plastic wrap and leave to set in the refrigerator or freezer for a minimum of 6 hours. I tend to do them overnight to be safe, or in the freezer if I'm in a hurry.

Optional blueberry coulis topping, see following recipe.

blueberry coulis

250 g (9 oz/2 cups) **frozen blueberries** (defrosted)

2 tbsp **irish moss paste** (see page 33)

60 ml (2 fl oz/¼ cup) **lemon** juice

1 tsp **vanilla extract**

75 g (¼ cup) **light raw agave**, **organic maple syrup**, **coconut nectar** or **light honey**

optional – 1 tbsp **freeze-dried blueberries**

Blend everything in a high-speed blender until smooth, let set in the refrigerator for 5–6 hours before using.

If using as topping for the blueberry cheesecake, try folding 155 g (1 cup) fresh blueberries through the coulis mixture, as pictured below.

strawberries & cream cheesecake

Strawberry cheesecake was my first recipe published in a magazine. It's still a café favourite but has gone through various alterations; we think this is the perfect strawberries and cream cheesecake experience.

Make time: 50 minutes + component recipes | Soak time: 2–4 hours | Setting time: 6–8 hours/overnight | Serves: 12–16 | Equipment required: blender, food processor

base

see blueberry cheesecake recipe page 242

cream filling

195 g (1¼ cups) **cashews** (soaked 2–4 hours)

320 g (11¼ oz/2 cups) **young coconut flesh** (if you can't get young coconut you can use another 235 g (8½ oz/1½ cups) of cashews)

250 ml (9 fl oz/1 cup) **almond milk** (see page 30) or just use filtered water

3 tbsp **lemon juice**

175 g (6 oz/½ cup) **raw honey**

pinch **sea salt**

¼ tsp **vanilla bean powder**

125 ml (4 fl oz/½ cup) melted **cold-pressed coconut oil** (see page 270)

3 tbsp melted **cacao butter**

strawberry filling

300 g (10½ oz/2 heaped cups) **fresh** or **frozen strawberries** (defrosted)

70 g (2½ oz/½ cup) **frozen raspberries** (defrosted)

2 tsp **vanilla extract**

90 g (3¼ oz/⅓ cup) **irish moss paste** (see page 33)

90 g (3¼ oz/¼ cup) **raw borage honey** or other light floral honey

3 tbsp **lemon juice**

80 ml (2½ fl oz/⅓ cup) melted **cold-pressed coconut oil** (see page 270)

topping (optional)

fresh or **freeze-dried berries**

edible flowers

To prepare the base:
As per blueberry cheesecake recipe on page 242.

To prepare the filling:
Drain the soaked cashews and rinse thoroughly. Blend all the cream filling ingredients except the coconut oil and cacao butter in a high-speed blender – be careful not to let it heat up. Blend until it's really smooth – if you coat the back of a spoon with the mixture you shouldn't see any lumps or texture in it.

Slowly pour in the coconut oil and cacao butter with the blender going until completely combined into the mixture.

Pour half the mixture into the cake tin. Set aside.

Add the rest of the strawberry filling ingredients except the coconut oil and blend until smooth. Slowly pour in the remaining coconut oil with the blender going until completely combined into the mixture.

Now pour the strawberry filling over the base cream mixture and, with a teaspoon, swirl them together until you get a nice marbling effect. Be careful not to get carried away, otherwise you will end up with an entirely pink cake and no white cream to be seen.

To finish:
Cover the cake with plastic wrap and leave to set in the refrigerator for a minimum of 6 hours (note that cakes incorporating Irish moss will not set properly if placed in the freezer). I tend to do them overnight to be safe, especially with this cake as it contains Irish moss.

Optional topping:
Fresh or freeze-dried berries with edible flowers.

All our raw desserts are packed with goodness; no fillers here so you will feel very satisfied with a small piece.

chocolate swirl cheesecake topped with chocolate bark

This is a very similar recipe to our berry cheesecakes, except it is filled with a delicious chocolate swirl to contrast with the cream. We have also added a little miso to it for an extra cheese-tasting element to the cream base. For the berry cheesecakes we use lots of lemon to create a cheesy flavour but with chocolate, lemon can be a bit conflicting in large amounts so we use miso here as well to balance that out.

We have topped it with chocolate sauce and chocolate sticks (see page 249) to make a very decadent chocolate cheesecake fit for a birthday celebration.

Make time: 50 minutes + component recipes | Soak time: 2–4 hours | Setting time: 6–8 hours/overnight | Serves: 12–16 | Equipment required: blender, food processor

base

120 g (4¼ oz/1 cup) **dried activated almonds** (see pages 27–28)

40 g (1½ oz/¼ cup) **cashews**

210 g (7½ oz/1¼ cups) **pitted dates**

65 g (¾ cup) **desiccated (shredded) coconut**, ground into a flour in your food processor

¼ tsp **vanilla bean powder**

¼ tsp **sea salt**

2 tbsp melted **cold-pressed coconut oil** (see page 270)

3 tbsp **cacao powder**

cream filling

continued on the next page …

chocolate filling

continued on the next page …

To prepare the base:
Blend nuts and dates together in a food processor until almost a couscous-like texture; add the remaining ingredients and pulse a few times until combined. The mixture should hold together well.

Add 1–2 teaspoons of filtered water if the mixture is too dry and crumbly.

Line a cake tin approximately 22 cm (8½ in) in diameter with plastic wrap. Press the mixture approximately 8 mm (⅜ in) thick into the base of the tin evenly and firmly.

Place the cake base in the refrigerator while you make the filling.

Organic pitted baking dates are what all our base recipes are made from, they are soft but not overly sticky or too sweet. If using medjool, use around 40 g (1½ oz) less as they are much sweeter and stickier.

cream filling

155 g (1 cup) **cashews** (soaked 2–4 hours)

270 g (9½ oz/1⅔ cups) **young coconut flesh**

185 ml (6 fl oz/¾ cup) **almond milk** (see page 30) or just use filtered water

1 tbsp **lemon juice**

1 tsp **white miso**

100 g (3½ oz/⅓ cup) and 1 tbsp **raw agave**

1½ tsp **vanilla extract**

pinch **sea salt**

80 ml (2½ fl oz/⅓ cup) and 1 tbsp melted **cold-pressed coconut oil** (see page 270)

2½ tbsp melted **cacao butter**

chocolate filling

275 g (9¾ oz/1¾ cups) **cashews** (soaked 2–4 hours)

160 g (1 cup) **young coconut flesh**
(if you can't get young coconut you can use another 235 g (8½ oz/1½ cups) of cashews)

250 ml (9 fl oz/1 cup) **almond milk** (see page 30) or just use filtered water

260 g (9¼ oz/¾ cup) **organic maple syrup**

2 tsp **vanilla extract**

80 g (2¾ oz/¾ cup) **cacao powder**

pinch **sea salt**

125 ml (4 fl oz/½ cup) melted **cold-pressed coconut oil** (see page 270)

4 tbsp melted **cacao butter**

topping (optional)

chocolate sauce (see following recipe)

chocolate sticks (see following recipe)

To prepare the cream filling:
Drain the soaked cashews and rinse thoroughly. Blend all the cream filling ingredients except the coconut oil and cacao butter in a high-speed blender – be careful not to let it heat up. Blend until it's really smooth – if you coat the back of a spoon with the mixture you shouldn't see any lumps or texture in it.

Slowly pour in the coconut oil and cacao butter with the blender going until it's completely combined into the mixture.

Pour the cream filling on top of the base and set aside.

To prepare the chocolate filling:
Drain the soaked cashews and rinse thoroughly.

As with the cream mixture, blend all the chocolate filling ingredients except the coconut oil and cacao butter in a high-speed blender – be careful not to let it heat up. Blend until it's really smooth – if you coat the back of a spoon with the mixture you shouldn't see any lumps or texture in it. Slowly pour in the coconut oil and cacao butter with the blender going until completely combined into the mixture.

Now pour the chocolate filling over the base cream mixture and, with a teaspoon, swirl them together until you get a nice marbling effect. Be careful not to get carried away with swirling or you will end up with an entirely light brown cake and no white and dark colour contrast.

To finish:
Cover the cake with plastic wrap and leave to set in the refrigerator for a minimum of 6 hours. I tend to do them overnight to be safe.

Optional topping:
Chocolate sauce with chocolate sticks.

Young coconuts have white or green husks – don't use the ones with brown husks. If you can't get young coconut, you can use another 195 g (1¼ cups) of cashews in this recipe.

chocolate sticks

We use these chocolate sticks to garnish our sundaes (page 266) and chocolate cheesecake (page 246) and as swizzle sticks for chocolate drinks. They provide a bitter chocolate accent; if you're after a sweeter chocolate, double the quantity of organic maple or raw agave.

When working with chocolate, always be careful not to let any water get into the mixture.

Prep time: 30 minutes | Setting time: 2–3 hours | Serves: 20 small sticks | Equipment required: chocolate moulds

80 g (2¾ oz/⅓ cup) **cacao butter**

1 tbsp melted **cold-pressed coconut oil** (see page 270)

3 tbsp **raw agave** or **organic maple syrup**

105 g (1 heaped cup) **cacao powder**

pinch **sea salt**

½ tsp **vanilla bean powder** or the seeds 1 **vanilla bean**

Melt the cacao butter and coconut oil in a double boiler (see page 270). Add the agave, cacao powder, sea salt and vanilla.

Stir gently until the mixture is well combined, at least 10 minutes. You want the temperature to stay around 41°C (106°F) to ensure a smooth, consistent chocolate that doesn't separate.

The coconut oil in the mixture prevents us tempering it like a traditional chocolate, but there are still benefits from reducing the temperature before using. To do this, place some ice in a bowl of water and make a cooling version of the double boiler.

Remove the top bowl from the double boiler and place on the iced water. Stir continuously to reduce the temperature evenly. Do this for approximately 1–2 minutes until the chocolate is around body temperature. (Test this by placing some on your chin just under your lip; it should not feel warm or cold.)

Place mixture into silicon chocolate moulds and place in the refrigerator for 2–3 hours or freezer for 1 hour until set.

Store in the refrigerator in an airtight container for several months.

chocolate sauce

A simple, versatile chocolate sauce you can store in the refrigerator for months. We use it to garnish our iced coffee milkshake (see page 102) and chocolate cheesecake (see page 246). It's really sweet, so use it sparingly.

Make time: 10 minutes | Makes: 2 cups | Equipment required: blender

105 g (1 cup) **cacao powder**

350 g (12 oz/1 cup) **organic maple syrup** or **raw agave**

pinch **sea salt**

1½ tbsp **vanilla extract**

3 tbsp melted **cold-pressed coconut oil** (see page 270)

Blend the cacao, maple syrup/agave, sea salt and vanilla extract in a high-speed blender until smooth. Add coconut oil with blender still running.

Store in a glass jar in the cupboard for 1 week or in the refrigerator for several months. If it's in the refrigerator you will need to get it out and leave it some place warm before using.

carrot cakes

These gorgeous little cakes will get everyone in the house excited about eating carrots. At Easter we change the name to Bunny Spice Cakes; they are a great alternative to sugar-laden chocolate eggs and hot cross buns.

Being a massive carrot cake fan, I was well pleased when we created this delicious version. Coconut, almonds and cashews stand in for the flour; fresh grated carrots and dates provide moistness; and cashews and coconut form the base of the rich, lemony frosting.

Instead of mini cakes, you could make one larger layer cake or the old-school square one we serve at the unbakery.

These stay beautiful and moist in the refrigerator for about a week.

Make time: 1 hour + component recipes | Soak time: 2–4 hours | Setting time: 30–40 minutes | Serves: 10 | Equipment required: blender, food processor

150 g (5½ oz/1¼ cups) **dried activated almonds** (see pages 27–28)

195 g (1¼ cups) **cashews**

205 g (7¼ oz/2¼ cups) **desiccated (shredded) coconut**

270 g (9½ oz/1½ cups) **almond pulp** (see page 270)

2 **medium carrots** (approximately 235 g (8½ oz/1½ cups) grated)

140 g (5 oz/1 cup) **currants**

1½ tbsp **cinnamon** plus extra for dusting

2 tsp **ground nutmeg**

1 tsp **vanilla extract**

2 pinches **sea salt**

1 tbsp **lemon zest**

80 ml (2½ fl oz/⅓ cup) **lemon juice**

180 g (¾ cup) **date paste** (see page 41)

115 g (4 oz/⅓ cup) **organic maple syrup, raw agave, or raw honey**

60 ml (2 fl oz/¼ cup) melted **cold-pressed coconut oil** (see page 270)

Blend almonds, cashews, and 115 g (4 oz/1¼ cups) of the desiccated coconut separately in a food processor until they resemble a 'flour' consistency.

In a bowl, add the nut pulp, 'flours', remaining desiccated coconut, carrot, currants, cinnamon, nutmeg, vanilla extract, sea salt and lemon zest and fold together with hands.

Blend the lemon juice, date paste, sweetener and coconut oil in a food processor or high-speed blender and set aside.

Now add the wet mixture to the dry ingredients and mix together with hands until it sticks together.

Line your mini cake, cupcake or regular cake tin with plastic wrap (note: you can get biodegradable versions of this).

Divide the mixture into however many layers you would like in the cake. We usually do three layers as pictured. Then divide the first layer between 10 mini cake tins or just make one layer in a regular cake tin.

Do the same with your frosting mixture once it has become firm.

Alternate the layers of cake and frosting in the cake tin, finishing with a layer of the lemon cream cheese frosting.

Dust with cinnamon and serve.

lemon cream cheese frosting

155 g (1 cup) **cashews** (soaked 2–4 hours)

160 g (1 cup) **fresh young coconut flesh**

150 g (5½ oz/½ cup) **raw agave**
or **organic maple syrup**

1 tbsp **nut cheese** (if you don't have nut cheese
add more lemon juice)

80 ml (2½ fl oz/⅓ cup) **lemon juice**

1 tbsp **vanilla extract**

pinch **sea salt**

250 ml (9 fl oz/1 cup) melted **cold-pressed
coconut oil** (see page 270)

Drain the soaked cashews and rinse thoroughly. Put the cashews, coconut flesh, agave, nut cheese, lemon juice, vanilla extract and sea salt in a high-speed blender, adding enough filtered water to blend until smooth – approximately 125 ml (4 fl oz/½ cup). If using maple syrup, the cream will be a darker colour.

With the blender still running, slowly pour the coconut oil in at the end.

Leave to set in the refrigerator or freezer for 30–40 minutes before using.

chocolate layer cake with coconut frosting

Layers of chocolate cake and light creamy coconut frosting make for a wonderful celebration cake. When raspberries are in season, sandwich them between the frosting and the cake.

Make time: 40 minutes + component recipes | Soak time: 2–4 hours | Setting time: 3–4 hours | Serves: 10 |
Equipment required: blender, food processor

wet

240 g (1 cup) **date paste** (see page 41)

80 ml (2½ fl oz/⅓ cup) **almond milk** (see page 30)

1 tbsp **vanilla extract**

60 ml (2 fl oz/¼ cup) melted **cold-pressed coconut oil** (see page 270)

3 tbsp melted **cacao butter**
(use coconut oil if you don't have cacao butter)

dry

360 g (12¾ oz/2 cups) **almond pulp** (see page 270)

180 g (1½ cups) **dried activated almonds**
(see pages 27–28), blended in a food processor
to a 'flour' consistency

65 g (⅓ cup) **organic coconut sugar**
or **organic maple syrup** (if using maple syrup add
it to the wet mixture)

180 g (2 cups) **desiccated (shredded) coconut**,
blended in a food processor to 'flour' consistency

3½ tbsp **golden flax meal**
(make by blending whole flax seeds in a blender)

160 g (1½ cups) **cacao powder**, plus extra
for dusting

pinch **sea salt**

coconut cream frosting

80 g (2¾ oz/½ cup) **cashews** (soaked 2–4 hours)

160 g (1 cup) **young coconut flesh**

125 ml (4 fl oz/½ cup) **almond milk** (see page 30)

1 tbsp **vanilla extract**

75 g (¼ cup) **light raw agave**

pinch **sea salt**

250 ml (9 fl oz/1 cup) melted **cold-pressed
coconut oil** (see page 270)

To prepare the cake layer:
Blend all wet ingredients, except coconut oil and cacao butter, in a food processor until smooth. Slowly add coconut oil and cacao butter and blend until smooth.

Place all the dry ingredients in a bowl. Using a fork or whisk, lightly mix until well combined and there are no lumps of almond pulp.

Add wet ingredients to the dry and mix with a fork or whisk until well combined but still fluffy; do not over-mix. Set aside while you make the frosting.

To prepare the frosting layer:
Drain the soaked cashews and rinse thoroughly. Put the cashews, young coconut flesh, almond milk, vanilla extract, agave and sea salt in a high-speed blender, adding enough filtered water to blend until smooth.

With the blender still running, slowly pour the melted coconut oil in at the end and set aside.

Line an 18 cm (7 in) round cake tin with plastic wrap. Press ¼ of the cake mixture into the bottom and pour ⅓ of the frosting on top.

Place in freezer for 30–40 minutes to set frosting, then press the next quarter of the cake mixture on top, followed by another ⅓ of the frosting and leave to set, repeat for the next layers, finishing with a layer of the cake mixture.

Leave to set in the refrigerator for 2–3 hours or until the cream has set.

To serve:
Dust with extra cacao powder, and serve with fresh raspberries when in season.

the perfect raw christmas cake

Christmas cake was never a favourite for me. It wasn't until I was in my early twenties and made an amazing macrobiotic version containing miso and dark beer that I realised how delicious it could be without the weird artificial almond essence and glazed cherries.

This is my raw homage to that recipe. It has become a Christmas favourite; we sell as many as the kitchen can make.

Make time: 2 hours + component recipes | Soak time: 2–4 hours | Makes: 2 cakes |
Equipment required: blender, food processor

cake

120 g (4¼ oz/1 cup) **dried activated almonds**
(see pages 27–28)

65 g (¾ cup) **desiccated (shredded) coconut**

75 g (½ cup) **brazil nuts**

1 **apple** (granny smith or braeburn)

1 tsp **lemon zest**

1 **orange**, zest and juice

3 **dried figs**

135 g (4¾ oz/¾ cup) **pitted dates**

130 g (¾ cup) **almond pulp**
(left over from nut milk, see page 270)

60 g (2¼ oz/⅓ cup) **sultanas (golden raisins)**

40 g (1½ oz/¼ cup) **currants**

90 g (3¼ oz/1 cup) roughly chopped **dried apples**

2¼ tbsp **cinnamon**

1½ tsp **ginger powder**

1 tsp **allspice powder**

⅓ tsp **clove powder**

¼ tsp **ground nutmeg powder**

pinch **sea salt**

2 tbsp **vanilla extract**

1 tsp **white miso paste (shiro miso)**

90 g (3¼ oz/¼ cup) **organic maple syrup**

3 tbsp melted **cold-pressed coconut oil**
(see page 270)

Make the frosting recipe first so it can set before making the cake.

Blend almonds and the coconut separately in a food processor until they resemble a 'flour' consistency.

Hand chop the Brazil nuts into rough 1 cm (½ in) pieces.

Chop the apple up into approximately 5 mm (¼ in) cubed pieces. Zest the lemon and orange and hand squeeze as much of the juice as you can get. Set aside.

In a food processor, or by hand, chop the figs up into approximately 5 mm (¼ in) cubed piece. Set aside. Blend the dates until approximately the same 5 mm (¼ in) cubed size as the figs.

In a bowl, add the almond pulp, 'flours', Brazil nuts, sultanas, currants, dates, figs, apples, spices, sea salt, orange and lemon zest and fold together with your hands.

Blend the orange juice, vanilla, miso, dates, maple syrup and coconut oil in a food processor until well mixed and set aside.

Now add the wet mixture to the dry ingredients and mix together by hand until it sticks together.

Divide the mixture into 2, shape with your hands into 15 x 15 x 7 cm (6 x 6 x 2¾ in) high square cakes and place in the refrigerator for 20 minutes.

Now ice the cakes with approximately ¾ cup of frosting per cake.

frosting

235 g (8½ oz/1½ cups) **cashews** (soaked 2–4 hours)

125 ml (4 fl oz/½ cup) **almond milk** (see page 30)

1 tbsp **vanilla extract**

75 g (¼ cup) **light raw agave**

pinch **sea salt**

435 ml (15¼ fl oz/1¾ cups) melted **cold-pressed coconut oil** (see page 270)

3 tbsp melted **cacao butter**

optional – ¼ tsp **natural almond extract**

decorating

1 tbsp **goji berries**

30 g (1 oz/¼ cup) **dried activated almonds** (see pages 27–28)

unbleached baking paper

string

Drain the soaked cashews and rinse thoroughly.

Put cashews, almond milk, vanilla extract, agave and sea salt in a high-speed blender, adding enough filtered water to blend until smooth.

With the blender still running, slowly pour in the coconut oil and cacao butter at the end.

Leave to set in the refrigerator overnight or the freezer for a few hours before using. It is easier to ice the cake when the frosting has hardened.

Optional decorating – place goji berries and activated almonds on top of the cake, cut a 30 cm (12 in) square piece of baking paper and tie up with string.

Once iced, it will store in the refrigerator for approximately 1 week.

buckwheat crackle

Traditional crackle is filled with puffed rice, hydrogenated shortening and icing (confectioners') sugar, leaving you with a negative nutritional experience. Our little bird version is equally delicious but full of the good stuff.

Crackle is all about the texture. Here, sprouted and dried buckwheat offers satisfying crunch, while the dates are chewy and the coconut-chocolate coating tastes decadent. This is a wonderful treat or breakfast snack; we often eat these for breakfast after our green smoothies.

Make time: 20 minutes + component recipes | Setting time: 1 hour | Makes: 10 | Equipment required: food processor

280 g (2 cups) **sprouted dehydrated buckwheat** (see pages 26–28 and 270)

90 g (3¼ oz/1 cup) **desiccated (shredded) coconut**

55 g (2 oz/½ cup) **cacao powder**

2 tbsp **carob powder**

160 g (1 cup) **pitted dates**

75 g (½ cup) **dried currants**

125 ml (4 fl oz/½ cup) melted **cold-pressed coconut oil** (see page 270)

60 ml (2 fl oz/¼ cup) melted **cacao butter**

1 tsp **vanilla**

pinch **sea salt**

12 g (⅓ cup) **freeze-dried blackcurrants** or **blackberries**

Place buckwheat, desiccated coconut, cacao powder and carob powder into a bowl and combine with your hands.

In a food processor, blend dates, currants, coconut oil, cacao butter, vanilla and sea salt until combined. The dates should be in small pieces and the mixture should be sticky.

Add the wet mixture to the dry ingredients and mix together with your hands.

Crush the freeze-dried blackcurrants/blackberries with your fingers and mix through.

Line a muffin tin with plastic wrap and push the mixture firmly into the tins. Fill them to the top.

Set in the refrigerator for 1 hour.

Remove from muffin tin and store in an airtight container in the refrigerator for up to 4 weeks.

apricot, almond & sesame muesli bars

Easy to prepare, these yummy apricot, almond and sesame muesli bars are a good snack to have on hand for those many occasions when you need to grab something quickly. They're nutritious, filling bites to eat and especially good in-between meals. The only drawback is you need to keep them in the refrigerator; if you wanted to make them so they would hold up in a lunch box all day you could dehydrate them for 24 hours before cutting.

Make time: 15 minutes + component recipes | Setting time: 1 hour | Makes: 10 bars (10 x 3 cm (4 x 1¼ in)) | Equipment required: blender, food processor

120 g (4¼ oz/1 cup) **dried activated almonds** (see pages 27–28)

225 g (8 oz/¼ cup) **whole golden flax seeds**

50 g (1¾ oz/⅓ cup) **sesame seeds**

zest 1 large **lemon**

90 g (3¼ oz/1 cup) **desiccated (shredded) coconut**

1½ tsp **cinnamon**

pinch **sea salt**

80 g (2¾ oz/½ cup) **dried apricots**

115 g (4 oz/⅓ cup) **raw honey**

65 g (¼ cup) **raw tahini** (if you can't get raw, you could use regular organic tahini)

60 ml (2 fl oz/¼ cup) melted **cold-pressed coconut oil** (see page 270)

optional – 40 g (1½ oz/¼ cup) **sour cherries** or **currants**

Pulse the almonds in a food processor until lightly chopped. In a blender, make the flax seeds into a flour and place in a bowl with the chopped almonds, sesame seeds, lemon zest, desiccated coconut, cinnamon, sea salt and sour cherries or currants if using.

Chop the apricots by putting them in a food processor and process until they are in small pieces. They should be sticky (this will help hold the muesli bars together).

Place the honey, tahini and melted coconut oil in a bowl and mix until combined.

Mix the honey and tahini mixture with the dry mixture until well combined.

Line a 20 x 15 cm (8 x 6 in) tin with plastic wrap or baking paper and spread the mixture out evenly. Place another piece of plastic wrap or baking paper on top and press down firmly to ensure it's packed well.

Place in the refrigerator for 1 hour until firm. Cut into 10 bars and store in the refrigerator between sheets of baking paper for 2–3 weeks.

ice cream

Our favourite vanilla ice cream recipe uses predominantly young coconut flesh in the base. Realising not everyone has access to young coconuts, we wanted to give you a few options for a nut-based version and a fruit-based version so you don't miss out on the delights of raw ice cream and can make some quickly with what you have on hand.

vanilla coconut ice cream & variations

Make time: 35 minutes + component recipes | Soak time: 2–4 hours | Setting time: 5–6 hours |
Makes: approximately 1 litre (35 fl oz/4 cups) | Equipment required: blender, ice cream maker

250 ml (9 fl oz/1 cup) **almond milk** (see page 30)

250 ml (9 fl oz/1 cup) **coconut water**

320 g (11¼ oz/2 cups) **young coconut flesh**

155 g (1 cup) **raw cashews** (soaked 2–4 hours)

150 g (5½ oz/½ cup) **raw agave**

pinch **sea salt**

½ tsp **vanilla bean powder**
or seeds of 1 **vanilla bean**

½ tsp **lecithin**

125 ml (4 fl oz/½ cup) melted **cold-pressed coconut oil** (see page 270)

This is a really well balanced vanilla ice cream using coconut as a base. The vanilla flavour works well as a foundation for you to create other flavours with. We have several options below.

Blend almond milk, coconut water, coconut flesh, cashews, agave, sea salt and vanilla extract in a blender until smooth; there should be no texture to it. Add the lecithin and coconut oil and blend until smooth. Add the vanilla bean powder and mix with a spoon until incorporated.

Chill well and put into an ice cream maker for 25 minutes or however long your brand of ice cream machine suggests. Will take approximately 5–6 hours to set depending on your freezer.

chocolate

Add 40 g (1½ oz/⅓ cup) cacao powder to the vanilla ice cream mixture when blending.

passionfruit

Fold in 80 g (2¾ oz/⅓ cup) of passionfruit coulis (see page 66) after processing through an ice cream machine.

blueberry

Add 80 g (2¾ oz/½ cup) defrosted or fresh blueberries to the mixture when blending. If you have freeze-dried blueberries and want a more intense blueberry flavour, add 4 tablespoons of crushed freeze-dried blueberries when blending.

strawberry

Add 75 g (½ cup) defrosted or fresh strawberries to the vanilla ice cream mixture when blending. If you have freeze-dried strawberries and want a more intense strawberry flavour, add 4 tablespoons of crushed freeze-dried strawberries when blending.

mint chocolate chip

Leave out the vanilla bean powder and add 8–10 drops of organic peppermint extract or essential oil to the ice cream mixture when blending (you should do this to taste as every essential oil or extract has a different strength). Fold in 45 g (¼ cup) cacao nibs after processing through an ice cream machine.

vanilla cashew ice cream

When you don't have access to coconuts, this cashew-based ice cream is a great alternative.

Make time: 35 minutes + component recipes | Soak time: 2–4 hours | Setting time: 5–6 hours |
Makes: approximately 1 litre (35 fl oz/4 cups) | Equipment required: blender, ice cream maker

500 ml (17 fl oz/2 cups) **almond milk** (see page 30)

310 g (11 oz/2 cups) **cashews** (soaked 2–4 hours)

150 g (5½ oz/½ cup) and 4 tbsp **raw agave**
or **organic maple syrup**

pinch **sea salt**

2 tbsp **vanilla extract**

1 tsp **lecithin**

8 tbsp melted **cold-pressed coconut oil**
(see page 270)

½ tsp **vanilla bean powder**
or seeds of 1 **vanilla bean**

Blend almond milk, cashews, agave, sea salt and vanilla extract in a blender until smooth; there should be no texture to it. Add the lecithin and coconut oil and blend until smooth. Add the vanilla bean powder and mix with a spoon until incorporated.

Place in the refrigerator until mixture is cool (adding a warm mixture to most home ice cream machines will prevent the mixture from setting correctly).

Process in an ice cream maker for 25 minutes or as per manufacturer's instructions.

Store in the freezer in an airtight container. Will take approximately 5–6 hours to set depending on your freezer.

strawberry ice cream (banana base)

Quick and cheap to make, this ice cream freezes a little harder than the others, making it ideal for popsicle moulds.
Dip your ice pops in chocolate (see page 249) then roll in crushed nuts – delicious!

Make time: 10 minutes | Setting time: 4–6 hours | Makes: approximately 1 litre (35 fl oz/4 cups) |
Equipment required: blender, ice cream maker

4 large **ripe bananas**

400 g (14 oz/2⅔ cups) **fresh** or **frozen strawberries**
(defrosted)

3 tbsp **raw agave** or **raw honey**

1 tsp **vanilla extract**
or a pinch **vanilla bean powder**

125 ml (4 fl oz/½ cup) melted **cold-pressed coconut oil** (see page 270)

1½ tsp **lecithin**

Blend the bananas, strawberries, honey and vanilla in a high-speed blender until the mixture is very smooth, then pour in the coconut oil and lecithin and blend again until everything is well mixed. Pour into popsicle moulds.

Place in the freezer to set – depending on your freezer the popsicles should be ready in 4–6 hours, or leave overnight. As this recipe has a reasonably high water content from the fruit, you will need to take it out of the freezer for 10 minutes before serving to soften it.

chocolate & raspberry ice cream sandwiches

The first time we made these at the unbakery, they were delicious but far too big. It was hilarious and slightly embarrassing to watch people so excited after the first few bites, then looking despondently at the remaining half. We now make them a quarter of the size and they are perfect!

Make time: 20 minutes + component recipe | Makes: 8 | Equipment required: food processor, ice cream maker

cookies

195 g (1¼ cups) **cashews**

55 g (2 oz/½ cup) **cacao powder**

2 pinches **sea salt**

4 **pitted dates**

1 tbsp **cacao nibs**

3 tbsp **organic maple syrup**

3 tbsp melted **cold-pressed coconut oil** or melted **cacao butter** (see page 270)

1 tsp **vanilla extract**

ice cream (see page 262)

Blend the cashews into a fine flour in a food processor. Add the cacao powder and sea salt and blend until mixed through. Add the dates and cacao nibs and blend for 10 seconds until the dates have been chopped finely. Add the rest of the ingredients until the mixture forms a pastry-like consistency.

Place the mixture between 2 sheets of baking paper and with a rolling pin, roll out until it is uniform and about 4 mm (³⁄₁₆ in) thick. Cut it into 6 cm (2½ in) circles with a cookie cutter. Transfer all of the cookies to a baking paper-lined tray and place in the refrigerator or freezer until firm.

Repeat with the scraps left over from the first round until all the mixture is used up or you have enough to make around 16 cookies (you need 2 cookies per sandwich).

Once firm, place 3 tablespoons of your choice of ice cream in between 2 cookies and press down. Shape around the sides with a knife or back of a spoon to get it looking uniform. We often use 2 different flavours of ice cream inside a sandwich, or add frozen berries like raspberries to a flavour like chocolate or vanilla ice cream.

Keep in an airtight container in the freezer in between sheets of baking paper for up to 1–2 months.

banana & cherry choc sundae

There are few occasions when I don't feel like ice cream, so I'm always thinking of different ways to use it. This sundae is so good, you won't want to share! On burger nights, we often make these as well for an all-American dining experience. I like to use tall glasses to serve this in, but other cups or bowls would work well. Place whatever you are using – cups or bowls – in the freezer for a few hours beforehand.

Make time: 5 minutes + component recipes | Serves: 2

4 tbsp **chocolate sauce** (see page 249)

2 **ripe bananas**

6 scoops **vanilla ice cream** (see page 262)

30 g (1 oz/¼ cup) **dried activated almonds** (see pages 27–28) or crushed **hazelnuts**

1 handful **cherries**

4 **chocolate sticks** (see page 249)

optional – for extra chocolate crunch add 1 tsp **cacao nibs**

Drizzle 1 tablespoon of the chocolate sauce in each chilled cup while rotating the cup as the chocolate sticks around the sides of the glass. Slice the bananas lengthways and place at the back of the glass.

Place 1 scoop of ice cream in the bottom and sprinkle on a few almonds and a couple of pitted cherries, then repeat with the other scoops of ice cream, almonds and cherries.

Drizzle with the remaining tablespoon of chocolate sauce, a few whole cherries, remaining almonds and 2 chocolate sticks.

glossary

Activated & Dried Nuts & Seeds
Many of our recipes call for dried and activated nuts and seeds. To make, soak or activate the nut or seed (see pages 26–27 for more specific details and soaking times for different varieties) and then dehydrate at 46°C (115°F) for 24–48 hours (bigger nuts like Brazil nuts and almonds take 48 hours to dry). They are ready when they are crisp to bite – very similar to a toasted nut (see page 28).

Almond & Other Nut Flours
For the majority of our recipes that call for nut flour we make a fresh flour from whole nuts. Firstly we activate/soak the nuts or seeds (see page 27), then dehydrate them for 24–48 hours depending on the nuts or seeds (see page 28). Using a food processor, we make them into a flour, being careful not to over-blend; you don't want to release any of the oils from the nuts or seeds. Store any fresh flours in the fridge to keep fresh.

Carob Powder
Made from the pod of a legume, carob has a similar flavour to cacao, yet not close enough to call it a flavour substitute. Some raw carob is available but it is hard to come by. A good, lightly roasted organic carob powder is a minimally processed product that still retains a lot of goodness. Carob is naturally sweet, low in fat, high in fibre, has calcium and no caffeine. We use carob in a few of our recipes. If you're sensitive to cacao or chocolate you could use carob as an alternative or use half carob, half cacao.

Cold-pressed Coconut Oil
When selecting coconut oil choose a good, organic, cold-pressed one with a neutral, light coconut flavour, as a strong-tasting oil will dominate the other flavours in a recipe. Using cold-pressed, good-quality oils is an important choice to make, for more details on why check out pages 16–17.

Dates
There are many different varieties of dates. Our recipes use a soft pitted baking date, slightly sticky and not overly sweet. Hard baking dates are the most common and can be soaked and used for date paste but will not work well in bases for your desserts.

Medjool dates and other gourmet dates are delicious but expensive. If using as a replacement to soft baking dates, remember they are much sweeter and stickier so you can use less of them.

Dehydrating
• The times we suggest for dehydrating are approximate – different dehydrators and climates will result in quicker or slower drying times. Think about what you are trying to achieve – if you're making crackers you want them to be crisp, if it's a bread you will want it soft and pliable to eat – so dehydrate up until it reaches the desired consistency rather than relying on exact times.

• Energy conservation/planning: To get the most out of your dehydrator you should try planning ahead, making a few recipes at a time so that you are utilising the space and not running it ¾ empty. We also plan to ferment and sprout when dehydrating in winter to use the warm heat to help the sprouting and fermenting process.

• Using an oven for dehydrating: it's possible to use your oven for dehydrating some of the recipes. The times will vary considerably to a dehydrator and will be something you need to experiment with as each oven operates differently

(generally it will dehydrate much quicker). Basic guidelines: set the temperature to its lowest settings (often this is around 50°C/122°F) on a fan bake setting, leave the oven door slightly ajar or use a foil prop (a screwed up ball of foil) if your oven door keeps wanting to close – this helps to bring the temperature down and keep the air circulating, removing the moisture from the oven.

• Don't mix sweet and savoury in the same dehydrator. The flavours will mix together and infuse each other.

Dehydrator Sheets
In our recipes we refer to dehydrator sheets. These are reusable silicon sheets that work like baking paper. Alternatively, use baking paper. Mesh sheets are the perforated dehydrator sheets that allow for maximum circulation and quicker drying.

Flax Meal
Made by grinding or milling flax seeds. In our recipes we use whole golden flax seeds, making the meal (also called flour) fresh in a high-speed blender or spice mill each time. This is because the oils in flax are very delicate and degrade quickly once exposed to air. Store leftover meal in an airtight container in the fridge.

Ginger Juice
Make by putting fresh ginger root through a juicer. If you don't have a juicer you can also make it in a food processor by chopping fresh ginger root into chunks and blending to a pulpy mixture. Place in a nut milk bag or muslin cloth and squeeze out the juice.

Green Superfoods Powders
We use green powders for providing colour to some desserts in the cafés and as a boost in smoothies. They're a great thing to have on hand when travelling and in the pantry for when there's no time to make a fresh green juice. Find a good, wholefoods, organic green powder – Synergy Company, Health Force Nutritionals and Matakana Superfoods all make excellent green powders that contain a wide range of nutrients in a wholefoods form, packed with vitamins, minerals and chlorophyll.

Korengo
This is soft seaweed that grows in New Zealand's oceans. It has a similar flavour to nori. We use dried korengo in many of our Asian dishes, you could use wakame as an alternative or, in some recipes, shredded nori sheet pieces.

Lecithin
Used in several of our cake fillings and ice creams, lecithin works as an emulsifier to help water and fat molecules hold together. It's also good for the health and function of nerve cells. The majority of lecithin available is highly processed, which makes this great ingredient a lot less desirable. An organic sunflower lecithin is the ideal choice or an organic non-GMO soy lecithin.

Maple Syrup
Use organic or 100 percent natural maple syrup. Read the label and check that the syrup doesn't contain anything else; there are many maple-flavoured syrups cut with less desirable, unnatural ingredients.

Melting Oils
Coconut oil and cacao butter are used throughout our recipes. In colder climates they will become solidified so you need to melt before using. To do

this make your own double boiler: take 2 bowls, place the butter/oil in 1 bowl and set aside. In the other bowl, place a few cups of almost boiling water; set the bowl with the butter/oil on top, being careful to not let any water get in your oil. It will take around 10 minutes for the butter/oil to melt depending on the amount you are using and the climate. Refresh with hot water if needed.

Nut Pulp
When making nut milks you will be left with a lot of nut pulp – not all of it needs to go to waste. Almond pulp helps make a spongy cake texture and is used in several of our cake recipes. Hazelnut and Brazil nut pulp can also be used as a replacement when you don't have almond.

Store for up to 2–3 days in the fridge or freeze it. You can also dehydrate it to make a version of almond flour – store in an airtight container.

Plastic Wrap
Ideally you should be able to source biodegradable plastic wrap made from plant-based materials, which you can put it in your compost bin at the end when finished. If you can't get biodegradable, try reusing the pieces that you do use.

Raw Cacao Powder and Cacao Butter
Made from whole cacao beans that have been ground, milled and pressed into a paste, which is then separated into cacao powder and cacao butter. This process is done under 46°C (115°F) to ensure all the goodness is intact. Most good health food stores will sell both products but, if not readily available, substitute them with a good-quality organic cocoa powder and butter.

Salt
We recommend sea salt, Himalayan or a locally harvested salt. Standard table salt is refined and doesn't provide the trace minerals found in natural, unrefined salts.

Sprouted Dried Buckwheat
This is buckwheat that has been sprouted as per the sprouting instructions on pages 26–27 and dried overnight at 41°C (106°F) in your dehydrator (see page 28). You can keep these dried sprouts in an airtight container for several months.

Tamarind Water
Made simply by soaking tamarind pulp in water for several hours, then mashing the softened tamarind with your fingers and straining through a sieve. Use the resulting liquid.

Vanilla Bean Powder
You can purchase vanilla bean powder in many specialist food stores. It should contain vanilla beans and nothing else. Make your own by grinding dried vanilla beans into a powder using a high-speed blender or spice mill.

Water
When water is required in a recipe, we use filtered or living water (spring or rain). Depending on where you live in town, supply water can contain a lot of chemicals and affect the result of some recipes – in particular it can have a spoiling effect during soaking and sprouting nuts and seeds.

Young Coconuts
These have a white, very light brown and sometimes green husk. Do not use older, dark brown coconuts. In these recipes, we use the soft, inner white flesh and water from the young coconuts. See page 34 for more details.

index

Gratitude

While the little bird unbakery and cafés – and now book – stem from my mad optimism, it is very much a collaboration between many creative and wonderful people. I'd like to take this opportunity to thank some of them with all my heart.

Jeremy Bennett designed this beautiful book. He's also an award-winning architect, the brains behind the little bird branding and the go-to guy for everything else (other than food preparation). As my husband, he has also been my greatest source of strength and inspiration through both difficult and good times.

Lottie Hedley took the photos in this book. Having seen some of Lottie's work, we tracked her down and we're so glad we did. Traditionally a documentary rather than food photographer, her images have a richness and story-telling quality, which was exactly what we wanted.

Xander Cameron is our head chef at the little bird unbakery. His background is in foraging, hunting and creating seasonal, organic food – he's worked in some great restaurants. I'm not sure what he made of his first interview with us; our ad hadn't mentioned that the café was raw. We focus on getting great chefs in the kitchen – then they can apply their skills to the challenge of creating exceptional raw food. Xander has done just that. I've shared some of his recipes in this book, so that you too can create more challenging and complex raw dishes at home.

Carter Were is one of the original little bird family. She joined us four years ago when we were a team of six making raw products and selling them to wholefood stores. She applied for the job from Sydney where she'd been experimenting with raw foods at home, particularly sauerkraut and sprouted bread, which she now makes for our cafés. Some of the sweet recipes in this book were developed by Carter.

Harry Were is a talented photographer (and Carter's twin) who assisted with the styling and photography in this book. Harry has an amazing eye, is drawn to the visual textures of nature – be it food, landscapes or people – and has created a cult following of the little bird unbakeries' Instagram account.

Rejina Yoon is our head unbaker. Formerly a ballerina in Korea and a business graduate, she eventually realised her true calling and trained as a chef. She now crafts beautiful cakes and sweet treats for our cafés every day and has contributed to some of the dessert recipes in this book.

I would need another ten pages to properly thank all those I'm grateful to (but I'm sure you would prefer recipes). So just a few more acknowledgements …

To my dear friend Rebecca who has kept me sane and helped with editing, I couldn't have done this without your support. To Nellie for being so radiantly healthy and inspiring me with your naturopathic and nutritional advice. To Maria for your fabulously thorough recipe checking and to Lucia and Nicole who worked late helping to test them. To Beatnik, our independent publishers who have been patient and supportive in our quest to create a book of which we're proud. To Simon James for generously supplying many of the beautiful homeware pieces in these photographs (I would encourage any fan of beautiful homeware to visit simonjamesdesign.com) and to Gidon Bing, an Auckland artist who hand-crafted many of the beautiful ceramics pictured – your pieces are inspiring to work with. To the little bird originals: Sophia, Seth, Dean, the aforementioned Carter and the two Nicoles for helping build a family and a supportive foundation for creating great food. To Karla, Suhayl, Grace and Crisley for continuing that legacy. As I write this book there are fifty-six people working at little bird creating raw, organic food. It amazes me – we have a big family! To Leila and Imelda for helping me when life was not a happy, healthy place and for constantly steering me back to the food. To our friend Graham who keeps us focused on what's important; your enthusiasm for food and cacao is always a joy. And to all our little bird customers: life is far too short to not eat good food – thank you for believing in that.

x Megan